You
can
Teach Online

Building a Creative
Learning Environment

You *can* Teach Online

Building a Creative
Learning Environment

Gary S. Moore

Kathryn Winograd

Dan Lange

Boston   Burr Ridge, IL   Dubuque, IA   Madison, WI   New York   San Francisco   St. Louis
Bangkok   Bogotá   Caracas   Kuala Lumpur   Lisbon   London   Madrid   Mexico City
Milan   Montreal   New Delhi   Santiago   Seoul   Singapore   Sydney   Taipei   Toronto

McGraw-Hill Higher Education

*A Division of The **McGraw-Hill** Companies*

YOU CAN TEACH ONLINE
BUILDING A CREATIVE LEARNING ENVIRONMENT
Published by McGraw-Hill, an imprint of The McGraw-Hill Companies, Inc. 1221 Avenue of the Americas, New York, NY, 10020. Copyright © 2001, by The McGraw-Hill Companies, Inc. All rights reserved. No part of this publication may be reproduced or distributed in any form or by any means, or stored in a data base or retrieval system, without the prior written consent of The McGraw-Hill Companies, Inc., including, but not limited to, in any network or other electronic storage or transmission, or broadcast for distance learning.
Some ancillaries, including electronic and print components, may not be available to customers outside the United States.

This book is printed on acid-free paper.

2 3 4 5 6 7 8 9 0 QPD/QPD 0 9 8 7 6 5 4 3 2 1

ISBN 0-07-245517-9

Editorial director: *Phillip A. Butcher*
Editor: *Craig Beytien*
Senior marketing manager: *Zina Craft*
Senior project manager: *Susan Trentacosti*
Production associate: *Gina Hangos*
Cover design: *Jennifer McQueen*
Cover image: *© Sergio Baradat/SIS*
Compositor: *ElectraGraphics, Inc.*
Printer: *Quebecor World Dubuque Inc.*

Library of Congress Card Number: 2001086602

www.mhhe.com

Preface

The intention of this book is to create a richly illustrated, Web-enhanced book providing easy-to-follow examples of pedagogy and tools useful to faculty in developing courses in the traditional and online classroom. It's more than a hands-on, step-by-step guide to putting your course online. There are easy-to-follow materials in each lesson that will reinforce the chapter objectives including boldfaced terms within the body of text followed by definitions or explanations. There is an extensive glossary of terms and a powerful index. Each unit features a rich inclusion of Web links to related material that provide a specific function such as a links to a chatroom, downloadable plug-ins, graphic files, and much more. There is a dedicated website for the book with numerous features including a Course Showcase that provides examples of online courses in many disciplines at (http:www.mhhe.com/ucanteachonline).

The book features the latest information in many areas not adequately covered in other competing texts such as: best practices as defined by regional accrediting commissions; faculty ownership of intellectual materials; copyright issues; methods of student assessment and course evaluations; methods for evaluating online course delivery platforms; theories of learning; implementing online courses; innovations in the online classroom including its use as a platform for student publication; methods to heighten student and faculty interaction; and locating and employing a variety of tools to enhance Web-based course materials.

Special thanks are given to the following people for their reviews and their suggestions which proved helpful in the writing of this book: Karen Vignare, Rochester Institute of Technology; Dr. R. Celeste Beck, Palm Beach Community College; Byron Finch, Miami University of Ohio; Jerry Post, University of the Pacific; Andrew Siegal, University of Washington; and Marilyn M. Helms, Dalton State College

A very special thank you goes to Craig Beytien, Director of Market Development at McGraw-Hill, and Jackie Fitzgerald, Director of Distance and Distributed Learning at McGraw-Hill, who made the intial contacts and nurtured this project and its authors to a product for which we can all be proud. More special thanks to Jennifer McQueen, Designer, and Susan Trentacosti, Senior Project Manager, at McGraw-Hill whose specific expertise helped to fashion the appearance and drive the quality of this book.

Finally, we thank CiTE, the Center for Internet Technology in Education which is a research consortium among eCollege.com and participating higher education institutions to explore current issues in online education. It is from this forum that the authors emerged and were inspired to write this book.

Table of Contents

TABLE OF CONTENTS

UNIT 3: IMPLEMENTATION/ EVALUATION

Unit 1

Introduction

1

The eruption of computers and online capacity into the world of learning has evoked in many a sense of foreboding and fear while others have welcomed this new technology as a valuable tool in the art of teaching. The early adopters or pioneers of this technology have already made significant progress in the use of the Internet and the World Wide Web for instructing courses completely online or for adding to their courses taught on campus. However, they represent only a very small proportion of the educational workforce in the world. There remains a need to present the technology and learning theories to those who stand along the edges waiting for a signal to step onto the field and begin the game. This book and its associated website (**http://www.mhhe.com.ucanteachonline**) will make this transition easier for most.. This book and its website have been prepared by those who have stepped into the game, suffered the bruises, and now tell their story of the successes and failures, the technical issues, and the pedagogy. We hope that this proves helpful in your journey.

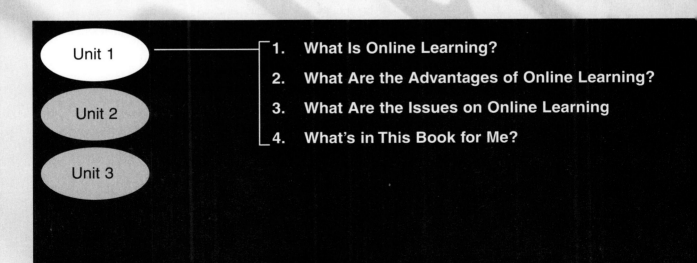

Unit 1
Unit 2
Unit 3

1. **What Is Online Learning?**
2. **What Are the Advantages of Online Learning?**
3. **What Are the Issues on Online Learning**
4. **What's in This Book for Me?**

Lesson 1
What Is Online Learning?

LESSON OUTLINE

1.1 INTERACTION IS THE CORE
1.2 GROWING A GIANT
1.3 THE FUTURE IS COMING

WHAT YOU WILL LEARN FROM THIS LESSON

YOU WILL BE ABLE TO:

1. Define what is meant by the term "online learning."
2. Describe the growth of online education and identify some of the growth factors.
3. Outline the growth in USA Internet connections and describe the increases in high-speed connections and potential new interactivity over the Internet.

LESSON 1: WHAT IS ONLINE LEARNING?

D
o you do email?" I remember hearing that question over and over again from teachers at a conference I once attended. Online teaching was equated with online email. And then I heard of a few hardy professors who had created something called "Web pages" in order to share their syllabi and lectures with their students outside of the classroom. Some spoke of "hypertext" and the astonishing concept of nonlinear reading—of the students creating their own learning experiences by choosing to click on words that were really gateways to other Web pages. It all seemed so impossibly futuristic.

That was 1998, just a few short years ago. Since then, teaching through the Internet has evolved at such a dizzying pace that it has earned its own spotlight in the pages of *The Chronicle of Higher Education*. Concerns about the technicalities of setting up an email listserv have blossomed beyond heated debates between education specialists over the ability or inability of learning communities to be formed in the purely online course into cautionary forecasts that if face-to-face courses in the traditional classroom do not use technology then students will be deprived of educational opportunities. Perhaps the latest statistics from America Online showing 7 million people logging on every day to the AOL chatrooms and staying logged on for an average of two and a half hours have suggested to some that the building of community in "virtual" reality may actually not be a problem.[1]

1.1 Interaction Is the Core

But what is **online learning**? Basically, it is distance learning modernized, akin to the rudimentary "by mail" correspondence course and the television satellite course that have been alternative means of education for decades now because of the flexibility and convenience they offer students. But instead of letters and televisions being the instructional mediums, computers, modems, and the Internet are the means by which teachers and students connect. And online learning is not relegated just to the genre of pure distance learning — the opportunities it offers in extending communication and the availability of resources outside of the classroom make it an exceptional enhancement to the traditional classroom.

1.2 Growing a Giant

What distinguishes online learning, and what is expected to spur the growth in the number of distance learning students from 710,000 in 1998 to 2.23 million in 2002 (**http://www.idc.com**),[2] is its online component — the technologies of the Internet. This technology allows for both **asynchronous** and **synchronous** networking, meaning that students and instructors can have both instantaneous and "staggered," more reflective interaction. The quantity and quality of interaction within a class, whether traditional or online, have been identified by The National Education Association as prime factors in the creation of a **learning community**, recognized as essential to effective learning.[3] Online learning, as **broad bandwidth** and Internet connectivity continue to improve, can also offer a variety of **multimedia** learning activities, ranging from streaming video and audio lectures to computer-simulated lab experiences, creating an interactive and engaging learning environment for students.

1.3 The Future Is Coming

The increased capabilities of Internet and Web-based distance learning are why the number of institutions offering Internet courses that utilize online asynchronous communication increased by 38 percent over the past three years, while the number of institutions offering pre-recorded video and two-way **video conferencing**, what were at one time considered the preeminent forms of distance learning, remained essentially the same.[4]

We still make jokes about the foibles of programming the VCR, but in reality, online teaching could not have evolved so quickly if not for the phenomenal growth in the numbers of people able to have skilled access to its technologies. Now, more than 50 percent of the 100 million in the United States have at least one personal computer (PC), and more than 4 million households are being added to this list every year. Many of these people purchasing computers are doing so because of the Internet.[5]

Despite concerns that computer technology and access to the Internet will be the new socio-economic dividers of our time, families with less than $30,000 in income made up more than one third of the new PC purchases.[5] In the education realm, the use of email in college courses has risen by five-fold since 1994, while classes using Internet resources have doubled in that time.[5] The number of colleges using the **World Wide Web** (WWW) for resources and class materials has expanded nearly six-fold since 1994.[5] Two-year colleges offering distance education courses are expected to rise from 50 percent in 1998 to over 85 percent in 2002 while four-year institutions offering distance education courses will likely increase from 62 percent in 1998 to 84 percent in 2002.[6] This phenomenon is reaching down even to the K-12 classroom in which classroom connection to the Internet has increased from 3 percent in 1994 to 63 prcent in 1999.[7]

But what technological advances have enabled us to even presume to offer learning experiences online that are equivalent to or even greater than what the traditional classroom has offered? Nearly all of this growth has been on the commodity Internet, that is, the Internet familiar to commercial (.com), government (.gov), organizations (.org), and academic institutions (.edu) around the world. There is now an explosion of high-speed "new generation" networks that permit data transfers more than 1,000 times faster than the commodity network. Although many of these, such as the Backbone Network Service (vBNS) and the Abilene network, are limited to universities and government agencies, there are new high-speed networks such as the Gemini2000 that will serve commercial customers as well.[6] Most ordinary people won't have access to such systems immediately, but there is the reality of faster connect times for many private citizens. Attracted by the potentially enormous customer base, cable and phone companies are aggressively marketing high-speed Internet access with cable or **digital subscriber lines** (DSL).[6] Such high-speed access greatly increases the sophistication of technologies available to the general public, including virtual reality and video conferencing. New software and improved server capabilities are making streaming video and audio available to current users with 28.5K modems. Faster connect speeds, new software, and improved computer technologies are opening up a vast new world of interactive distance learning opportunities. In the midst of these remarkable improvements in transmission speeds, there are equally astounding changes in the kaleidoscope of distance education. There are new educational providers, enhanced computer technology, newly developed software, regional educational collaboratives and alliances, and for-profit virtual universities. Harcourt General, a parent company to the textbook publisher Harcourt-Brace, is seeking to establish a for-profit virtual university that offers several degree programs completely online. The company has applied to the Massachusetts Board of Higher Education for permission to grant degrees up to the masters level.[6] The technology and business of the Web and online education are traveling at light speed as many of us sit aghast and breathless at what's happening. While the sophistication and power of computer and Internet technology increases, and the public at large continues to arm itself with the latest innovations, how can the educator prepare himself or herself to step into this new millennium of education and use these tools to effectively and creatively teach a dynamic, increasingly non-traditional student population? And why would he or she want to?

REFERENCES

1. **Access Magazine.** *The Denver Post.*
2. **Lau, S., et al**. "Online Distance Learning in Higher Education, 1998-2002." *International Data Corporation*, 1999 <http://www.idc.com>.
3. **Trinkle, D.** 1999. "Distance Learning: A Means to an End, No More, No Less." *The Chronicle of Higher Education*, August 6.
4. **Phillips, G.** "The Release of Distance Education at Post-Secondary Education Institutions 1997-98." *The National Center for Education Statistics*, December 17, 1999 <http://nces.ed.gov>.
5. **Greene, K.C.** 1999. "The Expanding Universe of Distance Learning: Distance Learning in Higher Education." *The Institute for Higher Education Policy for the Council for Higher Education Accreditation*, Washington, DC, 20036-1135, A1-A3, February.
6. **CHEA.** "Distance Learning in Higher Education." CHEA (Council for Higher Education Accreditation) Update, Part 2, *The Institute for Higher Education Policy*, June 1999.
7. **U.S. Department National Center for Education Statistics**. *"Internet Access in Public Schools and Classrooms: 1994-1999* (Report Date)." <http://nces.ed.gov>.

What Are the Advantages of Online Learning?

Lesson 2

What Are the Advantages of Online Learning?

LESSON OUTLINE

WHAT YOU WILL LEARN FROM THIS LESSON

YOU WILL BE ABLE TO:

1. Classify and compare the different types of students for whom online learning is important.
2. State and explain the opportunities for learning outside the classroom that online learning provides.
3. Describe and outline the advantages of online learning in reducing the issues of race and gender.
4. Explain the role of online learning in increasing student responsibility and interactivity.

LESSON 2: WHAT ARE THE ADVANTAGES OF ONLINE LEARNING?

According to the CEO of Cisco Systems, Mr. Chambers, the educational market is about to become "the next big killer application for the Internet. Education over the Internet is going to be so big it is going to make e-mail usage look like a rounding error" when measured against the total consumption of Internet capacity. [1] The driving force is a highly competitive global market that demands continually improving productivity. As geographical boundaries are ruptured by entire degree programs offered online by universities across the country, and, conceivably, the world, most academic institutions will have to keep pace by providing opportunities for rapid learning at lower costs and with greater accountability. Many large firms such as G.E., AT&T, IBM, and Cisco already offer online academies to train new employees and continually upgrade the skills of existing personnel. More and more universities are offering a combination of instructor-led courses and online learning based on restructured or reinvented curricula that offer the most interactive, stimulating, and pedagogically sound Internet courses. According to Mr. Chambers, those countries and schools that ignore this challenge will likely face the same fate of large department stores that predicted e-commerce would not flourish.[1]

But for those of us who still remember the heralded arrival of the Xerox machine in the department office as the "modernization of education," the thought of going "online" can seem overwhelming, and, frankly, superfluous. Excellent teaching has occurred for centuries now, without aid of computer or electronic file. What can Internet technology offer besides some "cool" factor for which the passing fancy of students will soon wane?

2.1 The Anywhere/Anytime Phenomenon and the Changing Face of Students

The Non-Traditional Student

Whether it is because of the ever-spiraling cost of higher education, or the dynamic needs of an Information Age workforce, the demographics of the traditional higher education student population are being broadened by an amalgamation of non-traditional students. Statistics in 1998 from the Department of Education reported an increase of 13 percent more part-time students, a 6 percent increase of students over 25, (a figure expected to increase between 1996 and 2000 by another 2 percent) and a 20 percent increase of female students,[2] which is particularly noteworthy given that females have become the leading users of the Internet for online learning.[3]

Because these non-traditional students are often campus-commuters, jobholders, and caretakers, online learning and its anywhere/anytime nature has become their panacea for educational opportunity. Even traditional on-campus students, as many universities which have adopted online learning programs have discovered, are filling out the rosters of online courses, for this very same reason.

Knowledge Workers

Technology creates dynamic corporate environments that demand adaptability and ongoing learning. Companies are looking for "knowledge workers," employees who possess specific high-level skills and have the ability and the desire to continue to learn as the technology becomes even more advanced.[4] Internet-based training accounted for $197 million in 1997, and this figure is predicted to grow to $5.5 billion in 2002 because of its effectiveness and flexibility.[2]

The Life-Long Learner

In tandem with this concept of the knowledge worker is the concept of the life-long learner. According to the Kellogg Commission on the Future of State and Land-Grant Universities, the Information Age has increased demand for education throughout an individual's lifespan. As far back as 1995, nearly half of the adult population was involved in continuous learning, learning deemed essential to both individual and community as the world draws closer together in a complex symbiotic relationship.[5]

The Homebound Student

The benefits of anywhere/anytime education extend to our marginalized student populations. As communities work to make public spaces available to those with disabilities, educational institutions work to make education available to those who are unable to attend school even when public spaces are altered to accommodate their handicaps. For many students with disabilities, the anonymity of the Internet classroom and its inherent flexibility and asynchronous environment that can allow all students time for reflection and preparation before participation can be advantageous. The ability to "write in" responses for those with speaking difficulties can make the difference between isolation and acceptance into a learning community. And for those wheelchair bound, simply not having the stress and exhaustion of commuting to campus can help them achieve their education goals. The World Wide Consortium's Web Accessibility Initiative is one of the largest research and information programs developed to provide guidelines on creating accessible websites and online courses (**http://www.w3.org**).

2.2 Extending Learning Opportunities

Communication Outside the Classroom Wall

Besides creating a flexible learning environment, online learning can virtually "extend the walls" of a classroom by creating communication opportunities for student and instructors and by increasing the availability of research resources both in and out of the classroom. A simple Web page can serve as an announcement board; communication tools such as an email list serve, a threaded discussion, or a chatroom can open up discussion forums outside of the classroom and increase opportunities for collaborations on group projects. The World Wide Web offers online newspapers, magazines and journals, and national news websites like CNN (**http://www.cnn.com/**), *Atlantic Monthly's* online publication, The *Atlantic Unbound* (**http://www.theatlantic.com/**), and *The New York Times* (**http://www.nytimes.com**). Students can access NASA online (**http://www.nasa.gov/today**/) and view an entire archive of space shots from the space shuttle and satellites, and the robot that ranged across Mars. Online instructors can create "hypertext links" to these Web resources within the text of their Web pages, creating non-linear learning experiences that encourage student-driven learning. Instructors can create their own archives of information for students in the online course, "publishing" exemplary student work for modeling and exemplifying the criteria for acceptable work in a course.

The World as a Classroom

Instructors who use Internet technology can also create a world-as-a-classroom experience for their students, taking students on virtual field trips to museums (**http://www.museumland.com/index.html**) and libraries like the New York Public Library (**http://www.nypl.org/**) and arranging online discussions with content experts. Those hardy instructors who are well versed in technology can even conduct class onsite in remote geographic areas. Even now there are several "roving" K-12 classrooms online (**http://www.quest.classroom.com**) where instructors on foot, bike, or boat explore countries around the world and "report" back on their exploits to students worldwide through audio, video, text, and images on their websites.

2.3 Creation of Collaborative Learning Environments

Community in the classroom can be an integral part of the learning process. Students who feel respected and valued by their peers will begin to interact on a deeper, more meaningful level, will be more open to risk-taking in learning, and will begin to engage in collaborative learning.[6] The ability and opportunity to grasp more complex concepts increase when individuals are part of a larger group that has the same learning goal and the members of that group are encouraging and constructively evaluative.[7] Often times, instructors are most effective when they nurture that community and the collaborative learning that arises from it.

One of the first questions that instructors new to online learning will raise is that of isolation. How can instructors and students nurture community when each is staring into their separate personal computer screens? Surprisingly, because of its very anonymity and the time that it allows for individual reflection, the asynchronous learning environment can create as strong a sense of community among students as can the face-to-face classroom, especially if the instructor designs the course around collaborative learning activities such as peer workshops and critiques, peer presentations, and shared student leadership in facilitating asynchronous and synchronous discussions.

Avoiding the Walls of Gender and Race

Interestingly, it has been suggested that gender and race biases in the traditional classroom, or the effects of anticipated bias, can be mitigated because, as of yet, the prohibi-

---

Leveling the Playing Field: Student Interaction in Online Education

Though the typical reason given for the non-traditional student's embrace of online learning is its anywhere/anytime nature, its intrinsic anonymity suggests another possible cause for student interest, particularly with female students. Fassinger's (1995) study on interaction in the traditional classroom is indicative of the well-documented gender-bias that women have confronted over the past four decades.[8] Testing the hypothesis that "women are disadvantaged in college because of professors' differential treatment of students by gender, " Fassinger observed that females were also "disadvantaged" by male students whom she found to participate and interrupt in class more often than the females in the class. What is especially interesting in this study is the female students' self-assessments that cited "poor formulated ideas, ignorance about a subject, and fear of appearing unintelligent to peers" as the reasons for their silence during times of interaction. And yet interaction has been identified in the traditional classroom, and especially, in the online classroom, as a "critical variable in Instructional theory" [9] because of the role it plays in the learning process, affecting both "critical thinking and intellectual development."[8]

Asynchronous communication in the form of threaded discussion appears to be the key to creating for both genders "instructional interaction." For the female student, threaded discussion can offer the twin shields of anonymity and physical distance from males who might dominate a discussion through both body posturing and oral interruption. It offers time for self-reflection, critical analysis and self-editing — all steps in the learning process that can validate for a female student the value of her contributions to a discussion.

A study performed by eCollege.com examined the impact of gender differences on student online communication behaviors.[10] Based on a survey of 1,380 students, of which 76 percent responded, the study provides evidence that an equal online forum for instructional interaction does exist between male and female students. For example, unlike the traditional classroom where female students appeared to be daunted by the physical presence of their male counterparts, in this particular study, females in the online classroom felt as involved as male students in opinionated discourse and questioning behaviors, and felt equally to the male students that the online discourse was educationally effective.

tive costs for two-way video conferencing via computer and Internet and the inadequacies of bandwidth have kept the online course generally text-based. The instructor may utilize audio and video in order to communicate with his or her students, but the students, generally, will not. Gender and race online are hard to determine and often become non-issues as students begin to identify each other through their writing styles and intellectual contributions to the course.

2.4 Increasing Student Responsibility and Interaction

Andragogy is a word that is replacing the still not quite familiar term of pedagogy in online learning. While pedagogy has to do with the practice of teaching children, **andragogy** is about adult learning. Online learning is still predominately a phenomenon of the non-traditional, adult student. Based on theories of learning as being the "construction of meaning through experience," andragogy has created a system of teaching that facilitates self-directed and individual learning.[11] This system of teaching is especially relevant in the online classroom, where instructors do not exercise the same kind of direct control and the students bring different expectations and motivations for learning. Active learning, as opposed to passive learning, has become a key concept in the online classroom.

2.5 Interactivity with Content

The learning paradigm of today is described as "information transfer," in which students simply receive the facts and information that their teachers wish to impart to them.[12] This terminology carries the negative implication of passivity in students, which for many suggests a real failure in our educational system. Greater hands-on learning, high interactivity with content, individualized learning paths, and active student learning are the ultimate outcomes envisioned by many in education. This would be the true adaptation of computer and Internet technologies into education.[13]

REFERENCES

1. **Friedman, T.T.** 1999. "Next it's E-ducation." *The New York Times*, November 17.

2. **U.S. Department National Center for Education.** 2000. "Statistics Projections of Education Statistics to 2008." (Report Date) <http://nces.ed.gov>.

3. **National Telecommunications and Information Administration.** 1999. "Falling Through the Net: Defining the Digital Divide." <http://www.ntia.doc.gov>.

4. **Hodgins, H. W**. 2000. "Into the Future: A Vision Paper." *American Society for Training and Development and the National Governor's Association*, February <www.astd.org>.

5. **Kellogg Commission on the Future of State and Land-Grant Universities.** 1999. "Returning to Our Roots: A Learning Society." Sept 1999, *National Association of State Universities and Land-Grant College*. <http://www.nasulgc.org/kellogg/learn.pdf>.

6. **Wegerif, R.** 1998. "The Social Dimension of Asynchronous Learning Networks." *JALN*, 2(1).

7. **Dede, C.** 1997. "Distance Learning to Distributed Learning: Making the Transition." *NCII Viewpoint*.

8. **Fassinger, P.** 1995. Understanding Classroom Interaction: Students' and Professor's Contributions to Students' Silence." *Journal of Higher Education*, 66(1), pp.82-96.

9. **Wagner, E.** 1994. "In Support of a Functional Definition of Interaction." *The American Journal of Distance Education*, 8(2), pp.6-29.

10. **Hoffman, K., and K. Winograd.** 1999. "Leveling the Playing Field: Student Interaction in Online Education." *eCollege.com*.

11. **Pratt, Daniel.** 1993. "Andragogy After Twenty-Five Years." *New Directions for Adult and Continuing Education*, Spring.

12. **Bork, A.** 2000. "Learning Technology." *Educause Review*, January/February <http://www.educause.edu>.

13. **Panel on the Future of American Higher Education.** 2000. *Educause Review*, January/February <http://www.educause.edu>.

What Are the Issues on Online Learning?

Lesson 3

What Are the Issues on Online Learning?

LESSON OUTLINE

WHAT YOU WILL LEARN FROM THIS LESSON

YOU WILL BE ABLE TO:

1. Identify some of the main concerns being published about the quality of online education.
2. Describe some of the issues in translating the traditional course to the online environment.
3. List some of the problems facing online instructors with regard to copyright and fair use of class materials.
4. Contrast the Internet access among economic lines, races, and the disabled.
5. State some of the mechanisms for retaining online students.
6. Identify some of the issues in the use of technology in teaching.

LESSON 3: WHAT ARE THE ISSUES ON ONLINE LEARNING?

A global rush to embrace electronic technologies and online learning, wisely, does not ensure immediate global acceptance. Debate over the online classroom flourishes. Despite recognition of the many advantages that online technology can offer to the process of learning, researchers and educators are concerned over the online classroom's comparable effectiveness to the traditional classroom.

3.1 Lack of Quantitative, Longitudinal Research

A national review of research and publications on online education by the Institute of Higher Education Policy concluded that many studies were flawed, citing a dearth of quantitative evidence and an overabundance of corporate sponsorship. The report questions the effectiveness of distance learning in higher education and whether it is equivalent to traditional classroom-based instruction.[1] The report raises questions about the skills required to use the technology, citing poor preparation of faculty and students to use this new technology; the quality of interaction between the instructor and the students, the cost of purchasing computers and technology, and the differences among students in how they learn.[2] Other educators have reviewed online courses and concluded most of those they reviewed still provide little in the way of interaction and consist mainly of posted syllabi or class notes [3] despite the advances in technology and Internet bandwidth which allow for the use of instructive multimedia and enhanced means of communication. Many fear that online education is simply about "fact-shoveling" and "training," and not about education, interactivity, and true engagement.[4]

3.2 I Have to Translate This?

For many instructors, the prospect of transforming traditional teaching practices conducted in a face-to-face classroom to the online environment is overwhelming. The problem is that most of us, especially at the college level, are accustomed to the use of lectures and textbooks that enhances our personal delivery styles in the classroom. Without a visible instructor in physical contact with students on a bi-weekly schedule, the online classroom demands the systematic design of many different learning activities that will engage students who have individual learning styles.

Many question how student and faculty roles online will be established; how assessment strategies will be established that can preclude cheating; how the heated discussion of the classroom will be emulated in the online classroom; and how students will be effectively motivated to learn. Though the successful and experienced educator will continue to employ elements that excite the imagination, involve problem-solving, and challenge creativity, the use of Internet technology in education is an evolving art, and well-supported standards and criteria must be established to ensure quality education. [5]

3.3 Intellectual Property Rights and Course Ownership

In regard to their professional careers, many faculty members express concerns over intellectual property rights for their online courses and how copyright and fair use laws translate to the online classroom. Do institutional administrators have the right to sell the materials created by instructors for online courses to another school? Especially if the institution provided that faculty member with specialized assistance that went well above what is normally provided faculty in the development of curriculum materials? The American Association of University Professors has recommended that contractual arrangements be made between faculty and administration prior to the start of a project because the advent of instructional technology has blurred definitions between pure "delivery service" and actual co-creation and, thus, ownership of an online course (**http://www/aaup.org/spcintro.htm**). [6] You may also want to try the following site for a wealth of information on this topic (**http://distancelearn.about.com/education/distancelearn/cs/intellectualright/index.htm**). Click on "Faculty Ownership and Control of Digital Course Materials" and read the article by Glenda Morgan, *Teaching with Technology Today*, January 25, 2000. Also click on "Intellectual Property Policies" and find links to actual policies used by institutions and organizations to resolve the intellectual property issues involved in distance learning.

The right to use materials created by others in an online course is another dilemma for the online instructor. Will the online instructor legally be allowed to scan an essay into his or her online classroom in order to "pass it out" to the students for a discussion as this same instructor did in the traditional classroom? Or import an image from the Web into the online classroom? Do the definitions of "restricted access" apply to the online class the same as they do to the traditional classroom? What does "fair use" imply? Answers to questions like these are still gray as experts and faculty and administrators hash out definitions and protocols.

3.4 Accessibility/ Feasibility of Online Education

Despite the encouraging statistics of low-income households purchasing computer equipment in order to access the Internet and its resources, the **Digital Divide** is a growing concern. Technology has been named the "new engine of inequality."[10] Sixty percent of households with incomes of $75,000 have Internet access while only 12 percent of those with incomes of $20 - 25,000 have access. 73.6 percent of the White and Asian populations of the U.S. use the Internet, while only 35.6 percent of Black and Hispanic populations do. This dearth of Internet access extends to the public schools of many low-income areas. While 74 percent of classrooms in low poverty are connected to the Internet, only 39 percent in high poverty have access.[10] Statistics like these become especially troubling given the statistics of Internet-based corporate training and the growing trend of universities establishing campuswide laptop adoption policies for their student body. Those unskilled at Internet and information technology will be at a disadvantage in both the job market and the education arena. This disadvantage extends to the disabled who could benefit the most from the opportunities that Internet technology extends. Only 11 percent of people 15 and above with disabilities have access to the Internet at home, while 31 percent of people without disabilities have access.[7]

3.5 Student Retention

A chairperson from a computer science department once approached me. Her department had designed a series of online courses. The student retention rate was as low as 40 percent and she was concerned. What were they doing wrong? Student retention in the online course is a major concern. Older students may become "lost" in the labyrinth of new technology; younger, more traditional students may become overwhelmed by the anywhere/anytime freedom of the online classroom and the personal responsibility and motivation that freedom demands. Attentiveness to the best practices in online course design; active and consistent instructor participation in the online course; prescreening of students for skill levels in the use of technology; and the availability of information resources and assistance throughout the course are some solutions to high online drop-out rates.

3.6 Technology vs. Teaching

Finally, the biggest issue continues to be that of "teaching vs. technology." Would the money being spent on implementing all of this technology be better spent on retraining teachers on the pedagogy of teaching? Is technology really making a difference in how well our students learn, or is rethinking and reassessment of our teaching practices in how we apply them to technology making the difference? Could technology finally supplant the teacher? One thing is clear in everyone's mind — information technologies have become such a driving force in every aspect of our lives, that, as William M. Daley, Commerce Secretary, states in announcing grants up to 12.5 million dollars to help bridge the Digital Divide: "Access and training, therefore, become even more essential so that all Americans have the ability to participate and benefit from the new economy." [8] This applies to students, teachers, and the population at large.

REFERENCES

1. **The Institute for Higher Education Policy**. 1999. "What's the Difference? A Review of Contemporary Research On the Effectiveness of Distance Learning in Higher Education." *The Institute for Higher Education Policy*, sponsored by the American Federation of Teachers and the National Education Association <http://www.ihip.com>.

2. **Fassinger, P.** 1995. "Understanding Classroom Interaction: Students' and Professors' Contributions to Students' Silence." *Journal of Higher Education*, 66(1), pp.82-96.

3. **Talbott, S.** 1999. "Who's Killing Higher Education? Corporations and Students: The Unusual Suspects." *Educom Review,* March/April <http:www.educause.edu>.

4. **Bork, A., and D.R**. **Britton, Jr.** 1998. "The Web Is Not Suitable for Learning, *Internet Watch*, 115-116, June.

5. **American Association of University Professors**. 1999. Special Committee on Distance Education and Intellectual Property Issues. Documents published in the May/June 1999 *Academe* for comment and then subsequently approved as policy <http://www.aaup.org/spcintro.htm>.

6. **Kaye, H., and Stephen Kaye, Ph.D**. 2000. "Computer and Internet Use Among People with Disabilities." *Disabilities Statistic Center* <http://dsc.ucsf.edu>.

7. **United States Department of Commerce**. 2000. "Commerce Announces $12.5 Million in Grants to Be Awarded to Help Close the Digital Divide." Press Release, 2000.

8. **Commissions on Higher Education.** "Draft: Statement of the Regional Accrediting Commissions on the Evaluation of Electronically Offered Degree and Certificate Programs." September, 2000, pp. iii-iv. <http://www. wiche.edu /Telecom/Guidelines.htm>.

What's in This Book for Me?

Lesson 4

What's in This Book for Me?

LESSON OUTLINE

4.1 PRACTICAL STEP-BY-STEP INSTRUCTIONS
4.2 LEARNING OBJECTIVES

WHAT YOU WILL LEARN FROM THIS LESSON

YOU WILL BE ABLE TO:

1. List the practical steps that this book covers in putting your course online.
2. Identify and list the learning objectives for the book.

LESSON 4: WHAT'S IN THIS BOOK FOR ME?

4.1 Practical Step-by-Step Instructions

Probably you have already begun to wonder about some of the realities of online teaching. If you cannot see your students, how do you know if you have engaged them in the learning process? How can you avoid the syndrome of "text online," which leaves many students cold and the whole reason for teaching online superfluous? How can you and your students communicate so as to create learning community? How can you test a student there in spirit and mind only? In the traditional classroom, how do you choose which activities and content to portion out to the online environment and which to the face-to-face environment?

In this book, we will help you answer those questions as you begin to create a preliminary skeleton of your class that you will then fill in with actual instruction, interaction, and the facilitation of collaborative learning. To begin, you will:

- Determine whether your class will be project-driven or time-driven, creating either week units or project modules.

- Put content from your traditional classroom into electronic form and decide on how best to present that content, whether as text, instructional multimedia, student-driven projects, or hyperlinks to resources on the Web.

- Create numerous activities and assignments for your students on a weekly or project-based agenda, balancing out instructor-led activities with peer group projects and reviews and self-learning opportunities.

- Create opportunities for many levels of communication, whether asynchronously or synchronously, between students, between you and students, and between students and the invited world at large.

- Develop assessment opportunities that run the gamut from self-tests, discussion participation, journal writing, formal assignments and projects, and timed exams.

You will learn from this book how to build these learning environments by employing technologies for the classroom and online. Using easy-to-understand language, creative illustrations and graphics, keywords in boldface with definitions, glossaries, a full index, and many other features, this book will bring you into the world of online course building. You will learn about enhanced instructional methods that will prove useful for the lecture hall and the WWW. This is a Web-enhanced book. We'll provide links to concrete examples of effective online course materials, new technologies, and useful tools.

4.2 Learning Objectives

When you complete reading this book and associated exercises you will be able to:

a. List and describe the different uses of online technology within and beyond the traditional classroom.

b. Use a computer and a browser to enter, search, and download Internet materials, and create and edit bookmarks.

c. Communicate both asynchronously and synchronously through email, threaded discussion, and chatrooms.

d. Discuss and evaluate common theories of learning and distinguish between instructor-centered versus student-centered learning.

e. Describe, list, and evaluate your current classroom materials.

f. Translate your traditional classroom materials to an online environment.

g. Create an online community of students and develop methods for keeping the students engaged in the online class.

h. Implement the online course.

i. List, describe, and employ various methods of student assessment in the online environment.

j. Describe and use evaluation methods for the course.

k. List, describe, and use a variety of innovations in the online classroom including its use as a platform for student publication, a heightened level for student and faculty interaction, communication with world leaders and top scientists, using the Web as an informational tool, and customizing the fluid course.

l. Locate, describe, and employ a variety of tools to enhance Web-based course materials including the adding of prepared course materials from publishers, music and sound, graphics and video, and interactive courseware.

m. Identify and discriminate among materials that may be published to the Web based on current copyright issues.

Unit 2

Development— Getting Started

2

There are are very few things we do in life for the first time that don't cause anxiety. Do you remember the first time you nervously pedaled solo on your two-wheeler, or negotiated across a busy intersection with your driving license still new in your wallet? Many faculty that begin the journey into online course development are intimidated because there appear to be so many skills and knowledge areas that must be mastered. It's much less imposing if the process is divided into small steps that are easily mastered and even enjoyable. It's really quite amazing to see teachers enthused over the student response to a threaded discussion topic or the discovery of a wonderful new website that fits in perfectly with their lesson plan. Before long, the modest steps pick up pace and excitement and lead to a marvelous journey of discovery. There are many places to begin this journey, but let's start with a basic understanding of the computer, the Internet, and the World Wide Web (WWW).

Unit 1

Unit 2

Unit 3

5. What Is the Online Environment?

6. What Are the "Tools of the Trade?"

7. What Are Online Course Delivery Platforms?

8. Will Your Teaching Style Translate?

9. Translating Content to Online

10. The Mechanics of Putting Your Materials Online

Lesson 5

What Is the Online Environment?

LESSON OUTLINE

5.1 THE BEGINNING (ABOUT COMPUTERS)
5.2 WHAT IS THE INTERNET?
5.3 THE WORLD WIDE WEB (WWW)

WHAT YOU WILL LEARN FROM THIS LESSON

YOU WILL BE ABLE TO:

1. Identify and define the major components of a computer including the microprocessor, expansion slots, and ports.
2. Define the terms RAM, ROM, CPU, MHz, MB, and OS.
3. Describe and use the Internet, the WWW, domain name, Internet host, TCP/IP, online service, search engines, ISP, and modems.
4. Identify and list the skills and software you should have to take or deliver an online course.

LESSON 5: WHAT IS THE ONLINE ENVIRONMENT?

5.1 The Beginning (About Computers)

Computers are your tools in the online environment just as a hammer and saw are tools of the carpenter. You will want to select the tools that make your online adventure more pleasurable and achievable. In this chapter you will learn information that will help to select those tools. In following chapters, we will guide you on how to apply those tools most efficiently in the online environment. You will be able to experience everything important to online learning at websites that we provide or link to along the way. There are many links in this chapter to download free files, obtain useful information, find Internet service providers, log on to sample chatrooms, and much more. We're appearing before a wide audience in this book, and some of you are well beyond these initial concepts. Some are not. All of you will need to know what's in these sections at some point in your online course development. I have found that even experienced computer users find sparkles of useful information glittering among the paragraphs.

The Computer — What's a MHz?

A computer is an electronic device that is told what to what to do by a set of instructions stored in its own memory. Computers can receive data in the form of words, numbers, letters, audio, or graphics and manipulate this information to create something such as a newsletter, a multimedia presentation, a spreadsheet, an audio clip, a Web page, or a database. The data is input into the computer through a keyboard, a mouse, a microphone, a drawing tablet, or from storage media (hard disk, CD-ROM, DVD-ROM, or Zip disk) (Fig. 5.1). The data is manipulated and then output to a printer, a speaker, monitor, or storage media (Fig. 5.2). Computers can also be used to communicate with other computers at a distance through a modem and so allow users to view Web pages, send files, exchange email, talk to each other in real time, and even see each other through the use of videocams.

Why do you need to know about a CPU? It is the heart of the computer. The **central processing unit** (CPU) or processor (Fig. 5.3) manages most of the computer operations, and when you purchase software, or use an online course delivery platform, or buy a scanner, then you need to know whether your CPU is compatible. All information coming into the computer passes through the CPU where it is processed. The processor in a **personal computer** (PC) is often called a microprocessor and includes a control unit, an arithmetic/logic unit, a system clock, and registers (Fig. 5.4).[1] Examples of microprocessors used in the PC include the Intel style Pentium® processor and the Celeron® processor, while the Macintosh employs a Motorola PowerPC® microprocessor (Fig. 5.5).

The **control unit** in the CPU manages most of the computer operations by obtaining an instruction, decoding it, and then carrying out the instruction and storing it if required.

DEVELOPMENT

HEADS UP
There are many websites mentioned throughout this unit that will provide downloadable free graphics, audio, animated gif files, and other useful items. Don't forget to visit our dedicated website at (**http://www.mhhe. com/ucanteachon line**) for hands-on experience.

Figure 5.1
Various types of
hardware for
inputting data into
a computer

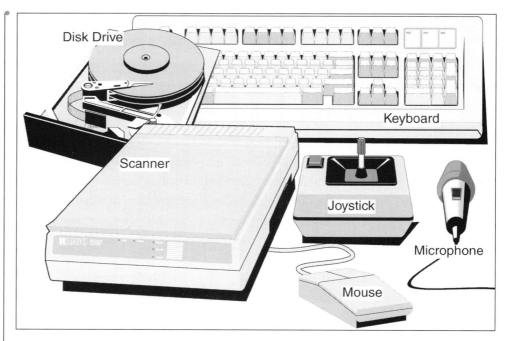

Figure 5.2
Output devices
(monitors, storage
media, printers)

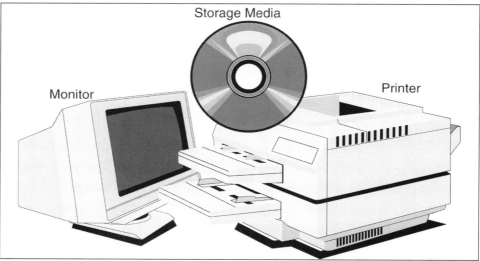

Addition, subtraction, division, or multiplication operations are performed by the **arithmetic/logic** unit of the CPU. Comparison operations (<, >, =) or logical operations (and, or, but, not) are also performed in this unit. The **registers** in the CPU are used to hold data and instructions temporarily while awaiting some operation. The computer operations require timing and synchronization that is accomplished by a small microcomputer chip referred to as a **system clock**. The clock generates electronic pulses that regulate the number of instructions passing through the CPU. Clock speed is measured in megahertz. One

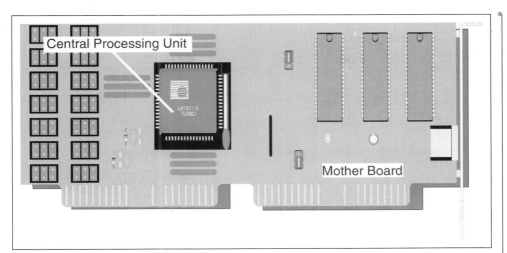

Figure 5.3
The central processing unit (CPU) is located on the mother board

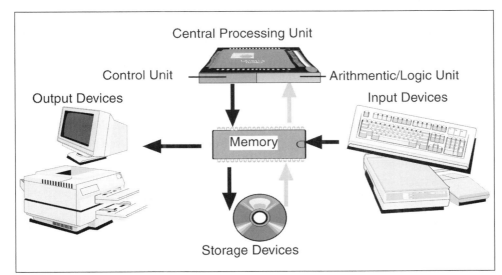

Figure 5.4
Organization of a typical microprocessor and its relation to other computer devices

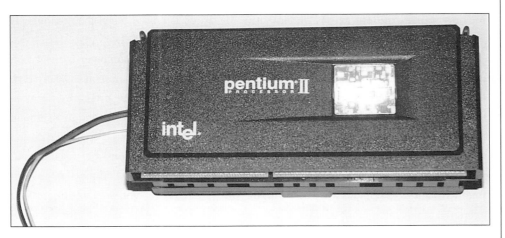

Figure 5.5
Example of a microprocessor. This is an Intel Pentium II©

Figure 5.6
Minimum system requirements for running Microsoft Office 2000

PC with Pentium 75 MHz or higher processor.	**Additional Items or Services May Be Required to Use Certain Features**
16 MB RAM for the operating system (Windows 95/98/2000) plus an additional 4 MB of RAM for each application running simultaneously.	14,400 or higher-baud modem recommended.
32 MB of RAM for the NT operating system plus an additional 4 MB of RAM for each application running simultaneously.	Multimedia computer required to access sound and other multimedia effects. Microsoft Mail, Microsoft Exchange, Internet SMTP/POP3, IMAP4, or other MAPI compliant software required to use email.
189 MB of available hard disk space.	Microsoft Exchange Server required by certain advanced collaboration functionality on Outlook.
CD-ROM drive.	
VGA or higher resolution monitor.	Some Internet functionality may require Internet access and payment of a separate fee to a service provider and local charges may apply
A Microsoft mouse or compatible pointing device.	

megahertz (MHz) is equal to one million pulses per second. The faster the clock speed, the more instructions may be processed per second. Clock speeds of 500 MHz are very common in PCs today, while clock speeds of more than 1000 MHz are already appearing in some CPUs. The CPU will run faster at higher clock speeds and so run programs faster such as word processors, graphics, and databases. However, peripheral devices such as printers and scanners do not increase their speed in accordance with the CPU clock speed.[1]

Computers have two types of memory. The system software is normally stored in nonvolatile memory known also as **read only memory** (ROM) which are maintained when the computer power is off. Application program instructions (word processors for example) and any data being processed by the application program are stored in volatile memory called **random access memory** (RAM) which is erased when the computer is turned off or loses power.

In order to run the program (i.e, Microsoft Word) when the computer is turned on again, the application program must be reloaded from a storage device such as a hard disk (usually the C drive). If the computer has sufficient RAM, several programs may run simultaneously which will be more efficient when needing to move back and forth among programs. Programs are continually being designed to perform more complex tasks and so consume more RAM. Therefore, as updated versions of programs are installed and multiple programs are run, there needs to be greater amounts of RAM. Typically, the minimum system requirements are printed on the software packages you are installing. As an example, the installation of Microsoft Office 2000 requires 16 MB of RAM for the operating system and 4 MB of RAM for each application running simultaneously and 8 MB for Outlook (Fig. 5.6). It is recommended that computers to be used in the home have at least 32 MB of RAM while those used in the office start at 64 MB of RAM.

The instructions that a computer must follow to upload the operating system are stored in ROM so that they remain intact when the power to the computer is off. The ROM instructions are recorded when the chip is manufactured so that the data (**firmware**) is permanent. The **operating system** (OS) is a set of instructions that manage and coordinate the hardware devices and run the applications software. Windows 95/98/2000 and MacOS-9 are examples of operating system software that have evolved into true multitasking operating systems supporting multimedia capabilities, networking environments, and Internet integration. You will have to know which of these systems you are running to determine compatibility with program software and online courses delivery platforms.

What's Inside?

So why do you need to know what's inside the computer? Hopefully you will never have to open up the case and look inside. However, you will certainly hear about expansion cards, disk drives, internal modems, and so forth. You may even have to install one of these at some time. I think it's important enough at least to familiarize you with some of the terminology. You never know when a student might ask you a question.

The metal or plastic case that holds the electronic components of the computer is referred to as the **system unit**. The system unit normally houses expansion slots where circuit boards may be inserted that provide additional memory, modem, video capture, sound, networking, and interface cards. Interface cards connect with scanners, external CD-ROM drives, and other devices. Installing expansion cards in recently constructed computers is simplified tremendously by **Plug-and-Play** technology that automatically configures expansion cards (or other devices) when the computer is subsequently turned on after the device installation. If you have a laptop computer, then you probably have an expansion slot where a PC card may be installed. **PC cards** can be used to add memory, sound, fax/modem, disk drives, and other capabilities. These cards are often referred to as **PCMIA** (Personal Computer Memory Card International Association) since they must adhere to a set of standards that allow interchangeability. The PC cards come in three thicknesses referred to as Type I (thinnest cards, usually memory); Type II (modems); and Type III (thickest, usually hard drives).[1]

Making a Connection

Whether you move your computer around, buy a new scanner or printer, or accidentally disconnect a cable, you need to make a connection to one or more ports on your computer. It's part of the knowledge base of becoming an online instructor. Located on the

Figure 5.7
Examples of vari-
ous types of com-
puter connections

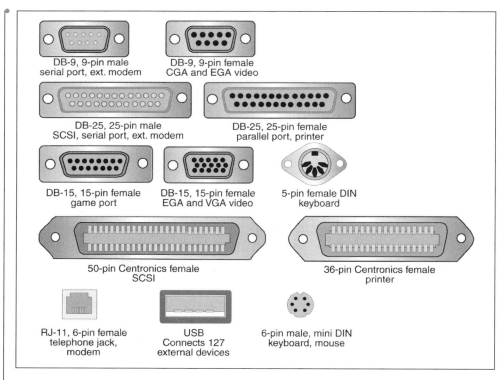

back of most system units are a variety of **ports** that serve as connection points or interfaces to external devices such as a mouse, monitor, printer, speakers, microphone, scanner, drawing tablet, modem, or other peripheral devices. The ports come with different
types of connectors that join the peripheral devices to the computer via a cable.
Connectors are normally referred to as **female connectors** (holes to accept pins of male
connectors) or **male connectors** (exposed pins). Examples of various types of connectors
are shown in figure 5.7. It is important to understand the shorthand or naming convention
used to identify connectors (i.e., *DB-9, 9 pin male*) since most certainly you will be
applying these connectors to some peripheral device.

The **Universal Serial Bus** (USB) can connect up to 127 different external devices by
connecting them serially one to another in a chain sometimes called a daisy chain. Most
new digital cameras, joysticks, DVD-ROMs, and other devices come with a USB connector and also support Plug-and-Play technology and Hot Plugging. **Hot Plugging**
means the device may be plugged in while the computer is running and will be recognized
by Plug-and-Play so that it will automatically configure the device for immediate use.

The **Small Computer System Interface** (SCSI: pronounced *skuzzy*) port is a high-
speed parallel port used to attach external devices including printers, disk drives, and
scanners. The SCSI port can support up to seven devices that are daisy chained together.

Another type of port is the 1394 port that is similar to a USB and can connect multiple devices with Plug-and-Play capability including printers, digital cameras, CD-ROMs, DVD-ROMS, printers, and hard disks. These ports along with USBs are gaining in popularity because of the improved function over serial and SCSI port connections.[1]

Making a Decision (What to Buy?)

So what computer should you get? You're going to be doing online work. If you are using a PC, your minimum requirements should be 32 MB of RAM, a Pentium II processor, a 28.8 kbps modem, and a sound card. If you're going with a Macintosh, you should have at least a MacOS 8.0 operating system, a Power PC® processor, 32 MB of RAM, a 28.8 kbps modem, and speakers (Table 5.1).[1] The more RAM, the faster the processor, and the higher the Internet speed connection you can afford, the better will be the overall experience with your online course development.

Macintosh	PC
PowerPC processor MacOS 8.1 or later 32 MB of RAM or more 28.8 kbps modem or faster (high-speed cable connection would be ideal) Sound card Speakers	Pentium II or faster Windows 95/98/2000/NT 32 MB of RAM or more 28.8 kbps modem or faster (high-speed cable connection would be ideal) Sound card Speaker

Table 5.1
Recommended minimum hardware for instructing or taking online courses[1]

Skills You Should Have to Start

You will need certain basic skills to develop and manage a Web-based course (Table 5.2). [2] This book provides information on many of those skills. If you aren't comfortable with any of the recommended skills, then you should contact your information technology (IT) people at the business or school where you work to see if they offer basic courses in these areas. Very often there will be adult education courses in computer basics offered by a nearby two-year college. When you are comfortable with some of the basic operations, then your experience with online learning can begin.

Software You Might Want

You will need certain software to develop materials for your course or to read, listen, or view materials on the Web (Table 5.3). [2, 3]   Many of the software applications are plug-ins and come at no cost. These plug-ins make it possible for your browser to play streaming audio or video, read certain file types (PDF), view 3-D, activate live voice chat and

DEVELOPMENT

Table 5.2
Recommended minimum skills for instructiing or taking online courses[2]

Computer	Word-Process	Email	Internet
Write down and understand your computer type (i.e., PC); hard disk size (in MB), memory (RAM), and software programs.	Select and open a current word-processing program Microsoft Word or Wordperfect.	Send and receive email messages. You must have an email account with your ISP who will also provide you with an email address.	Type in URL and navigate to specific websites. Move backward and forward to visited sites, use links, scroll bars, bookmarks, and refresh tools.
Organize files, rename files, navigate (locate) programs and files, open and close files.	Create and format paragraphs and documents, cut and paste text, and change fonts.	Create and organize an electronic address book in your email program. Create mailboxes for groups of students or certain interests (projects).	Use search engines such as Yahoo!, Dogpile, AltaVista, and others. Identify sites with relevant information and bookmark those sites.
Load files from the Internet or CD-ROM.	Name and save documents as files.	Create filters that steer incoming email into certain mailboxes.	Create and organize bookmarks.
Perform routine maintenance on your computer such as updating anti-virus software, and running utilities programs such as Norton or similar programs built into Windows98/2000/NT.	Save files in different formats such as .rtf, .doc., and .txt.	Attach files to email and open email attachments.	Maintain recent versions of Web browser by downloading latest versions off the Web. Activate certain features of your browser such as "cookies."

display many other multimedia files. Some of the software is expensive (in the range of $600) and requires sophisticated skill levels with a steep learning curve. These programs are for those who have the interest and ability to create illustrations, animations, video clips, audio clips, and other multimedia materials. Certainly most faculty will want to have many of these done for them. They can obtain many of these materials accessing pre-existing course materials and template libraries or seeking out graphic designers and multimedia specialists on their campus.

Software	Available at	Purpose
Acrobat Reader **Plug-in**	Free on the Internet at **http://www.adobe.com**	View, print, and move around in PDF files that appear similar to the printed version complete with page layout and graphics.
Internet Explorer	Free on the Internet at **http://www.microsoft.com/ie/download**	Web browser
Netscape	Free on the Internet at **http://www.cgi.netscape.com/cgibin/upgrade.cgi**	Web browser
Shockwave Flash Player **Plug-in**	Free on the Internet at **http://www.macrome-dia.com**	Allows user to see dynamic and interactive multimedia, streaming audio, and graphics created with Macromedia Flash.
Realplayer G2 **Plug-in**	Free on the Internet at **http://www.real.com**	Reads streaming audio and video files allowing fast, live, on-demand high-quality audio and video viewing.
Quicktime **Plug-in**	Free on the Internet at **http://www.apple.com**	A plug-in for the Apple computer that permits a Web browser to display animation, play music and video, and present 3-D virtual reality.
Ichat **Plug-in**	Free on the Internet at **http://www.acuit.com**	Allows Web access to thousands of chatrooms permitting live synchronous communication with voice.

Table 5.3
Recommended software[2]

DEVELOPMENT

Table 5.3
Recommended
software[2]

Software	Available at	Purpose
Microsoft Office Suite (Word, Excel, Powerpoint)	Your school bookstore, computer software retailer, online e-store. There is a cost.	A collection or suite that includes a word-processor, a spreadsheet program, and a graphical presentation application. Highly recommended.
Macromedia Freehand, Flash, Authorware, Fireworks Powerpoint)	Your school bookstore, computer software retailer, online e-store. There is a cost.	For advanced users who wish to create their own multimedia presentations on the Web.
Adobe Photoshop	Your school bookstore, computer software retailer, online e-store. There is a cost.	An image editor useful in editing and modifying scanned images for the Web. This is often provided with newly purchased scanners.

5.2 What Is the Internet?

The Internet refers to an international system of interlinked computers that all use a specific set of communication rules known as **Transmission Control Protocol/Internet Protocol** (TCP/IP). This protocol makes the transmission of data possible among almost any type of computer and transmission system including cables, telephone lines, or satellite. The TCP/IP standards determine how the digital information is formatted, how the messages find their target, how widely different computers can talk with each other, and the ways in which software programs must connect with the information being sent over the Internet. Every message is separated into small discrete data packages along with a header that contains the addresses of the sender and the targeted receiver. Think of entire messages as a caravan of identical cars with numbers on top that follow a sequence (i.e, 100, 101, 102, etc.). The cars become separated at an intersection and take different routes. They all arrive at their destination where they line up in sequence in the same way they started. TCP/IP represents the rules that allow data messages to do the same. They must all arrive at the final destination and be reassembled into the original sequence or message. The data packets travel over telephone lines, optical cables, or even via satellite through the Internet host computers that monitor this electronic highway. The packets are sent along until they reach their intended destination (determined by the Internet address) and are reassembled for delivery to the intended recipient. If you are doing online work, you are depending heavily on this system. Sometimes the transmission of data is very fast, and sometimes it becomes quite sluggish, just as traffic jams on the Interstate occur at certain times of the day.

How do the packets of information know where to go? A universally accepted set of rules provide a naming system to specifically identify any computer in the world. Every host computer has a unique address known as an **Internet protocol** (IP) address. The IP address is a combination of a domain, subdomain, and individual computer address. The IP address consists of four groups of numbers separated by a period. The numbers in each group may be from 0 to 255. As an example. **206.132.104.77** may represent an IP address. If you would like to know the IP address of your particular computer go to **http://www.whatismyipaddress.com**. However, numbers are usually difficult to remember or associate with a particular recipient so a host name that corresponds to the number is usually used (for example, **http://www.ecollege.com)**. This corresponding text version contains the **domain name**. This address represents a critical component of the **uniform resource locator** (URL) which the Web uses to find resources. Every domain also has a **top-level domain** that identifies the organizational type operating the site (Fig. 5.8). There have been seven top-level domain names. Recently, several more have been released (Table 5.4). These domain names are registered and stored on a **domain name system** server (DNS servers) where the domain names are translated into an IP address for correct routing to the destination computer.[3]

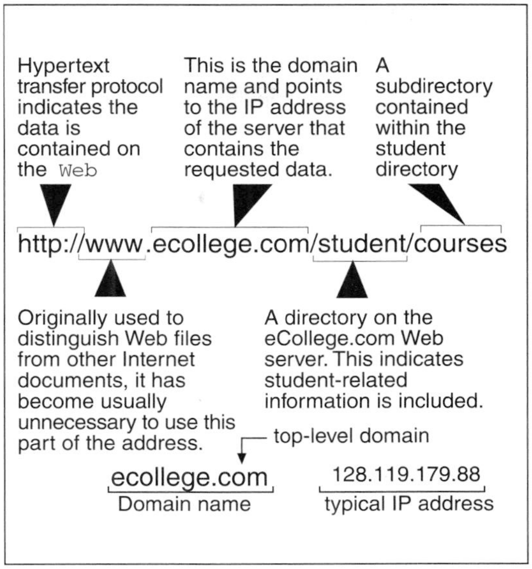

Figure 5.8
How domain names work

Table 5.4 Current and newly released top-level domain names

Current Names		Newly Released	
Extension	**Use**	**Extension**	**Use**
.com	commercial	.arts	arts and culture
.edu	education	.firm	business or
.gov	government		agency
.int	international	.info	information
	organization		services
.mil	military	.nom	personal or
.net	gateway or		family
	host	.rec	recreation/
.org	non-profit		entertainment
	organization	.shop	online retail
		.web	Web activities

How the Internet Started

The Internet was originally developed in 1969 through the efforts of a Department of Defense group known as the Advanced Research Projects Agency (ARPA). They built a system that allowed scientists and military personnel to collaborate by way of computers at a distance. They also designed into the system the ability to continue functioning even if large parts of the system were destroyed. Other government agencies joined this effort and integrated their high-speed computers into the network thereby becoming a **host**. The hosts were directly connected to the network and could store and transfer data at high speed (much like a superhighway) while permitting other computers to connect along the major arteries much like side roads. The system of high-speed host computers became known as the **backbone** of the Internet. The Internet backbone has been hosted by commercial firms and corporations since 1995. The structure of the Internet is an independent and largely public system that depends on the cooperation of government, commercial, and educational organizations along with cable, satellite, and telephone companies.

Connecting to the Internet

Although the Internet is a cooperative entity and no single agency or person controls it, there are costs associated with constructing and maintaining the computers and connections. Some of these costs are passed onto users. In order to connect to the Internet you need a computer that links by cable, telephone lines, or satellite to an **Internet service provider** (ISP). The ISP has a permanent connection to the Internet and normally charges a fee to the temporary user. This is not the case for most faculty and many businesses that supply a free connect service to their employees. There are also companies such as *Yahoo.com* and *Hotmail.com* that provide free email accounts. Most companies charge a fee for connection. The fee for those connected to a commercial service is usually a fixed monthly charge with unlimited use. Other ISPs charge an hourly rate beyond a preset monthly time limit. There are many national and numerous local ISPs. These services should all provide access to a local telephone or cable service that allows you to connect to the Internet without long distance charges. Many of the ISPs provide additional services to their members including chatrooms, information, news, sports, weather, financial information, games, places to create and store your own website, and even travel guides. Such ISPs become identified as an **online service**. National online services include America Online (AOL), Microsoft Network (MSN), and numerous others. You should be aware that AOL, Compuserve, and Prodigy are national ISPs that provide an internal Web browser that may be a modified or older version of Internet Explorer (IE). Such modified browsers may not support all of the features of your online course delivery platform. Therefore, you should plan to use recent versions of IE or Netscape. If you are using a national ISP such as AOL, Compuserve, or Prodigy, you can switch to IE and it will function through the connection you make. For a listing of ISPs try the following URL (**http://www.thelist.com**). Reliable ISPs may also include AT&T at (**http://www.att.net**) or Earthlink at (**http://www.concentric.net).**

What Will You Need to Connect to the Internet?

Once you have your personal computer in place, you will need to have a physical link to the Internet and the software to decode and interpret the signals arriving and leaving your computer. There are four common types of communication devices that transmit data, instructions, and information. These include a modem, cable modem, network interface card (NIC), and multiplexer (MUX). The type of connection you and your students make to the Internet will be very important in determining your speed of transmission and therefore the types of materials you may choose to use online. As an example, a faculty member from another college said she wanted to show her class an online movie clip but the pictures were choppy and unclear. I suggested the transmission speeds were slow and she should have the students view this in the computer labs where they would be connected to high-speed transmission lines. It worked! She was delighted at the quality of picture and sound. The connection speeds to the Internet are quite important in determining what limitations you may have in delivering online course materials. The following examples provide information that is valuable in making decisions about the type of physical connection you make to the Internet.

Modem

There are dozens of manufacturers of modems. These modems may be an internal modem that is an expansion card residing within your computer or an external modem that sits outside of your computer and normally attaches to a serial port on your computer and to a telephone outlet with a standard jack and cable. The modem converts the digital signal of the computer to an analog signal that can be transmitted across telephone lines (MODulation) and a modem at the other end reconverts the analog signal back to a digital signal (DEModulate). The rate at which this data processing takes place is measured in kilobytes per second (Kbps). Modems connected to standard telephone lines operate at up to 56 Kbps. The faster the rate of information transfer, the more rapidly files, messages, and data can be sent among computers connected by modems. Typical dial-up telephone lines seldom allow for a full 56 Kbps transmission rate. The dial-up connection is temporary, and the quality of the connection is varied because the phone company switches lines based on telephone traffic. It is possible to obtain much faster transmission speed over conventional phone lines by using an **integrated services digital network** (ISDN). The ISDN can carry from three to twenty-four signals. The small business or individual can usually obtain a three-signal ISDN called a Basic Rate Interface (BRI) for under $60 a month. If you have a digital line that carries multiple signal such as an ISDN line, you will require a multiplexing device that tags each stream of data and then combines those streams into a single stream for transmission across telephone lines. Another multiplexer at the receiving end separates the signals base on the tags and delivers the data to the intended device.If the phone is also to be used on the same line, a specially adapted telephone will be required. Another alternative is the **digital subscriber line** (DSL) that incorporates a technology which is able to transmit a greater number of bytes per second on a standard twisted-pair cable. The transmission of data can be faster than ISDN and is generally more costly averaging $60 to $110 per month.Check with your ISP to see if they offer this option. There are also T-1 and T-3 digital carrier lines that are capable of transmitting up to 1.5 Mbps and 45 Mbps respectively, but they cost about $1,000 and $10,000 per month. This is generally out of the range of most professors and students.

Cable Modem

Many cable television (CATV) providers now provide a service and equipment to transmit data over coaxial cables that bring the Internet signal into the home. A cable splitter divides the signal between the television and the cable modem attached to the personal computer. Both internal and external cable modems are available with transmission rates of 500 Kbps to 2Mbps. These transmission speeds are 10 to 40 times greater than over the typical telephone line. This means that you will have very fast download and upload times, excellent videoconferencing, and multimedia capabilities. Cable services now reach more than half of all American homes. However, not all cable companies also provide this Internet service. Check with your local cable company to see if such a service is provided. The rates are currently from $30 to $60 a month.

The LAN

Many schools and businesses maintain a local area network (LAN) that requires a network interface card (NIC) that is either an expansion card or a PC card. The NIC is designed to work with a specific set of protocols such as Ethernet, and is also designed to accept specialized connectors standardized for fiber-optic cable, twisted wire, or coaxial cable. The University of Massachusetts provides optical cables to offices and student dorms throughout the campus. This is ideal for rapid data transmission, but it does require a special PC or NIC card.

5.3 The World Wide Web (WWW)

The Language of the Web

When you become an online educator you will be using the World Wide Web (WWW). The WWW is just one of many services available on the Internet and was introduced in 1990 as a collection of electronic hyper-linked documents residing on computers around the world. The Web page or website (a collection of related Web pages) is accessed by typing in its specific address within a browser. The address is known as the URL and normally includes the protocol, domain name, path, and even a document name. The majority of URLs begin with the letters http:// which stand for **hypertext transfer protocol** and identifies this as a Web page with a specific communications protocol required to transfer such pages. Web pages must be formatted in a set of standard codes collectively called **hypertext markup language** (HTML). These codes are rules that manage the appearance of colors, fonts, text styles, digital images, sounds, animations, and links within the Web page. A document shown in HTML with all the codes in place is shown in figure 5.9. This figure shows the page before the browser interprets the code and displays the page as it was intended to be seen.

You don't need to be fluent in HTML programming language to write Web pages. There are a wide variety of HTML editors avaiable that give you the ability to create dynamic Web pages with little or no knowledge of HTML. These editors have automatic programming features that do all the complicated HTML work for you behind the scenes while you use familiar tools and actions to build your Web pages. You will be able to see the graphics, colors, text, buttons, and other features as you construct the Web pages. Periodically you can use the same software to view the construct Web page(s) in a typical browser. Some of the popular HTML editors include Macromedia Dreamweaver®, Claris Homepage®, Adobe Frontpage®, and Netscape Composer®.

Browsers

The two most commonly used browsers are Netscape Communicator® and Microsoft Internet Explorer®. One or the other of these browsers is normally provided when: (1) you purchase a computer; (2) subscribe to certain ISPs; or (3) purchase certain types of software. You may decide to use one or the other of these browsers. The most recent version

DEVELOPMENT

 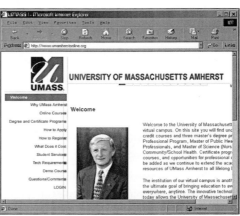

Figure 5.9
 A document shown in HTML code (left) and its appearance when displayed by a browser (right)

of each may be downloaded from the Web at no cost to you. In order to download the latest version of Internet Explorer go to (**http://www.microsoft.com/ie/download)** and follow the directions for "saving the program to disk." The current version of Internet Explorer at the writing of this text is 5.5. Save the file (**ie5setup**) to your desktop as an application, so you will be able to easily locate it when the download is complete. Once the download is finished, you can click on the installation program (ie5setup) and installation will proceed automatically. Similarly for the Macintosh, you will need to click on the download file titled "IE installer."[3, 4]

Downloading the latest version of Netscape follows a similar pattern. The latest version of Netscape at the writing of this text is Netscape 4.72. The upgrade location for Netscape is (**http://cgi.netscape.com/cgi-bin/upgrade.cgi**.) Netscape will analyze your current browser and recommend a later version if appropriate. Follow the instructions to download the Netscape program for free. Save the file to your desktop where you will be able to easily find it. Write down the name of the file. It may resemble something like **cc32e45.exe**. Close any open files and click on the setup file for installing Netscape.[1, 4]

The Web pages must be stored on a computer or server that sends out the requested Web pages to your computer. When you type the desired URL into your browser and request the Web pages from the service, the pages are sent to your computer. Normally you enter a website at the beginning or **home page**. The Web pages are normally linked to other Web pages or files through hyperlinks allowing a user to move from the topic of interest to another following the links as branches in a tree based on your interest or selection. Links on the Web may appear as underlined text or differently colored text, highlighted images, animated buttons, or other graphic images. When you point to a link, the URL for the link normally shows up in the browser window in the **address bar**. Click on the link and you may be taken to: (1) another section of the same page; (2) another page in the same website; (3) another website altogether anywhere in the world; or (4) to a file to download. Simple pages will load quickly, while more complex ones with many graphics or multimedia presentations will load more slowly. Keeping your eye on the task bar will tell you when the document has completely transferred (downloaded) to your computer. When downloading is complete, the words "document done" or "done" will usually appear in the task bar.

Browsers normally have many functions beyond simply reading Web pages and linking to the next one. As an example the Internet Explorer browser has a number of functions all of which may be accessed by the buttons in the toolbar. Included among these functions are email, audio and video conferencing, saving the URLs of favorite sites with bookmarks, document sharing, Web searching, creating and editing pages, and even Web shopping. If you want to know more about Internet Explorer try taking a tour at the following URL (**http://www.microsoft.com/windows/ie/tour/**).

Search Engines and Portals

Many websites and browsers provide access to information through **search engines**. Search engines are used to locate websites with topics of interest by typing in key words or phrases and then pressing the designated key to submit the search request to the appropriate server. There are numerous search engines. Some are designed to search within a website while others will search large parts of the Internet. Still others such as (**http://www.dogpile.com**) simultaneously search many engines. Dogpile.com is a leading **metasearch** service that integrates several medium and large Web search and index guides into a single service by providing a single launch point. Websites such as Dogpile.com, Yahoo!, AltaVista, Netscape Netcenter, and Lycos offer multiple services such as search engines, weather, news, sports, yellow and white page directories, chat rooms, and emails. Such websites are often called **portals**. Entering the words <online course> will return a list of websites (hits) that contain the words entered into the search field. In this case, the metasearch engine returns with hits based on the combined words <online course> and on the words individually <online> and <course>. The search may be narrowed by placing commas before and after the search phrase. The search is then based only on the combined words found within the commas. Many search engines use Boolean logic (and, or, but) providing a powerful tool to limit searches to specific subjects. A detailed explanation of Boolean search logic may be found at (**http://www.albany.edu/library/internet/boolean.html**). Many of these sites are organized into directories of special topics or interest such as arts and humanities, business and economy, education, entertainment, recreation and sports, and so forth. These categories help to find information on a particular topic more easily.

Mainstream browsers such as Netscape® and Microsoft Internet Explorer® come equipped to display many of the multimedia elements on a Web page. However, more advanced multimedia features including streaming audio and video and interactive multimedia such as voice may require additional add-on programs or **plug-ins** to be used with the browser. These plug-ins are normally downloaded for free off the Web and extend the capability of your browser. Examples of common plug-ins, their uses, and the websites from which they may be downloaded are shown in Table 5.3.

REFERENCES

1. **Shelly, G. B., T. J. Cashman, M. E. Vermaat, and T. J. Walker.** 1999. "Discovering Computers 2000, Concepts for a Connected World." *Course Technology*, One Main Street, Cambridge, MA 02142.

2. **ECollege.** "How to Design, Develop, and Teach an Online Course." *Handbook. eCollege,* System 3.0.eCollege.com, Denver, Colorado.

3. **Soper, M. E.** 2000. "Deciphering Domain Names." *Internet Basics, Smart Computing Learning Series*, Vol. 6, Issue 1, pp. 29-33.

4. **Hannah, H**. 2000. "Configuring and Setting Up Web Browsers." *Internet Basics, Smart Computing Learning Series*, Vol. 6, Issue 1, pp. 61-63.

What Are the Tools of the Trade?

Lesson 6

What Are the Tools of the Trade?

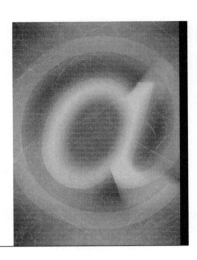

LESSON OUTLINE

6.1 USEFUL TOOLS FOR ADDING ZIP TO WEBSITES
6.2 INTERACTIVE TOOLS

WHAT YOU WILL LEARN FROM THIS LESSON

YOU WILL BE ABLE TO:

1. Identify, define, import and use the most common image, sound, and video formats used in the construction of websites.
2. Describe and use interactive tools such as email, chatrooms, threaded discussions, mailing lists, and white boards. You will also be able to transfer files using email or FTP.

LESSON 6: WHAT ARE THE TOOLS OF THE TRADE?

6.1 Useful Tools for Adding Zip to Websites

Images (Still and Animated)

Excitement and interest in an online course can be increased dramatically with the use of images. Images are also an excellent instructional tool. I use numerous line drawings and photographs in my online courses that support the course materials much as they would in a richly illustrated textbook. Students can download detailed class notes from my courses materials. Throughout the notes are numerous links to figures that the students may choose to view and/or download as well. Nearly all of the students download the notes, and many also download and print out the detailed figures. I also use extensive animations at the front end or introductory portions of each unit. These animations are designed to be relevant to the topic and often humorous to attract student attention. You don't need to know how to create animations. You can obtain them free along with Web objects or graphics at hundreds of websites. For a comprehensive listing of 100 of the top websites offering copyright free graphics and animations try (**http://www.clipart.com**).

Figure 6.1
Typical use of JPEG using photographic material with many fine shades

Most browsers recognize several graphic forms including the commonly used **JPEG** (pronounced JAY-peg) and **GIF** (pronounced jiff) formats. Both of these formats compress the file size so that download times are faster. Generally it's a good idea to limit the image file size to 60K or less since larger files will slow the downloading of Web pages and lead to student frustration. I use JPEG (Joint Photographic Experts Group) files for images having numerous subtle color transitions such as photographs (Fig 6.1). I'll explain later in the book those specific steps,

equipment, and software you will need to create such images. When I create line drawings or illustrations, or use them from copyright-free sources, they normally have fewer color transitions and are ideally compressed as GIF (Graphic Interchange Format) files (Fig 6.2). Files created in GIF are usually much smaller than JPEG, and it is in this format that many of the animations are created (animated gifs). If you would

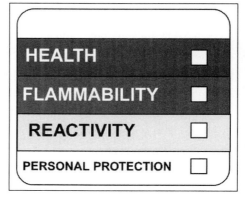

Figure 6.2
Typical use of GIF using few colors and sharp contrast

DEVELOPMENT

like to see an animated GIF try (**http://www.clipart.com**/). Animated GIFs are created using an animation software package such as Macromedia Fireworks (now in version 3.0). Multiple images are linked together and played in sequence giving the appearance of motion much like flipping through a series of drawings on a pad of paper. You can find animations, graphics, hard to find HTML, Javascript, Java Applets, and other resources to build your Web page at (**http://www.bellsnwhistles.com**). You may also purchase large collections of copyright free Web objects, animated GIFs, Java buttons, photos, and videos on CD-ROMs. Try the following website (**http://www.xoom.com**). to purchase a 5-set CD-ROM collection called the Web Empire, or go to (**http://www.animfactory.com/**) for purchasing CD-ROM collections of animations and clip art suitable for Web design projects.

Audio

I also use audio in my online courses. I like to use a lively music piece in the introduction, but most of the audio files are narrations associated with the slides that accompany the class notes. I also inform the user that clicking on the right mouse button (PC) allows them to turn off that sound file for that session. These narrations may play by clicking on the Realplayer icon and the linked sentence. The audio files used on my site are in **.wav** format, although the Web recognizes **.au** files as well. Audio files tend to be large, and although I adjust the size of the files downward by converting them to mono and reducing the sound quality by half, the typical one- to two-minute audio narrative file is still 1.5 to three megabytes. If you needed to download these entire files before playing them, you would certainly become frustrated. Fortunately, a technology has been developed that instantly begins to feed (stream) the audio file into your computer so that it plays immediately from the beginning while downloading the next parts in sequence. This process is known as **streaming audio** and is normally supported on the Web by a plug-in called Realplayer. A free version of the basic Realplayer plug-in is available at (**http://www.real.com**). Click on the icon that reads "Free RealPlayer." You may be asked to fill out some information including your operating system (Windows 95, 98, 2000, NT, Mac); your CPU (Pentium 486, Pentium II, Pentium III, PowerPC); your connection (28.8 modem, cable modem, etc.); language (English, German, French); your name and email address. You may begin to see why lesson 5 has some importance to this process. Download and save the file to your desktop. The file is likely to have a title such as *rp7-standard-setup.exe*. Click on this setup file and follow the installation procedures.

Streaming audio is also used to broadcast live radio shows, music, concerts, and even live lectures. If you have a sound card and an updated browser with a Realplayer plug-in go to (**http://www.real.com**) and listen to a live radio show or music. You can also use Web-based audio and a microphone to converse with people just as you would a telephone.

There are a number of programs that allow you to do this for no cost beyond the Internet connection. You can find examples at (**http://www.ichat.com**). I use audio conferencing or **livechat** on my website. You can install a livechat capability on your website at no cost by simply cutting and pasting a few lines of HTML code into your Web page from the following location (**http://www.hearme.com**). I have live discussions with many students at different locations including England, Japan, San Diego, and Nova Scotia. Students who don't have a microphone can also type in their question or comments. There are more advanced versions of this conferencing capability. You may already have access on your computer to Microsoft Netmeeting. This is available as a component of Internet Explorer. A **Wizard** guides you through the setup process and allows you to audio and or video conference with many other participants using a microphone and videocam. In addition to conversing live, many of the videoconferencing software applications allow you to display illustrations and photographs, type in messages, and even see video images of those who have videocams attached to their computers.

Video

Internet video conferencing is made possible by **videostreaming** technology.[1] Later versions of Netscape and Microsoft Internet Explorer browsers support Realvideo or related browser plug-ins such as **RealPlayer**. RealPlayer 8 is the most recent streaming media player available at the writing of this text from (**www.real.com**). Such plug-ins allow you to view live video images or video clips by streaming the data over the Internet so that video and sound begin playing immediately without having to first download megabyte-sized files. The videos are normally compressed into **MPEG** (Motion Picture Experts Group) format to further reduce the size of the files allowing for faster transmission of digitized video. If you are interested in viewing video or even live television over the computer go to (**www.real.com**).

6.2 Interactive Tools

Email

The Internet began by transmitting messages and files through a computer network. The transmission of such messages and files became known as email. The use of the Internet for email transmission is still among its most used services. Email is a very effective way to communicate with students. You can use email to:

1. Create distribution lists for your class that allow you to send announcements and updates to the entire class simultaneously or to subgroups within the class.
2. Create replies that load automatically for students, such as "I received your assignment."
3. Create mailboxes or folders for each student and set up the mail program filter to

direct incoming assignments or messages into each student mailbox or into an assignment mailbox.

4. Create form emails for those messages that are sent routinely, such as student grades, late assignment notices, change of exam dates, and so forth.

5. Send messages and attach documents and other file types to individual students or to the entire class.

6. Send messages to individual students in order to add a personal touch.

In order to send and receive email you will need to have a software program, a physical connection to the Internet, and an ISP. The connections and ISPs have been discussed earlier in the chapter. There are numerous software programs available to support email, but two of the most commonly used ones are Eudora and Microsoft Outlook. You will need an email address that is normally obtained when you subscribe to the service through your ISP. The address is a combination of a username and a domain name (Fig 6.3).[2] Incoming emails are placed in your assigned **mailbox** or storage location that resides on the host computer connecting you to the Internet. The message arriving at your mail server is transferred to **POP3** (Post Office Protocol) server that stores the message(s) until opened by the recipient. When you send a message, it is transmitted using a protocol referred to as **SMTP** (simple mail transfer protocol) that manages the routing and delivery of your message.[1] The majority of email programs support the attachment of audio, video, graphics, and text files to the email for transmission to the recipient. The programs will normally encode the attachment files to a binary format for transmission over the Internet, and then it is decoded at the other end when received. This requires that both the sender and the receiver have email programs that provide adequate coding/ decoding capabilities.

Figure 6.3 The email address is a combination of user name and a domain name

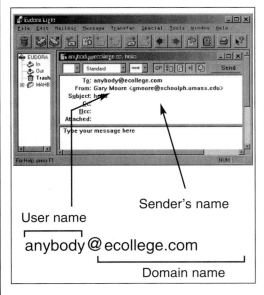

User name

Sender's name

anybody @ ecollege.com

Domain name

In order to attach a document you must begin by addressing the new message. Each email program has a slightly different way of attaching a message. Many email programs have a paper clip icon. That you can click on to attach a file. I use Eudora so I click on the word *Message* and then scroll down to *Attach file*. If you are using Outlook then click on Insert at the top of the menu and choose File. You will be asked to locate the file. Follow the paths back to your file, click on the file, and then click on "open" or "attach." You will know if the message is attached by viewing an icon of the attachment or it may appear as a text message after the word "Attached." Once attached, the program will return you to your email.

Most attached documents may be opened by double-clicking on the associated icon or text string. If that doesn't work it may be necessary to open the program in which you wish to view the file. As an example, if the attachment is a Microsoft Word file, you would open Word and click on "File" from the top menu bar and choose "Open." You would follow the directory path to the drive where your mail program files are stored ("C" drive for most) and find a folder named "attachment" or "attached files." Here you would select the document you want to open. If your program doesn't open the file, it may be that the file was created in a program that you do not have residing on your computer or do not have the necessary translators to convert the file. In such cases you may need to contact the sender and ask that a different version be sent. My suggestion is that you ask to be sent a version saved in rich text format (RTF). Saving a document in RTF is as follows. Open the document within the word processor program (i.e., Microsoft Word), click on "File" and then "save as." Scroll down the "save as type" screen until you see **Rich Text Format** (*.rtf) and click on it. Type in a name for the file and select a directory where you would like it saved. The file should have an .rtf extension and may then be attached to the email. The file will conserve the original formatting and may be opened by most word-processors operating on most computers. In a similar way it may be advantageous to save graphic files in a JPEG, GIF, or TIFF format so they may be opened by the browser. If you have a complex document that contains text and graphics together such as a newsletter, you might wish to save it in a **PDF** (portable document format). You will need a software program that supports the conversion of files to PDF. You may also purchase a program specifically to create PDF from Adobe.com called Adobe Acrobat. A plug-in program called Adobe Reader is required to read PDF files, but is available at no cost from (**http://www.adobe.com**).

Transferring Files

Building a website or online course requires the transferring or exchanging of files. Even if you have a service that does most of this for you, there will be times when you want to change, add, or alter files within your course. You will want to have some control over this process. Some platforms such as eCollege.com have a document sharing feature that allows both instructor and students to upload and download documents, images, spreadsheets, HTML pages, and small programs.[4] Students can download documents from the instructor or other students to view, build, or revise them. These documents can then be uploaded to a central site where changes may be viewed. Most hosts use a standard protocol for the transfer of files known as **FTP** (file transfer protocol). When you wish to upload or **post** Web pages to a Web server you will accomplish this through a software program that supports FTP. As an example many Web page authoring software packages such as Claris Homepage or Macromedia Dreamweaver allow you to post your completed Web pages to the Web server using a built-in FTP program. There are also stand-alone FTP software programs such as FTP Explorer that facilitate the uploading and downloading of files to the FTP server. FTP Explorer allows me to store files, upload, download, and perform a number of other functions in the management of this site.

When you download files off the Web such as plug-ins or updates, then you probably are using an FTP, although it may be invisible to you. Sites that allow you to download free software use an anonymous FTP that allows anyone to transfer the files. The system I store my website files on is limited by use of a username and a password assigned to my user account.

Chatrooms

Most online educational programs support some form of real-time interaction among students and/or faculty. This ability to communicate with one another at the same moment is called **synchronous** communication. The environment or channel in which you are communicating is called a **chatroom,** and you need a software program (chat client) on your computer that connects you to chat server. There are numerous free chat client programs available for this purpose. Some chatrooms are completely text-based and require you to type your messages to be read on-screen by chatroom participants. Other chatrooms feature real-time audio and allow you to carry on a conversation among multiple distant persons much like a teleconference. Students and instructors normally enter the chatroom at a pre-selected time to discuss course questions or issues. Some instructors use this medium to hold office hours. Chatrooms can be used for group discussions. Many chatrooms allow you to type in a URL that immediately redirects the participants to that new website. Many chatrooms allow the instructor special privileges such as muting students, disconnecting students, or even assigning special privileges to guests. This is an excellent medium for inviting special guests to participate with your class while they remain in their own country, office, or home.

Try downloading free chatroom software at (**http://www.hearme.com**) or at (**http://www.ichat.com**). Your browser may support conferencing or chatroom capabilities. You may already have access on your computer to Microsoft Netmeeting. This is available as a component of Internet Explorer and supports chatroom and videoconferencing capabilities.[3] You can communicate in the chatroom by typing a message that displays to all the other participants in the same chatroom. You may also communicate in many chatrooms by talking over a microphone, much as you would in a conference call on a telephone. Here's an idea. Kristin Hirst at "Distance Learning" supports a chatroom

on the subject of distance education at (**http://distancelearn.about.com/education/dis
tancelearn/mpchat.htm**). Stop on by on Tuesday afternoons from 1:00 to 3:00 pm
Central Daylight Time. This site also provides you with useful information and an index
of previous chats about distance learning.

Each participant is identified in the chatroom by a name they type in when they enter.
Some chatrooms allow you to choose different font styles and colors to increase the individuality. It takes a few seconds for a typed message to load and appear on the recipient
screens so that it is not instantaneous and it is good etiquette and sensible to wait a few
seconds for responses. The typed comments and questions are not always dated and saved
to a file (or archived), but may be lost when the chatroom session is ended.

When you are communicating by voice, only one person at a time is electronically
cued to talk. This prevents a lot of confusion. Some chatrooms allow you to select images
of famous people, cartoons, or animals to represent your identity while you are in chatroom to protect your anonymity. There is often a leader in the chatroom who can electronically remove guests who don't practice good netiquette. Netiquette is a cyber term
standing for Internet etiquette. There are hundreds of websites devoted to the discussion
of proper behavior while surfing the net. You might try (**http://www.albion.com/neti
quette/corerules.html**) for an interesting trip through the netiquette maze. Generally
you want to follow the same standards of behavior online that make you a good citizen in
your school or business. Don't participate in "flame" wars or "spamming." **Flames** are
abusive or insulting messages that get sent back and forth. **Spams** are unsolicited email
messages that are sent to numerous recipients at once. Don't use vulgarities online.
Respect others' online time and don't tie up the Internet connection when you are not
actively using it.

If you are using a microphone, it may be a challenge to set it up and have it
work perfectly the first time. You can obtain some help at the following URL,
(**http://www.mscomm.com/~twoton/**). If you are using Microsoft Netmeeting, the wizard will automatically guide you through the setup, testing, and use of the microphone.

Threaded Discussions

Think of an ongoing email that that allows students to log in at different times, locate
the topic of interest, and respond to it. Their response will be posted along with their
"name" and the date of their posting. Threaded discussions allow students to post comments to a discussion topic, react to other students' comments, share ideas, and even
upload text and graphics files for others to share. The online discussions take place **asynchronously** so that students can enter and leave at the time of their choice. I use the
threaded discussion to post a question or challenge for each chapter (unit). The students
are expected to respond within the week. The responses to that topic are displayed below

the topic with a time and date stamp along with name of the responder. Since all the postings are listed, each of the students may see the responses of others and benefit from the more thoughtful analysis that is possible when time is not a factor in responding. Threaded discussions may be sorted by topic, dates, or author. The entries may also be expanded so that the full text of all the entries may be displayed while also permitting the entire threaded discussion to be printed.

Mailing Lists

A mailing list is a collection of email addresses collected under a single name. I collect all my student names and email addresses and then create a single email address with all of the names entered in the address book under that single identity. When I want to communicate with my class, I compose a message, attach a file if I want, and then with a single click send the message off to an entire class. Some mailing lists allow to you select one or more individuals within the list by checking off their names on the screen and then sending the email. There are numerous mailing lists to which you may subscribe. You can use your browser search function to locate lists that may be of interest to you. Once you find one, you will be asked to **subscribe** to the list by sending along your name, email address, and other requested information to the person that manages the list. If you "pass" the entry requirements, then you will be added to the list and will receive periodic postings from the organization in your email. The list manager may be using a software program that specifically manages such lists. The commonly used program is called ListServ. Should you decide at some point that you no longer want receive emails from this organization, then you will have to unsubscribe to it. The procedures for doing this normally accompany each email that you receive from them. If not, you will need to send an email directly to the manger of the site requesting your removal.

Whiteboards

This is a window that appears on your computer screen during a video conferencing session that allows you to draw on the screen much like a chalkboard or whiteboard in the classroom. The notes and drawings you produce may be viewed at once on the screens of all the participants. Many whiteboard programs offer a variety of simple drawing tools that permit the user to offer a lecture style presentation while illustrating points on the whiteboard. You may also capture windows or portions of windows and place them on these snapshots on the whiteboard where you can draw over them to point or circle relevant objects.

A summary of the features and uses of the more commonly used interactive tools for online teaching is provided in Table 6.1. This is not inclusive. There are other interactive tools that are not yet commonly used in online instruction including video conferencing and live Webcasting. These tools require significant bandwidth, and it may be months to years before there is sufficient numbers of participants with this capability to justify wide use of these advanced technologies.

Tool	Features	Uses
Email	An asynchronous tool that allows you to send or receive messages at any time to one person, a subgroup, or an entire class. Documents and other file types may also be attached and sent.	1. Respond to individual student questions or concerns. 2. Make class announcements. 3. Encourage class to collaborate on projects using email. 4. Send out documents, graphic files, or other file types to the class.
Threaded Discussion	An asynchronous tool that allows you to post assignments to an entire class. Documents and other files types may also be attached and sent. These remain in a central site where the class may view the questions/assignment and respond at flexible times. The responses are recorded and may be viewed by the instructor and class members.	1. Post periodic discussion questions to which students are required to respond. 2. Post assignments for peer review. 3. Post graphics, tables, pictures at the site and ask students to describe, explain, or comment on the posted materials. 4. Use the site for student collaborative projects.
Chatroom	A synchronous tool that requires all participants be present online at the same time. The chatroom may be typed text, live voice, or a combination of the two. Many chatrooms also support document sharing, whiteboarding, and posting URLs so that participants may view the same website simultaneously. Some chatrooms support video conferencing as well.	1. Allows small group collaboration. 2. Experts at-a-distance may be invited to present to the class. 3. May be used by instructor for advising and holding office hours. 4. Provides high level of interaction but often not as useful as threaded discussion in inviting thoughtful students to respond.

Table 6.1 Features and uses of commonly used interactive online tools

DEVELOPMENT

REFERENCES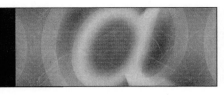

1. **Shelly, G. B., T. J. Cashman, M. E. Vermaat, and T. J. Walker.** 1999. "Discovering Computers 2000, Concepts for a Connected World." *Course Technology*, One Main Street, Cambridge, MA 02142.

2. **Soper, M. E**. 2000. "Deciphering Domain Names." *Internet Basics, Smart Computing learning Series*, Vol. 6, Issue 1, pp. 29-33.

3. **Hannah, H**. 2000. "Configuring and Setting Up Web Browsers." *Internet Basics, Smart Computing Learning Series*, Vol. 6, Issue 1, pp. 61-63.

4. **ECollege.** "How to Design, Develop, and Teach an Online Course." *Handbook. eCollege,* System 3.0.eCollege.com, Denver, Colorado.

What Are Online Course Delivery Platforms?

Lesson 7

What Are Online Course Delivery Platforms?

LESSON OUTLINE

7.1 INTRODUCTION
7.2 COMPARISONS OF COURSE DELIVERY PLATFORMS
7.3 EXAMPLES OF COURSE DELIVERY PLATFORMS
7.4 SHARING AND COMPATIBILITY

WHAT YOU WILL LEARN FROM THIS LESSON

YOU WILL BE ABLE TO:

1. Compare and contrast the majority of available online course delivery platforms.

2. Describe and appraise five online course delivery platforms including WebCT, eCollege, Prometheus, Blackboard, and McGraw-Hill PageOut.

3. Define and describe the SCORM and IMS project for producing standards related to the development of shareable courseware and learning objects.

LESSON 7: WHAT ARE ONLINE COURSE DELIVERY PLATFORMS?

7.1 Introduction

The remarkable growth in distance learning using online technologies is opening pathways for new e-businesses. As accredited schools for higher education enter the arena of online education, they are facing competition from for-profit entities that exist as virtual universities offering degrees completely online. At the same time, there is an increasing demand from higher education, K-12 instructors, and corporate training specialists for technical assistance in making the transition to online education. Companies offering such technical assistance provide a range of services that extends from course delivery systems to full service providers that create virtual online campuses, providing faculty training, marketing, student help desk services, and online college administration services. These companies are competing to produce products that make it easy for faculty to produce and deliver effective online courses. Some platforms are more intuitive and easier to use than others. Most of them provide course templates that are simply filled with course content by the faculty member. Some platforms require the faculty to know limited HTML language while others have built-in Web authoring tools. Such tools allow you to create sparkling Web pages without the need to know HTML. The HTML is created in the background by the authoring software. You can choose colors, fonts, backgrounds, graphic files, and other features without having to leave the course delivery platform. Some platforms allow the faculty to introduce JPEG, GIF, and animated GIF files. Some will support multimedia capabilities, including streaming audio and video. The pedagogically advanced platforms provide a variety of synchronous and asynchronous tools, including email, threaded discussions, bulletin boards, and newsgroups. Many provide synchronous tools including chatrooms, voice chatrooms, whiteboards, and even video conferencing. Most advanced platforms provide some mechanisms for online testing and evaluation. They allow faculty to post a variety of exam types, randomize the test questions for each student, limit the time available to each student to take the exam, and automatically grade objective exams. These platforms often allow the faculty to track the progress of students, graphically display the time spent on the computer performing certain tasks, and maintain an electronic grade book that permits the entry of objective exams and subjectively graded papers and reports. Some companies/platforms provide a variety of administrative functions. They may support online registration, online fees handling, student support, and even faculty support.

7.2 Comparisons of Course Delivery Platforms

Because there are presently more than 60 online providers of course delivery plat-

DEVELOPMENT

forms, it would be difficult to review them for all of these categories prior to selecting one for use in your company or on your campus. Educators and administrators could easily be overwhelmed investigating these online course delivery platforms. Fortunately there is good news. There are a number of websites that offer an evaluation of online course delivery platforms. Among the most useful and objective of these is provided by Bruce Landon at (**http://www.ctt.bc.ca/landononline**). The site sponsor is the Centre for Curriculum, Transfer and Technology. A partial listing of course delivery platforms arranged alphabetically is provided in Table 7.1. Most of these platforms are available for comparative analysis at the Bruce Landon website. I have included two additional platforms.* There are several other sites available that provide reviews of online courseware and these are listed in Table 7.2.

A project to provide a useful Web tool for the comparative evaluation of online course delivery platforms was undertaken by Bruce Landon in collaboration with the B.C. Standing Committee on Educational Technology, the Centre for Curriculum Transfer and Technology, the Office of Learning Technologies, and the Center for Learning Technologies at Mt. Allison University. The project provides quantitative and qualitative data on online instructional software applications (**course delivery platforms**). The terms instructional software applications and online course delivery platforms are often used interchangeably. The whole field of online education is filled with overlapping definitions and ambiguous terminology because it is an immature and rapidly expanding area. For our discussion, I prefer to use the term online course delivery platform since most applications today have expanded to include many functions. The evaluation data used on the Langdon website was obtained by soliciting raters from across North America and some participants outside of North America. Information was also gathered from software vendors and from examining case studies at various educational institutions. National peer reviewers also provided input into initial development of the site. You can obtain more information on the development and use of this site at (**http://www.ctt.bc.ca/landononline/back grn2.html**). The software platforms that were evaluated ranged from very elaborate, full service systems to those with very limited functionality. Most of the sites presently available for comparative analysis on the Web can be seen in Table 7.1. A comparison table for all applications is available at (**http://www.ctt.bc.ca/landononline/choices.html**). Clicking the mouse on the abbreviation of the application in the first row (application homepage) will open the URL for that company homepage. Since many of these companies make frequent upgrades it is a good idea to visit homepages of those companies that interest you. This is also a good place to try out many of the platforms. If you mouse click on the category row (i.e., Web browser), it will take you to a comprehensive notes page in the Landon website where information is provided in several categories of performance. Comparisons of the platforms are divided into (1) learner tools and (2) support tools.

Course Delivery Platforms

Asymetrix ToolBook	McGraw-Hill PageOut*
Authorware	Pathware
BlackBoard	Phoenix Pathlore
Cu-Seeme	Prometheus*
Digital Trainer	QuestionMark
Docent	Serf
ECollege.com	Symposium
Edusystem	The Learning Manager
First Class	Top Class
Generation	UniLearn
Intralearn	Virtual-U
Knowledgesoft	WebBoard
Learning Space	Web Course in a Box
Learnlinc	WebCT
LUVIT	

Table 7.1
A partial listing of providers of online course delivery platforms arranged alphabetically

Sites For Reviewing Online Courseware

Alaska
Distance learning for the rest of us
http://www.uaa.alaska.edu/newmedia/web-based-learning.html

Beaumont
CM & CMS, Review, evaluation, adoption, training/support & deployment
http://bio444.beaumont.plattsburgh.edu/West/cms.html

Murdoch
Comparing software for online teaching
http://cleao.murdoch.edu.au/asu/edtech/webtool/compare.html

UMD
Evaluation and selection of Web course management tools
http://sumil.emd.edu/webct

UTK
Review of leading asynchronous Web-based course delivery systems
http://www.pemba.utk.edu/weblearning/reviewasynch.htm
Review of leading synchronous Web-based course delivery systems
http://www.pemba.utk.edu/weblearning/reviewsynch.htm

Virginia Tech
Survey of online education tools
http://www.visc.vt.edu/succeed/wwwframework/survey.html

British Columbia
Online educational delivery systems: A Web tool for comparative analysis
http://www.ctt.bc.ca/landononline

Table 7.1
Websites that evaluate online course delivery platforms (Adapted from B. Landon, 2000, "Online educational delivery systems: A Web tool for comparative analysis." (**http://www.ctt.bc.ca/landononline**)

The learner tools are subdivided into Web browsing, asynchronous sharing, synchronous sharing, and student tools. The support tools are subdivided as shown in Table 7.3. If you want a definition of a category term (i.e., voice_chat) you can mouse click on that term while viewing the website, or look at the glossary of terms provided in Table 7.4.

Table 7.3
Categories of features / tools used to compare course delivery platforms (**http://www.ctt.bc.ca/landononline**)

Learner Tools		Support Tools	
Accessibilty Bookmarks Multimedia Security	**Student Tools** Self-assessing, Progress tracking, Searching, Motivation build- ing, Study skill build- ing	**Course** Course planning Course managing Course customiz- ing	**Administration** Installation Authorization Course customiz- ing Registering
Asynchronous Sharing Email Newsgroups BBS file exchange Threaded discus- sion*		**Lesson** Instructional design Presenting infor- mation Testing	Online fees han- dling Server security Resource monitor- ing Remote access Crash recovery
Synchronous Sharing Chatroom, Voice chat Whiteboard, Virtual space, group browsing Teleconferencing		**Data** Marking online Managing records Analyzing and tracking	**Help Desk** Student support Instructor support
		Resource Curriculum man- aging Building knowl- edge Team building Building motiva- tion	

*Not listed in the categories on the Landononline website.

A glossary of the terms developed by Landon for these categories is provided in Table 7.4. Reviewing these terms is useful in understanding the spectrum of capabilities offered by online course delivery platforms

Glossary of Terms For Categories Used in Landon Website

Accessibility. Accessibility for persons with disabilities entails providing for a universal text version without relying on frames, tables, or images.

Administration. Administration tools include all those setup and maintainance tasks involved on the server side of the application and extending to setup/configuration of client side software to work properly with the server side application. Some of these tasks may be carried out by instructors in some situations.

Analyzing_and_tracking. Analyzing and tracking tools include facilities for statistical analysis of student-related data and the facility to display the progress of individual students in the course structure.

Application_sharing. Application sharing includes the running of an application on one machine and sharing the window view of the running application across the Web. There may also be provisions for sharing mouse control of the application.

Asynchronous Sharing. Asynchronous sharing refers to the exchange of data and files where the correspondents are not online at the same time.

Authorization. Tools that assign access and other privileges to specific users or user groups.

BBS_file_exchange. Bulletin Board Service is the facility for downloading files and upload\posting files over the Web.

Bookmarks Bookmarks identify Internet locations, and this category covers the creation, display, management, and updating of bookmarks.

Building_knowledge. Building knowledge includes facilities to accumulate and share the knowledge gained by individual instructors through their experience with distance education. Examples of knowledge building include the range from simple Q&A files to extensive database style data warehouses of tips, workarounds, and class exercises.

Table 7.4
Glossary of terms used for categories listed in the Bruce Landon website

DEVELOPMENT

Building_motivation. Building motivation includes facilities for self-help and possibly other help (buddy system) to encourage and enhance morale.

Chat. Chat includes facilities like Internet Relay Chat (IRC) and similar text exchanges.

Course_customizing. Course customizing includes the facility to change the structure of the course and its assignments, exams, etc. This may include guides, templates, and related product suport and training.

Course_managing. Course managing tools include facilities to enable instructors to collect information from or about students related to their progress in the course structure and to permit/deny access to course resources.

Course. Course tools are facilities that facilitate the instructor's tasks related to bringing course materials together and managing the student's use/access of those materials.

Course_monitoring. Course monitoring includes facilities that provide information about the usage of course resources by individual students and groups of students.

Course_planning. Course planning tools are facilities that enable at least initial course layout and or structuring.

Crash_recovery. Crash recovery tools include facilities to recover from communications or server hardware failure without loss of data. These are tools in addition to the tools provided by the operating system.

Curriculum_Managing. Curriculum management includes tools to manage multiple programs, to do skills/competencies management, and to do certification management.

Data. Data tools includes tools for marking online, managing records, and for analyzing and tracking.

Email. Electronic mail using the Internet protocols unless noted otherwise.

Group browsing. Group browsing involves a group tour of websites with a shared browser window and some interaction capability between the members of the group and at least the tour leader.

Help desk. Help desk tools are facilities that assist the technical administration personnel in handling trouble calls and requests for technical assistance.

Installation. Server installation includes both software setup tools and installations related services provided by the vendor.

Instructional_designing. Instructional designing includes facilities to help instructors create learning sequences.

Instructor_support. Instructor support tools are facilities to assist technical support personnel in providing technical assistance to instructors using the application.

Learner Tools. Tools/facilities used by the student learner at their location, the client side of distance education.

Lesson. Lesson tools are those facilities that facilitate the development and deployment of instructional sequences smaller than a whole course, like assignments, modules, topics, etc.

Managing_records. Managing records includes facilities for organizing and keeping track of course-related information.

Marking_online. Marking online includes facilities that support the marking of student generated material while online.

Motivation_building. Motivation building includes self-help tools and other facilities that provide direct encouragement to overcome difficulties that impede or impair student performance.

Multimedia. Multimedia includes the support for images, audio, video, and VRML files.

Newsgroups. Newsgroups facility includes Usenet newsgroups and like functions.

On-line_fees_handling. Online fees handling includes tools to accomplish credit card transactions.

Presenting_information. Presenting information includes facilities for formatting, displaying, or showing course material over the Web.

DEVELOPMENT

Progress_tracking. Progress tracking includes some facility for the student to check marks on assignments and tests.

Registering. Registering includes online registration and/or linkage with existing registration systems.

Remote_access. Remote access tools include facilities to do application system administration from more than one machine.

Resource. Resource tools includes tools for building knowledge, team building, and building motivation among instructors.

Resource_monitoring. Resource monitoring includes the facility to display the disk space and CPU resources devoted to the application while it is being used.

Searching. Searching includes the facility to locate parts of the course materials on the basis of word matching beyond the user's current browser page.

Security. Browser security refers to the support for secure transactions on the Web and to verify the security of downloaded code.

Self-assessing. Self-assessing includes practice quizzes and other survey style assessment tools that may or may not be scored online.

Server_security. Security tools are used to prevent unauthorized access and/or modification of data. This can include a wide range of approaches and methods.

Student Tools. Student tools include applications that cater to the special needs of tele-learners.

Student_support. Student help desk support tools include facilities to facilitate the tasks of an operator responding to requests for help by student users of the application.

Study_skill_building. Study skill building includes facilities that support effective study practices, which can range from simple review tools to mini courses in how to study.

Support Tools. Instructor tools are facilities primarily intended for use by instructors, markers, and course designers.

Synchronous Sharing. Real-time information exchange.

Team_Building. Team building includes the facility for instructors with common interests to communicate in a way that facilitates their forming a sense of group/team identity.

Teleconferencing. Teleconferencing includes audio conferencing.

Testing. Testing includes facilities to assist in the making up of practice quizzes, tests, exams, and other assignments.

Threaded Discussion.* An asynchronous learning tool simulating traditional classroom discussion by allowing students and faculty to post comments to a discussion topic, attach files for sharing, and respond to faculty questions. The discussions are "threaded" because each response is time and date stamped and all responses may be sorted by topic, dates, or author. * Not a category evaluated in the Landononline website

Video conferencing. Video conferencing includes broadcasting video to those without a video input device.

Virtual space. Virtual spaces include MOOs, MUDs, and virtual meeting rooms.

Voice_Chat Voice Chat enables two or more to communicate via microphone and speaker conference call style over the Internet connection in real time.

Web Browsing. Tools for viewing HTML documents.

Whiteboard. Whiteboard facility includes a shared text window that may also support shared drawing.

DEVELOPMENT

The Landon website provides three options for comparing online educational delivery applications:

1. Option one is designed for those who have narrowed their choice to one or two applications or for those who want to quickly review technical and instructional specifications without first entering criteria. You may enter the name of the application (i.e., WebCT) and a complete list of technical and instructional specifications will appear for comparison or evaluation.

2. Option two allows you to review by criteria. You can check a box next to those features most important to you (see Table 7.2) and select up to 10 platforms to be compared against those criteria.

3. Option three is useful if you wish to set your own weights and values to the criteria to determine how scores for applications compare. You select which criteria are important enough to rate the applications to be compared for those selected criteria. The weighted average scores are computed and displayed on a customized form.

7.3 Examples of Course Delivery Platforms

Since you now have Web access to numerous sites for comparing and visiting online course delivery platforms, it isn't necessary to compare all of them here. Instead, I will provide an overview of a few systems that are among the most widely used and compatible with the **Online Learning Centers** provided by McGraw-Hill. Online Learning Centers are pre-formed digital supplements in each of 38 subject areas (Table 7.5). The digital supplements include lecture materials, self-grading quizzes, interactive exercises, Powerpoint slides, and other key supplements. These digital supplements give you complete ownership in the way digital content is presented to the class and are also compatible with the WebCT, Blackboard.com, eCollege.com, McGraw-Hill PageOut platforms, and Prometheus platforms. Other publishers also produce digital supplements that are compatible with one or more of these platforms and you should communicate with the publisher of your textbook to determine if they can provide Web ready digital materials that are compatible with your platform. What this means is that you can place your course online with very little development time since all that upfront work has been done for you. You just have to select the right textbook and publisher. Since more publishers are entering this digital arena continuously, there's a good chance that your subject matter is adequately covered by one of these publishers.

McGraw-Hill Online Learning Center Categories	
Accounting	Geology
Anatomy and Physiology	Health
Anthropology	History
Arts	Management
Astronomy	Management Information Systems
Biology	Marketing
Chemistry	Math
Communication	Music
Computer Information Technology	Nutrition
Computer Sciences	Operations and Decisions Sciences
Criminal Justice	Political
Economics	Physics
Engineering	Physical Education Science
Engineering Graphics	Psychology
English	Sociology
Finance	Student Success
Genetics	Theatre
Geography	World Languages

Table 7.5
Online learning center categories for McGraw-Hill textbooks (Each category has several learning centers)

WebCT

WebCT is an interactive course management system developed in the computer science department of the University of British Columbia.[1, 2] WebCT was recently acquired by Universal Learning Technology and now is used in nearly 1500 institutions in 57 countries with over a 6.9 million students. It is a Web-based educational environment that provides the structure of the course including color palette, buttons, course templates, and page layout. It is designed so that you may load in your educational elements without the need to know HTML. You and your students access the course materials through a Web browser such as Netscape or Internet Explorer. There is no other software for you or your students to install except possibly for browser plug-ins (See Table 5.3 in Lesson 5). WebCT provides interactive communication features including email, chat, and bulletin boards. It also provides tools for grade management and testing (quizzes, surveys, self-tests).[2] Tools are available for organizing course content and developing student Web presentations. Individual student login names and passwords provide security through restricted access to sensitive sites such as grades. Password restriction is especially important when dealing with copyrighted materials. Permissions to use copyrighted materials are usually much easier to obtain when it can be shown that access is restricted by password protection to individual students. If you would like to test drive the WebCT course development platform, go to **http://about.webct.com.** You can see a demo or actually teach your course free online for 120 days to as many as 50 students.

WebCt also offers an e-Learning Resource Pack, or e-Pack that is a set of fully customizable online course materials developed by WebCT content providers for instructors. You may select from hundreds of prepared online course materials produced by nationally known authors of widely used textbooks. This is an excellent solution for faculty who want to begin using an online course component immediately. These materials are also available on the WebCT site to demo, evaluate fully, or adopt. The Online Teaching & Learning Community of WebCT is a place for you and other online educators to share resources, strategies and observations about improving your ability to teach and your students' ability to learn.

eCollege

The eCollege site is accessed at (**http://www.ecollege.com**) with Internet Explorer 5.0 or later. The platform from eCollege is now used in nearly 180 institutions with several thousand students. These institutions offer degree programs and single courses. Its course platform allows the creation of units of instruction and extends the opportunity for content "chunking," providing the structure of the course including color palette, buttons, course templates, and page layout. The eCollege platform easily accommodates the use of Instructional Multimedia, supporting streaming audio and video, and the delivery of JavaScript, Flash, and other multimedia programs over the Internet. Nearly any popular multimedia type may be submitted to eCollege for uploading to their streaming servers or uploaded by the instructors themselves. The newest version of the eCollege system, 4.2, offers the ease of an authoring tool that can be accessed by a simple tab switch, allowing the instructor to quickly move back and forth between the course view and the authoring view of his or her course. Its authoring tool contains a Visual Editor that allows you to create the Web pages of your course, including colorful fonts and styles, vary backgrounds, and insert graphic images without having any knowledge or use of HTML. Further, you will see those changes on the screen as they are made. Through an arrangement with Microsoft, documents created in Microsoft Office, such as PowerPoint, Excel, and Word, can be uploaded into the eCollege course with no HTML conversion necessary. You and your students access the course materials through a Web browser such as Netscape or Internet Explorer. The eCollege course shell offers both asynchronous and synchronous communication tools, including threaded discussion, chatroom, document sharing, and a journal. Instructors may easily form collaborative groups in their course, automatically making accessible to each group private email functions, threaded discussions, document sharing areas, and chatrooms. Instructors and students alike may email their students as an entire class, in smaller groups, or individually, directly from the course homepage without accessing an external program. In 4.2, they may also email their students private messages from the threaded discussions. Instructors may also attach files to those emails. Individual student login names and passwords provide security through restricted access to sensitive sites such as grades. The eCollege system supports seven types of online testing including matching, true/false, multiple choice (with one or more possible answers), short answer, essay, and oral exams. Instructors may create test banks, develop a pool of questions and randomize the questions for each person taking the exam. Students may view their personal grades, take practice exams, and view instructor comments on those exams or quizzes.

A wide variety of authoring tools is available. You can select start and end dates for the course and each unit, provide a course description, and select enrollment options. You can add as many content items to each unit as you wish and rename or delete any content item. You may check course activity for each student, time access to individual units and content items within those units. You and your students each have access to a calendar that can display both course events and individual personal events. Support is offered to the instructor within the 4.2 system in the form of a start-up wizard, tutorial, context-sensitive help pages, and design tips.

One of the many strengths of eCollege is its support system for educational institutions including: course development services including instructional multimedia, instructional design services, a help desk that operates 24/7, server security, resource monitoring, and online tutorials and online evaluation services. The course development services of eCollege provide the technical support for converting materials to the Web. They support encoding audio and visual files, working with images, slide shows and the translation of text to the web. The instructional design team provides assistance in content delivery, unit layout, and perspectives on learning styles and basic pedagogy. Additionally, they provide online tutorial courses that walk you through the course creation process, instructor-led online workshops and certificate courses. Students have access to the 7/24 hour help desk and an orientation course. The eCollege system requires a username and password combination to use all system features and so provides security on their server for all users.

There are three main products produced by eCollege that include eToolKit, eCompanion, and eCourse. The eToolKit program is a set of online communications tools that allow you to easily create a secure and private online enhancement for your traditional course. The eCompanion option is designed for faculty who teach in a classroom and want to use the power of the Internet to make teaching easier and better and offers a full series of communication tools and content presentation options. The eCourse option is designed to promote the maximum interaction possible in the online environment for a completely

Web-based course. If you would like to test drive the eCollege course development platform, go to (**http://www.ecollege.com**). You can see a demo or actually use many of the eCollege features free for a semester.

Prometheus

Prometheus is a Web-based software that that uses an open source code designed on a standard database that permits the direct integration of the system into existing administrative architecture (**http://www.prometheus.com**). This means that the university or business has extraordinary flexibility in modifying Prometheus to their design. They can restrict permissions to multiple layers across the campus, and even permit unlimited growth on the user base.

Prometheus provides a self-guiding "Q and A" workflow that guides the instructor with little effort to creating a course by selecting from a variety of templates. Fields can be renamed, reorganized, and removed as desired by the instructor. There are user interfaces that allow the user (student) to customize the appearance to each individual taste. The system provides options for threaded discussions, chatrooms, and file sharing. You can request and access library reserves online. The system supports streaming audio and video, slides, narrated slides, and links to spots in videos on CD-ROM. Prometheus comes with an equation editor to create math and science equations with the need to know HTML code. It is customizable, allowing you to control the fonts, the background and the functions. You can rename, reorder, or completely remove course information. The system allows you to send and track email and announcements. There is also contextual help, meaning that there is extensive and specific help online with one click away from each page.

Online testing is supported with multiple-choice, true-and-false, short-and-long answer questions. Test questions may be generated randomly for each person taking the exam. The true/false and multiple-choice questions may be graded automatically and results entered into the electronic grade book. For additional information and a trial run of the system go to (**http://www.prometheus.com**).

Blackboard

Blackboard is a Web-based course delivery system that is now used at more than 3,300 colleges, schools, companies, and state associations throughout the United States and in 70 countries. The most recent version is Blackboard 5 that features many useful portal and administrative capabilities. Blackboard supports most multimedia including streaming audio and video. It supports email, file sharing, chatroom, voice chat, and whiteboard. It supports progress tracking with numeric grades and/or text comments. The course site permits the analysis of individual performance or the entire class by viewing statistical graphs and charts generated online by the course software. The system supports quiz/survey and test generators that allow the instructor to create matching, multiple-choice, multiple-answer, true/false, fill in the blank, ordering, short answer, and essay questions. Questions may be pooled, administered randomly, and timed. Grading of objective questions may be performed online.

Blackboard.com provides a number of support systems for online instructors including an online community of instructors, tips from the "User's Corner," an Academic Resource Center, the option to teach online for free, and the option to take an online demo course for free. The Resource Center is a free, value-added service from Blackboard that offers academic resources for instructors and students including: current news about specific academic categories and disciplines, a research area containing thousands of articles organized into specific disciplines, featured links to useful external websites screened and summarized by the editorial staff of Blackboard, instructor and student communities organized according to academic categories, and a customizable environment through which the instructors may control the features presented. Blackboard has thousands of courses online. You may browse some of them online if they belong to the Featured Course List. They have a featured CourseSite titled "Introduction to Distance Learning" designed especially for teachers. This is an excellent way to see how a distance course functions from the eyes of a student. Taking this course will give you experience in navigating through an asynchronous distance learning course, entering an online discussion, taking an online quiz, participating in a chatroom, and developing an understanding of the technology used in distance learning. You may wish to visit this site. They also have courses in many other areas. Check them out at (**http://www.blackboard.com/course sites.html**).

PageOut

PageOut is McGraw-Hill's custom course delivery platform used by over 26,000 professors that provides you with your own personal website complete with a unique URL for your course. PageOut is free with the adoption of Mcgraw-Hill textbooks. PageOut requires no prior knowledge of HTML and no design skills. Instead, it offers a series of templates that you fill in with your course information and then select one of the 16 course designs available. Although usually taking less than an hour to complete this part of the process, the finished website provides an interactive syllabus that allows you to post content to coincide with your lectures. This content may be of your own creation or from the book's Online Learning Center. There is an online grade book, automatic storage of quiz and test grades, posting of grades to individual students, a discussion board, and the option for students to construct and build their own Web page. If you don't want to take the time to place your own course materials on the Web, you may send them to McGraw-Hill. They will assign you an online training specialist who consults with you for 30 minutes by phone and will use PageOut to create your online course website after you mail your materials to them. The Distributed Learning and Knowledge team will incorporate course content from the Online Learning Center germane to your textbook. Students will find interactive exercises, quizzes, current and relevant articles from leading periodicals with full-text articles online, peer reviewed and refereed content, and optional research and study skills. Additionally they will provide training in online teaching for your own development including email support, a toll-free hotline, Web support sites, and training classrooms at educational conventions.

7.4 Sharing and Compatibility

SCORM

One of the faculty members at my university recently asked me what would happen to all of his course materials if we were to change to a different course delivery system. The answer was that we would probably have to redo everything to adapt to the new system. A similar problem was also of concern to the Unites States Department of Defense. They are looking for a standardization process that permits courseware to be reusable, portable, accessible, and durable. The concept was to develop small packets of reusable and sharable course content that could be easily located and retrieved from a repository. This would increase the ability of persons to find and move entire courses or have adaptive learning systems that can assemble content to meet the needs of learners on demand. The Department of Defense (DOD) and the White House Office of Science and Technology Policy (OSTP) launched the Advanced Distributive Learning (ADL) initiative in November of 1997. This initiative is a component of the national strategy to promote affordable and high-quality education and training opportunities. The Institute for Defense Analysis (IDA) then established the ADL Co-Laboratory to provide an open and collegiate environment for evaluating and demonstrating ADL tools and prototypes, and sharing data on these efforts among government agencies and the private sector. The ADL Co-LAB was formed to provide the backbone for the development of guidelines, certification procedures, and shared courseware objects in a collaborative environment among government and private groups.

ADL began working with key industry leaders and standard-setting organizations to identify critical technical interface points around which standards for Web-based learning technologies could be developed. The meetings resulted in the development of ADL's Sharable Courseware Object Reference Model (SCORM). You can obtain details on SCORM at (**http://www.adlnet.org**). The ultimate goal of ADL is to encourage technologies that make it possible for a learner to custom-assemble content based on their own personal needs and pace. SCORM is still being evaluated as of the summer of 2000 but actual products may be available before the end of the year. A number of companies have signed onto the SCORM initiative and will intend to provide small, reusable, sharable course content that can be retrieved from several interoperable repositories.

Additionally another effort is simultaneously developing to facilitate the retrieval and discovery of online learning resources. A global coalition of educational institutions, commercial organizations, and government entities adopted specifications for the interoperability of distributed learning resources. This organization is known as IMS (Instructional Management Project). Information on IMS may be found at (**http://www.imsproject.org**).

IMS

The release of a set of specifications using metadata tags designed to describe education resources was recently announced by IMS.[3] Metadata tags are currently imbedded in Web materials to permit their retrieval by search engines. The IMS metadata search fields include learning level, users support, educational objectives, copyright information, price code, learning object, and many other fields in addition to those currently existing such as author, subject, and publisher. The learning object is a discrete "chunk" of data that

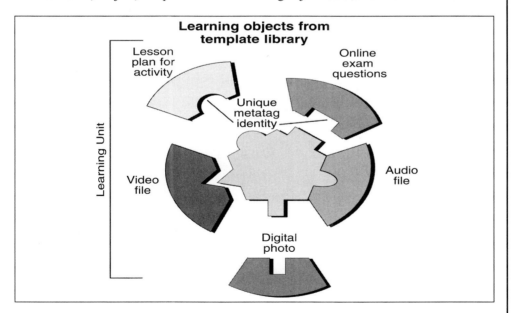

Learning objects from template library

Lesson plan for activity · Online exam questions · Unique metatag identity · Audio file · Digital photo · Video file · Learning Unit

Fig. 7.1
Learning objects with unique metatags may be assembled from template libraries to create custom learning units

is part of a learning module. It could include video, audio, text, email, slides, case studies, collaborative activities, or any medium that can be digitized (Fig 7.1). The metadata specification contains a dictionary of fields and values organized into groups or sets that become attached to these learning objects. The imbedded IMS metadata will help insure that distributed learning resources and Internet learning products will work on a variety of IT platforms. The metadata specification (**www.imsproject.org/metadata**) benefits the learner seeking information with a metadata aware search tool both when the search is on the Web or offline on a CD-ROM or DVD-ROM encyclopedia. Content developers who have implemented the IMS Learning Resources Metadata Specification will have simplified the search for learning resources because the metadata allows users to specify the search terms. This means that a learner or student will be able to use a search engine or metadata enabled software program to seek out learning materials throughout the Web with these tags attached. Developers and students will be able to access content libraries containing all types of materials on medical, defense, industrial, K-12, and higher education content. The specifications are being made available free of charge to the general public. The IMS Metadata Specification is available at (**http://www.imsproject.org**).

Both ADL and IMS are now coordinating activities to promote the development of software specifications and the implementation of interoperable learning resources and systems.[4] The ADL Co-Lab is integrating work from IMS and other groups into SCORM. You should be aware of these rapidly developing worldwide standards since they will have an impact on the development of Web-based course materials and perhaps on the availability of your personally developed course content as well. I don't have an answer for you about the distribution of these materials, copyright issues, or compensation. You may want to visit the sites mentioned above to gather more information on these developing strategies to produce a global learning environment.

REFERENCES

1. **Fister, S.** 2000. "Web-Based Training on a Shoe-String." In *The 2000/2001 ASTD Distance Learning Yearbook*. Mantyla, K. New York, McGraw-Hill, pp. 76-86.

2. **Peterson, D.** 1999. "Observations on a Web-Based Course Management System." *OIT*, Newsletter of the Office of Information Technologies, University of Massachusetts, Amherst, Vol. 5: No.1, pp. 32-34.

3. **News Release.** "IMS Announces Metadata Specification for Distributed Learning." San Jose, CA, August 20, 1999
    <http://www.sbu.ac.uk/litcc/lt/1999/news1621.html>.

4. **PR Newswire.** 2000. "ADL Co-Lab and IMS Close Implementation Gap for Online Learning." Madison, Wis. August 8, PRNewswire, <http://www.zdnet.com>.

DEVELOPMENT

Will My Teaching Style Translate to the Online Classroom?

Lesson 8

Will My Teaching Style Translate to the Online Classroom?

LESSON OUTLINE

8.1 STAND AND DELIVER
8.2 WORKSHOP-BASED INSTRUCTION
8.3 LAB-BASED INSTRUCTION
8.4 SELF-PACED TUTORIAL
8.5 INTERDISCIPLINARY TEAM TEACHING
8.6 WHERE ARE YOU IN THE COURSE?

WHAT YOU WILL LEARN FROM THIS LESSON

YOU WILL BE ABLE TO:

1. Identify the various types of teaching styles and select the one(s) to use.
2. Match your teaching style with the types of online delivery possibilities that most closely match.
3. Design a curriculum for online presentation that best meets your teaching style.
4. Demonstrate how to use collaboration in the online environment.
5. Construct an online teaching experience that reveals much of your personality.

LESSON 8: WILL MY TEACHING STYLE TRANSLATE TO THE ONLINE CLASSROOM?

The answer is definitely yes. Your teaching style <u>will</u> translate to the online classroom. First, you absolutely can and will use your experience of teaching your course traditionally in your online class. Second, the instructional materials that you've developed and assembled for your traditional class will still be valuable to you. Teaching online is not simply about utilizing technology. It's about good teaching. And what does good teaching come down to? Whether live or "virtual," it's about expertise, passion, communication, organization, and empathy for your students.

In this section, you will consider this question: "What makes my traditional course successful?" Do you rely on lecture style? Are in-class discussions the backbone of your course? Do you place importance on building relationships with your students? Do you create workshop scenarios in which your students become responsible for instruction? Answers to these questions will help you establish your overall approach to creating the online course.

8.1 Stand and Deliver

Lectures

Lecturing in the online classroom is as possible as it is in the traditional classroom. You could videotape a lecture and simply upload it into your course; or you could speak into a tape recorder and then upload an audio file. This type of course design and development could certainly save you a lot of time and give your online students the same kind of experiences you are giving your traditional students. But have you ever watched a video online? It's not like TV. And have you ever tried sitting in front of a box, listening to a disembodied voice for 50 minutes or so? It's not the most effective way to learn <u>anything</u>.

But, your students do want to hear you. They are taking your class because they want to know your ideas and understand the course material from the perspective of your expertise. Even if they aren't sitting in a classroom with you three times a week, they want to know who you are. Lecturing is an important component of your online teaching strategy, but you must approach it with judiciousness and restraint. Rather than a 50-minute monologue, your lectures might take the form of short PowerPoint presentations with streaming audio, or focused 5-minute video clips; or even text online that contains images and hyperlinks. Before you begin preparing your online lectures, ask yourselves these two questions and be prepared to answer them:

1. How does my lecture delivery of this material help students to better learn content they could otherwise get from a textbook, a collaborative project, or through a discussion group?

2. How can I best convey my personality and my passion for this content in an online lecture?

Answering these two questions will help you determine how to limit your lecturing online so that it is most effective. It will also allow you to begin considering alternative ways for teaching your course that could enhance the effectiveness of your lecture and help you work on "humanizing" your online course, something essential in this technology-driven age.

Tips for Creating the Online Text Lecture

If your course has a lecture component, you undoubtedly have lecture notes in one form or another. These might be actual notes or handouts you give your students to fill in as you lecture. Perhaps you use overhead transparencies to assist in structuring your lectures. To simply transfer your notes to online Web pages could result in online material that is confusing to your students or incomplete. Better for the online text lecture to write mini-lectures that reflect your voice and style and can serve as models for your students for the kind of writing you expect from them in your course. Here are a few guidelines for turning your traditional classroom notes into online text lectures:

- Focus on bringing out your personality in the lecture.
  - Use an informal, first person perspective — as if you were talking to the class, or better, to each student individually.
- Gravitate to anecdotes, stories, and situations to bring the facts to life. Let the textbooks cover the facts.
  - Combine lecture notes in the form of PowerPoint or text with streaming audio.
  - Write well: model for your students the kind of writing you expect from them.
- Be as concise as possible. Avoid forcing the student to read the equivalent of a textbook online.
- Use "white space" and insert graphics or pictures that reinforce the content.
- Use the power of the Web. Include hypertext links to sites that augment your lecture. Just be sure the students know how to return to your lecture so you don't lose them! With the power of programming, you can also open these supporting sites in a smaller window if that suits the lecture. This will lessen confusion for your students, as they no longer will have to suddenly jump out of your lecture to visit other sites.

Using Multiple Learning Materials (Video, Audio, Slides, Guest Speakers, Exams)

The joy of teaching online comes from the technology that allows you to present content to your students in many different ways and to have it all available to you with just one "click." Text lectures are one way to present content, but too many and you have created a "text online" scenario. At that point, you begin to wonder why you shouldn't just turn the course into a correspondence course by mail.

As we said before, with the audio and video capabilities of the online environment, it is possible to put a video production of your lectures online, to create audio clips, PowerPoint, and lab simulations. With the right technology, you can even broadcast a live lecture to your students and allow your students to interject questions in real time. Some enhancements to "text online" are fairly simple to implement and quite reliable. But be aware that with more synchronous interactivity comes more difficult and expensive implementation that can also be more unreliable, making it frustrating to both you and your students. Before using the technology, you need to understand all the ramifications and implications for you and your students that come from that choice.

So how do we make intelligent choices? The first consideration must be the effectiveness of implementation. Students will be very tolerant of setup difficulties if the result is an experience in learning that otherwise couldn't be accomplished. Our choices may be limited by the available services. Check to see if video or audio streaming is possible. If not, using something like audio .wav files may be an option, but their use dictates shorter clips since the longer loading times to the students' computers must be taken into consideration. A long load time will disrupt rather than reinforce the lesson.

There's also the alternative of mailing a set of videotaped lectures, audio tapes, or CD-ROMs to your students. The advantages include the ease-of-use and availability of the VCR for students, the reliability and quality of tape, and the capability on most campuses to create quality recordings. For instance, fast motion clips such as wave experiments in physics will display more smoothly on conventional videotape. This solution also solves the problem of needing support personnel to convert video to the online environment, which can be complex.

Though these are certainly viable options to putting everything online, don't forget that in putting everything online, you are creating an integrated environment for learning. A well-designed unit of study stimulates the learning process by drawing the student into the material.

Tips for Video Online

- Use shorter video segments that are two to ten minutes long and that get right to the heart of the subject to maximize the value of this tool. Organize these clips within the Web lecture using hypertext links connected with normal text.

DEVELOPMENT

- Avoid lengthy sections of video where you are talking to the camera, or where the video is focused on a still image. A picture accompanied by an audio clip could more efficiently handle these settings since it loads faster, isn't as susceptible to Internet bandwidth limitations, and requires much less hard drive storage space than audio.

Let's put together a strategy for using video and audio that would effectively translate your traditional lecture to the online environment.

- *Introduction* – Use a two-minute video clip to introduce the main points of today's lecture. Take this opportunity to show enthusiasm for the topic and to place emphasis where appropriate.
- *Lecture Topics* – Begin each important point with a text statement or introductory paragraph pertaining to this topic. Where appropriate, insert graphics or pictures. Add an audio clip to reinforce or further explain the topic. Video (if well performed) is most powerful in delivering impact to the topic, but audio can be very effective for offering anecdotes to reinforce the material. If you have multiple video and audio clips, avoid creating merely a list of links to these clips. By building them into a textual context, you can better lead the students from one clip to the next. An alternative method is to create a slide format where each screen features navigation buttons to the next screen. This type of slide show can nicely display key points, and automatically play video or audio clips. Programs like Microsoft's PowerPoint are designed to build this kind of interface.
- *Discussion* – Within the lecture, you may want to include links to discussion questions. By going to questions from within the lecture, your students will be more likely to respond with a perspective that better fits that moment of the lecture. This can also be applied to supporting websites. Be sure to provide navigation directions to your students on how to return to the lecture.
- *Conclusion* – Often, a written conclusion will suffice. Using audio or even video to add impact is an option.

If you are starting with a set of notes, arrangements must be made to create the audio and video clips. Begin by consulting with your support staff. Find out what capabilities are available for video and audio on the Web. Based on these capabilities, create a plan that spells out where in each section you will employ audio or video clips. Determine how you feel most comfortable in recording these clips. Is it possible to videotape your traditional lectures from which you can use excerpts? Do you feel comfortable standing in front of a camera and delivering the material in a natural way? Can you do acceptable audio clips by checking out a cassette recorder and recording them in your office? In answering these questions, you will gain a better perspective of the time and effort the online course may require for development.

Guest Speakers. Online technology gives you the opportunity to invite guests across the world to visit every one of your classes, time and again, without having to travel or to even actually be there at a given time. You can invite your guest speakers to submit audiotapes or short videotapes, still pictures and written mini "lectures," to take part in chatroom discussions, or to monitor threaded discussions. And their contributions can become a permanent part of your course.

Midterms and Exams (Objective Quantitative Assessments)

You can deliver midterms and final exams online. You can create time and date-accessed exams that "open" the exam on a given day for a certain number of hours and that allow students to take the exam for a given period of time. This flexibility, which can be as limited or comprehensive as you want, can allow students to take the tests when they feel most prepared, and during their peak performance times for the day. You can also create "answer wizards" online that will automatically grade your objective quantitative assessments with consistent accuracy, and return the results over to your students as soon as you want. It is even possible to build a better assessment tool by creating interactive testing where the next question is based on the quality of the prior answer.

There are, however, difficulties inherent in the online assessment arena. Perhaps the two biggest concerns for online instructors are technology breakdowns and student cheating.

What happens when the technology doesn't work? Taking tests online requires stable, reliable technology. A system down on the final day of the testing window will surely have panicked students asking for extensions. There is also the unavoidable student computer crash that will bring requests by students to retake an exam. How can we meet these special needs without providing an unfair advantage? As done in the traditional classroom, an alternative test online can be provided. Or a time extension can be allowed for completing the exam. An oral test could be given over the phone, or online with a chat application. A set of essay questions or a paper could be assigned. As you can see, the online solutions parallel our traditional solutions.

How can I prevent my students from cheating? Just as there are many ways of cheating in the traditional classroom environment, so are there online. The philosophical discussion about who the cheater is really hurting and what message is sent when we become draconian in our attempts to prevent cheating applies as well, but there are some common practices for curbing cheating.

Besides timing access and duration of a test, create test pools and "randomize" the questions that are given out to each student. Make your test open book, but create enough questions of enough complexity so that to successfully complete the course, the student must be completely familiar with the materials beforehand. For tests that require absolute verification of the test take — often necessary for certification testing — make arrangements with regional test centers for proctored exams and require your students to go to these regional centers.

For essay exams, include in the instructions that the essays must be in the student's own words. This clearly defines parameters for the student. Next, include a number of sub-elements to the question (Table 8.1). This will make it obvious if the student has anticipated the question and created the essay answer in advance, since the answer will not include important elements, or will be poorly organized.

Essay answers suspected of being copied and pasted from the Internet can be easily checked. Open a search engine such as AltaVista or Hotbot, copy and paste a student sentence into the search box. Be sure to use the concatenation device (usually a "+" symbol) between each word to limit the search results. This situation can become a learning experience for the student by exposing him or her to a critique of the poor organization and omitted areas of the plagiarized site, despite the student's assumption of good writing style and accurate facts there, and the lack of proper citation in the student's essay (which obviously would have exposed the cheating).

Finally, much of the pressure to cheat can be alleviated by restructuring the course to place more value on a variety of activities including threaded discussions, journals, searching and critiquing websites, and various individual and group projects. This restructuring has the added advantage of keeping the students more involved in the course as well as creating a learning community within the course which can help to leverage information into knowledge. Exams then will become only one component of the final grade for course. For more details, see our section on Portfolio Assessment.

Table 8.1
Typical essay question and an online essay question with sub-elements.

AN ONLINE ESSAY QUESTION
1. Discuss the major periods of Bach's life and music. **Online Essay Question**: 　　Discuss the major periods of Bach's life and music. For each, include two major works and a form or style upon which he focused. Also add a significant influence for each period.

8.2. Workshop-Based Instruction

A colleague of mine and I realized shortly after we started working with online courses, that much of the teaching practices done in the writing workshop are the practices considered best for the online classroom—group discussion, peer critique, and group collaborations. While many instructors at first worry that these activities in the classroom will
be lost online, they quickly realize that group discussion and peer work become the great
strengths of the online class.

Group Discussion

Discussions online can take place through chatrooms, threaded discussions, and
email. To guide the discussion, the teacher acts as facilitator — asking provocative questions and bringing out responses from the quiet members of the class or simply managing
the process of the discussion.   Initially, the online instructor is most excited by the
prospect of using the chatroom for class discussions because it most closely emulates the
give and take exchange of the classroom, though those exchanges are made typically
through written text and not verbally. (There are chatrooms available that allow for audio
discussion.) The discussion can be logged to a file for later evaluation if a portion of the
grade depends on involvement. To augment this discussion, there are applications that provide a common whiteboard so that documents and illustrations can be shared in real time.
Finally, there are even applications with audio and video capabilities to do video conferencing. Chatrooms work especially effectively for small group discussions, though larger
discussions can be handled through good management and prior rule setting. Chatrooms
can be used for student presentations and for peer analysis as well.

But there is the issue of real-time demands countering the flexibility offered to the
non-traditional online student. Synchronous discussion requires the student to be time-
bound for a portion of the course. The instructor will have to schedule the discussion times
as part of the course schedule, or work with the students to find a time for discussion.
These online discussions must be carefully organized to maintain order. While one student
is busily typing a lengthy answer, the discussion may have turned to other topics. Not only
does the student feel sheepish when the offering doesn't seem appropriate, he or she will
have missed some of the other entries. Because of this, the chat can be quite confusing to
follow, though there are ways to control the chatroom, which we will discuss later in this
book. Lastly, because of the real time nature of the chatroom, if students have technical
difficulties, they are likely to miss important elements of the class.

What typically happens in an online course is that the instructor discovers the wonders of the threaded discussion. The threaded discussion soon becomes one of the most
important tools in the online course for instruction. Threaded discussions can be used
purely for group discussions, or for peer group critiques, or for assignment submission,

which allows the rest of the class members to see and learn from each other's work. Threaded discussions are asynchronous — the instructor creates a topic for discussion and allows the students a period of time to respond. Or the instructor creates a "place" for the students to introduce their own discussions. These discussions will typically last anywhere from a couple of days to the entire term. This allows students to respond when it is convenient for them, and gives them the time to create as reasoned and lengthy a response as they would like. They can read the other entries and respond. The application will group responses with the original posting, hence the threaded aspect. Unlike chatrooms, threaded discussions give students a chance for reflection and then refinement of their work and response before posting. It allows you to model appropriate styles and sophistication of response. It allows you to turn over the learning to the students themselves. Most instructors discover that by the time the discussion is complete, the question has been thoroughly answered. Use of the threads for group collaboration and peer critique work creates an instructional tool that again allows for the students to take on the responsibility of learning for themselves and will encourage the growth of learning communities in your course, considered a key element to an effective online course. Managing threads is an art to be learned by most new online instructors because it can seem overwhelming to read and respond to 25–30 initial student responses and all the responses to responses that students will make to each other. In some ways, giving up control of the threads is the best way to manage them. This we will explore later in the book.

Email offers another forum for discussion. Using email to facilitate discussion is what "listservs" are all about. Every time a student responds to a discussion, that response is sent automatically to everyone on the listserv. The DEOS listserv is famous and old in Internet time. This listserv is on distance learning. The problem with email discussion is that emails can get lost; the number of emails can be overwhelming; the discussion takes place outside the confines of the course. But, while not synchronous, messages can be "pushed" to recipients rather quickly and, for some students, checking their personal email is a more daily occurrence then entering your course.

Peer Critiques

Peer critiques of work can occur through any of the communication tools used to enable discussions. Peer critique and feedback are important components of a workshop-based course. Online, these strategies in instruction encourage active learning. Threads are most useful for peer critiques because they allow members of the class to learn from each other and begin to emulate the best in each other's work. It also will allow your students to learn evaluation and analysis. Set up clear expectations for peer critiques from your students and grade them as you would any piece of writing for the course. Nothing is more frustrating for students than the peer critique that reads: "Sounds good to me."

Collaborative Projects

Just as communication is facilitated online, projects can be assigned and space given for collaborative projects. Remember to account for the asynchronous nature of the course when assigning a time frame for projects, since communication is a longer process. For that extended time, however, students often build more effective teams and better results thanks to the more calculated communication that comes with written messages, devoid of non-verbal influence. Also, the teacher can more closely monitor teams without influence since the students don't "see" the authority figure looking over their shoulder. Of course, this assumes the teacher maintains a hands-off attitude during the course of the project.

8.3 Lab-Based Instruction

If ever there were an area that strikes fear in an online coordinator, it would be how to develop courses that feature associated labs. How can you do hands-on labs in the computer's "virtual" environment? How can "home" labs be properly supervised? Is an otherwise online course worth doing if the students are required to meet periodically in a traditional lab environment? We'll discuss each of these issues in the following sections.

Hands-On Experiments

There are four common approaches to hands-on experiments in the online course. The first response of faculty is to avoid conversion as much as possible – require students to meet periodically to perform the experiments required of the course. By setting full-day intensive sessions, this requirement can be fulfilled in as little as one or two days. The disadvantage of this is that experiments may not be as timely as in a traditional course, and it requires students to meet at a specific location at the same time. The experiments however can be performed under the direct supervision of the instructor. This also provides an opportunity for members of the class to meet.

A compromise option is to arrange for proctored experiments. The proctor must have expertise and experience (such as a high school or college science instructor) as well as a facility. This can be accommodated through reciprocal arrangements with other institutions, but is certainly no small feat. Properly executed, this arrangement provides for the supervision and facility needs, as well as the scheduling flexibility desired by the students.

Many courses are being developed with an ancillary lab kit so that students can perform experiments at home. The labs are usually designed to produce a specific result that can be reported to the instructor via the course shell. A correct result means that the lab was done correctly. Design consideration must include cost factors, since expensive dedicated measurement devices will not be available or practical to purchase. With ingenuity, many lab situations can be simulated in this manner.

Finally, virtual experiments built within the computer course shell can boast the best integration with other aspects of the course. As one of the greatest hurdles to providing a core curriculum online, educational design companies are giving more and more attention to designing virtual experiments knowing that there is a ripe market for well-done products. And for the technically astute, programs like Director can allow you to create your own online lab experiment. For instance, one of my colleagues used Director to create a simple online experiment in the relationship and reactivity between different liquids. Using pictures to denote what the final result of the experiment should look like, he created an experiment that enabled students to click on various liquids, which would then "fill" a flask. Properly done in the correct order, the student's virtual flask would look the same as the pictured flask.

8.4 Self-Paced Tutorial

For many years, computers have provided an effective format for step-by-step tutorials. New screens pop up as tasks are accomplished, and animated examples paint themselves to the screen demonstrating an otherwise difficult-to-describe task. There's a lot to be said for the self-paced nature of computerized tutorials, especially when combined with the communication tools available to create a learning community. Applying this technology to exercises and experiments allows the instructor to "walk" students through complex principles. More and more, experts in education and technology are suggesting that self-paced tutorials online allow for self-assessment and competency-based progression. Content materials are especially effective when combined with instructor-led materials and cohort learning. The self-paced tutorials allow students to reach the same level of competency in a course before moving forward in higher cognitive tasks. The instructor is freed up from having to teach basic materials that need to be learned by rote memory, and can concentrate instead on helping students with higher knowledge applications.

8.5 Interdisciplinary Team Teaching

No one can deny that the wealth of information available on the Internet is one reason why so many are "going online." But the explosion of the World Wide Web has as much to do with communication and collaboration, whether that is between students and professionals or buyers and sellers. This environment lends itself to expanded educational models – bringing together faculty from a variety of disciplines to create core curriculum learning communities where knowledge providers and learners interact with each other on multiple levels in a course shell designed to accommodate interdisciplinary learning. "The more the merrier" isn't a phrase usually associated with the classroom, but it applies to some extent in this situation as the discussion is complemented by the diversity of multiple faculty and additional learners. Building an interdisciplinary, team-taught course online will require team-based decision making, and at least as much work as all the courses combined would have if conceived individually, but the result will be an exciting learning opportunity for students and faculty alike. Additional and perhaps more formidable challenges await those who haven't yet developed a structure for learning communities or team teaching, but this new online environment may provide the catalyst for just such an implementation.

8.6 Where Are "You" in the Course?

Don't let technology take over the experience of learning for your student. Your course is more than a "box" and content. Even if your students never have a chance to meet you in person, you can create for them the person that you are online.

Mini Lectures

Take advantage of the technology that now allows you to place audio and video lectures online. Since it taxes the Internet to its fullest, it is best to use these opportunities to bring out your personality, show your enthusiasm, and share anecdotes that reinforce the content. Remember that this is your opportunity to bring out your personality. Reciting facts in a droll monotone is a waste of potential and valuable resources. Write with style and asides.

Video and Audio Intros, Photo

Get your course started right by introducing yourself to your students. With a short audio introduction accompanied by a picture of yourself, or a short video, your students will more quickly become involved with the course as they realize there is a "real" person teaching the course and sense your enthusiasm. Or have some real fun—some instructors will put up a fake picture of themselves such as a movie star or model or animal, and introduce "themselves."

Instructions

You will be a central part of the course as you give students information about the course, and as you guide the students along. Speak to your students directly. Send weekly update emails to your students regarding the course. Model appropriate responses to threaded discussions for them. Explain chatroom etiquette. Direct your students to view particularly interesting threads. Don't just create your course ahead of time and then participate in it marginally when it has gone "live."   Be a constant presence to your students through email, announcements, additions to the course itself, and threaded discussion responses.

Modeling

Modeling is an extremely important aspect of keeping "you" in the course. Students will immediately look up to you as the instructor, and will pay special attention to your contributions in the chat, email, and threaded discussions. While you want to allow plenty of "space" for your students to develop their thoughts and share with each other, don't ignore these communication opportunities. A well-placed message or response, which exudes your personality as well as lends special insight, will further motivate and direct your students as the discussion continues. Modeling extends also to the lectures you create, to the discussion questions you formulate, to your parameters surrounding a successful assignment completion.

Adding the Individual "Fun"

Is your course "fun?" No matter what the difficulty of the content itself, translating the fun of your course is a responsibility you should take seriously. With audio and video, this can be accomplished quite naturally. Animations, cartoons, and graphics will speak to your humorous taste and provide a light moment. Send greeting cards. Put additions into your course that directly relate to particular students in your course. For example, a Japanese student once remarked in a thread that he was feeling quite lonely since he had moved to the U.S. to attend school. (Of course, if he had known about online course programs at the time, he could have stayed in Japan!) For fun, I went out on the Internet and found a site that contained haiku and pictures written and drawn by Japanese school children. I then created a link just for this student in the next unit of the course for a surprise. Just remember, as you are putting in your "fun," that text communication can easily be misconstrued. Use extreme care especially when attempting sarcasm. The humor is usually lost in the attempt to explain the sarcastic statement. Humor can be a two-edged sword, but for those who use it well in the traditional classroom, there is no reason to back away in the online world. For the rest of us, there are other ways we make our classes enjoyable if no less difficult. Analyze these assets and devise ways to recreate the atmosphere you want online — your students will appreciate it!

REFERENCES

1. **Chute, A. et. al**. 1999. *The McGraw-Hill Handbook of Distance Education.* McGraw-Hill.

2. **McLaughlin, M. and R. Sheizaf**. Ed., *Journal of Computer-Mediated Communication.* <http://icmc.huji.ac.il>.

DEVELOPMENT

Translating Content to Online

Lesson 9

Translating Content to Online

LESSON OUTLINE

WHAT YOU WILL LEARN FROM THIS LESSON

YOU WILL BE ABLE TO:

1. Appraise what is effective content, identify the needs of your students, describe and demonstrate methods of instructor interaction over the Internet.

2. Plan and construct how you will present and teach your course online.

3. Define and demonstrate the elements of good Web page design.

4. State and explain the elements of best online course design practices.

5. Formulate and construct your course content to an online environment.

6. Outline the basic issues with regard to copyright and fair use issues.

LESSON 9: TRANSLATING CONTENT TO ONLINE

9.1 Introduction

Online technology is for many of us a foreign medium of instruction. It can create new kinds of teaching and learning experiences; it can change the roles of teacher and student; it can demand modifications of our class materials so that we create interactive learning environments on the World Wide Web and not just static information resources. But you will discover that much of what you did and used in the traditional classroom you will do and use in the online classroom. Consider these three questions:

· What are the most effective ways to present your course materials to your students?
· How will your students communicate to you their mastery of the course material?
· What are the most effective and practical ways for you to keep in close contact with your students in order to give them the feedback and interaction necessary to make your course successful for them?

Familiar questions, aren't they? As you developed your course for the traditional classroom, you were probably answering these very same questions. And the general answers for the online classroom you will find are not that different.

Effective Content Presentation

In a traditional classroom, you may have a syllabus, textbooks and additional reading materials, slide shows and videos, audio recordings, graphs and charts, lectures and assignments, tests and review materials. This same content, in an online course, can be presented to your students through outside text readings, "live" links on your course page to websites that contain textual documents, visual materials, audio and video recordings or to Web pages that contain your own personal lectures, notes and papers. Slide show/audio lectures can be developed for your course that your students merely have to "click" on to view and hear; graphics, tables, maps can all be made a part of your course pages.

The big advantage in an online course is that there is free access to so many materials online that you can easily link out to these materials and make them a permanent part of your course. For example, in a unit on surrealism in poetry, I included Web links to live audio recordings of poets actually reading their own works, Web links to general information about surrealism, Web links to Breton's treatise on surrealism, and Web links to surrealist paintings by such artists as Dali to help my students get the "feel" of surrealism. This ability in an online class to have free access to so many different materials has become a "perk" for me in designing my courses. In a sense, I can now design my own "texts" and not be fettered by the fear of overburdening my students with the cost of too much material. I'm going to give you plenty of useful hints in the following paragraphs about creating an online course, but you should know that there are many useful websites available for assisting you in this effort. I have provided a partial listing of such sites in Table 9.1.

Assessing Your Students

In your traditional classroom, you probably had your students take tests, complete short assignments, write in journals, engage in class discussions, complete projects, and write final papers. In the online classroom, you can create timed and secured multiple choice, t/f, short answer, matching, fill in the blank, and essay exams which can include automatic feedback for the students and computerized scoring for objective questions. Students can respond to discussion questions that you post on the threaded discussions. They can post journal entries that you can read and comment on within the actual entries. They can post papers online or email them to you privately. They can engage in "live" discussions in the chatroom.

Instructor Interaction

In the traditional classroom, you may see your students once, twice, three times a week. Your students will meet you during office hours. You see your students; you talk to your students; you form good relationships with your students. This leads to what I feel is the biggest challenge in creating an online course. If I don't have daily face-to-face contact with my students, how can I create rapport with my students that will lead to a better learning environment for them? You can extend your personality into the course through your writing style., personal greetings by email, making a personal phone call, meeting students face-to-face at the beginning of the course, sending electronic greeting cards (**http://www.bluemountain.com/**), or sending a small prize that recognizes outstanding performance. You can order custom pens from (**http://www.orderpens. com/home_pens**/) for about 40 cents each with your own message on it. I put the words "*I am soooo...smart*" all over the pen and give it students who demonstrate that characteristic. My students value them as priceless.

Interaction between students and professor is essential in the online course, but it can be overwhelming for the professor trying to keep up with 25 students. You need to make firm decisions beforehand on the number of times a week you will respond to email messages, how you will respond to threaded discussions, journal entries, and exams.

But how does all of this come together in an online course? And what special considerations do I need to make because I am designing a course in the online environment?

Websites
Cyberprof:/ University of Illinois **http://ntx2.cso.uiuc.edu/wss/services/cyberprof/index.html** eCollege.com **http://www.ecollege.com** Filamentality **http://www.kn.pacbell.com/wired/fil** This is a do-it-yourself, fill-in-the-blank site that starts you off by picking a topic, then searching the Web, and assembling relevant websites that may then be turned into appropriate activities for students. Try it out…it's great for a template. Intro to Instructional Design/ Univ. of Iowa **http://www.uiowa.edu/~idt/courses/7W120** Learning Over the Internet **http://www.unc.edu/cit/guides/irg-38.html** Learning Space / Lotus **http://www.lotus.com/home.nsf/welcome/learnspace** PBS Adult Learning Systems Onlime / teleWeb Courses **http://www.pbs.org/adultlearning/als/** Resources for Creating Online Courses **http://www.cet.sfsu.edu/online-resources/webbased.html** Resources for Developing On-line Courses in a Box / Concordia University **http://www.csp.edu/courses/** The Node **http://thenode.org** A "not-for-profit" organization that promotes effective uses of Internet-based technology. It offers rich resources on instructional design, and pedagogy and community forums (that are timely and on going). The Web Course Development Home Page / Univ. of Louisville **http://dossantos.cbpa.louisville.edu/cbpa/webcourse/index4.htm** Web-based Instruction Resource Site **http://www.personal.psu.edu/faculty/w/d/wdm2/research.htm** WebCT Course Tools **http://homebrew.cs.ubc.ca/webct/**

Table 9.1
Web sites useful in assisting you to develop online courses

DEVELOPMENT

When I started creating my online course and then teaching it, I knew nothing and had very few resources to help me. Everything I learned was by, sometimes, painful experience. But because an online course is basically a series of Web pages, understanding not only some of the principles of instructional design, but Web page design, can help you answer some of your questions, before you experience "trial by fire."

9.2 What Is Instructional Design?

Instructional design is something you have probably been doing for years now for your traditional classes without even realizing the terminology behind what you are doing. It is simply the formal planning of a course and the creation of activities and events in a course that will help your students to learn. These can be both activities that you direct and activities that you ask your students to do independently or as collaborative groups. Creating activities and presenting your content in ways that motivate your students to learn on their own become especially important online since you may no longer have that "captive audience" sitting in front of you three times a week. There are three basic stages to instructional design. [1]

Determining the Needs of Your Students and Your Goals for the Course

What do your students know already, what do you want them to know by the end of your course, and what guidance and help do you need to give your students in order to help them achieve your goals and theirs?

Just as in the traditional classroom, you can create prerequisites for your course, develop entrance exams, and **self-assessment tools** online to help determine if the students have the prior knowledge they need to successfully complete your course. Specifically for your online course, you also want to assess your students' skills in technology and to provide them with information and training resources if needed. The **goals** and **learning objectives** for your course may be ones determined by you or standard goals determined by your institution. Regardless, determining up front what you want your students to achieve in your course will make the planning of your course that much easier. And presenting them upfront to your students will help them focus. Just be sure in writing your learning objectives that you write directly to your student audience; that you give parameters for determining whether the objective has been met in a measurable way; and that these objectives should be met within the duration of the course. (Note: "should" as opposed to "will." We do not have ultimate control over the learning success of our students.) In determining your goals, don't forget to consider what "roadblocks" you and your students might face in the course, which online can often include the technology itself, the autonomous nature of the online environment, and yours and your students' skill with technology.

Planning How You Will Present and Teach Your Course

At the heart of instructional design is the development of instruction that encompasses the creation and presentation of content. In order to instruct, you must have content and effective formats for presenting that content. You must also determine the sequence of instruction—what will you do and present first, and then next, and then next?

Robert Gagne, a preeminent voice in instructional design and learning theory, suggests there are nine **instructional events** that prompt the necessary conditions for learning to occur. (See Table 9.2) These instructional events can help you determine the content needs of your course and the most effective ways for your students to receive and/or discover that content and to be engaged and motivated by it.

Assessing Your Students and the Effectiveness of Your Course

This is the creation of assessments that will help you determine if your students have learned what you wanted them to learn. It is also your overall evaluation of the course and how well your instructional events created opportunities for learning. Besides creating the standard student evaluation form to help determine the overall effectiveness of an online course, some instructors establish standard exit exams that can be used for comparative analysis between classes and/or **portfolios** of accumulated work.

9.3 What Are the Practicalities of Good Web Page Design?

Identifying Needs

A major part of instructional design in the early stage of identifying needs and objectives for a course is the determination of resource availability and the issues involved in using those resources. Since online courses are created through Internet and software technology and are essentially a series of linked Web pages, understanding the basics of good Web page design is essential in designing your course and formatting your content. Don't be alarmed if you have no desire to do this. Remember in Lesson 7 that many course platforms provide templates that make it unnecessary for you create Web designs if you don't want to. However, some the principles mentioned here will still be important as you fill in the templates.

In creating an online class, you are creating a series of linked Web pages. Web page design is both visual and textual and it makes concessions to the present capabilities surrounding online technology. For instance, because of Internet connection speed and bandwidth issues, a video online does not come across the same way as a video on TV does. Audio and picture may not match; movement can "stutter"; the video itself can be the size of a matchbox. Creating too "rich" a Web page or section of your online course by incorporating too many images or animations can slow down the amount of time it

Table 9.2.
Gagne's nine instructional events that prompt the necessary conditions for learning to occur

Gagne's Instructional Events

Gaining Attention: the purpose of this event is simply to arouse your students' curiosity. You might ask leading questions, create scenarios online demonstrations, or point to Web pages that are "mysterious" at first and then explained later (or later presented again to the students with instructions to them to now explain significances and underlying concepts).

Informing the Student of the Objective: this event gives scope and meaning to the unit of instruction from the very start. You may list learning objectives and/or describe in detail the intended assessment assignment for the unit that will measure what learning has occurred

Using Recall: "scaffolding" or building upon prior knowledge and experience is an effective teaching method. You may begin with some review of prior materials, create self-assessment tests covering materials from required pre-requisite materials, establish parallels to common knowledge constructs, and/or provide hypertext links to basic background materials. You can then make correlations to new materials.

Presenting the Stimulus Material: this is simply providing students with the materials to be learned or providing the means by which students can actively discover the materials to be learned. You can create short audio/video lectures, PowerPoint presentations, text examples, links to the WWW, projects, and experiments that ask students to search out materials and then present these materials to the class.

Providing Learning Guidance: this event directly addresses the concept of "instructor as facilitator." Rather than "telling" students everything in lecture or discussion, you create opportunities for self-learning or group collaborative learning through discussion questions, listings of resources for study and exploration, and the creation of small, progressive assignments that allow for ongoing evaluation and assistance in individual student understanding. Given the autonomous nature of the online environment and the added demands in managing an online class, providing opportunities for student-led learning can be especially important.

Eliciting the Performance: typically this is the "show me" event. You create assignments or tests that evaluate comprehension or ask for group or individual presentations.

Providing Feedback: in this event you acknowledge the correctness or degree of correctness of the performance. Prompt and consistent feedback is essential in the online environment, whether it consists of threaded discussion responses, email comments on papers and assignment, or real time conferencing through the chatroom. Feedback can be both individual and general to the group. Feedback can also be automatically generated through programs like JavaScript. For example, a student can click on multiple answers to a quiz and a "pop-up box" can give immediate feedback. Objective tests can be created in which answers can be automatically and immediately graded.

Assessing Performance: in this event, you must decide whether the "performance" truly indicates that real learning has occurred. Some online instructors will create multiple assessment strategies in order to determine validity and reliability of performance outcome. Assessing performance can include proctored exams, online exams, graded projects, term papers, class participation, threaded discussion, or even laboratory or field experiments performed at a distance.

Enhancing Retention and Transfer: this event asks students to apply their newly acquired knowledge to other learning situations. You can create course-long projects that are culminations of overall learning in the course. Or require end of the course portfolios that show progress in the course through items such as essay rewrites, compilation of quizzes, and self-evaluation essays.

takes your students to access that portion of your course or "download" it. Besides issues of Internet connection speed and bandwidth when designing your course and creating content, you must also consider these issues:

Scrolling

"Page breaks" in a text document on the Web only exist so far as how big your computer monitor screen is, or to be more precise, what your **screen area** is. Screen area has to do with the number of "pixels" or dots that make up what you see on your screen. If you increase the screen area, you can have more information appear on your monitor. If there is more information than what can appear on your screen, or for example if your document is "longer" than your computer screen, then you are given the functionality of "scrolling" through the document by clicking on a scroll bar that appears on the side of the computer screen. (Content on the Web can also be wider than your screen area. A scroll bar will appear on the bottom of your screen to allow you to scroll from side to side.) As you scroll, your document seemingly moves "upward," allowing you to see additional text. For some, any kind of scrolling is a deterrent to not just reading comprehension, but motivation to even read through an entire document.   Reading online, for the unpracticed, can be difficult. To create Web pages with a small amount of material is one way to solve the scrolling problem, but too many bits can be annoyingly sketchy to your students and create disjunction in the information being presented. Long documents can be split up into different focused parts or "chunks" and made into "external pages." External pages are Web pages linked to a main Web page through hypertext links. Usually blue font distinguishes hypertext links and these links can be words or phrases within a text document. I prefer to include long text documents as PDF or RTF files that can be downloaded off the Web site and printed by the student. My students prefer this option when they print out my detailed class notes. They place them in a three ring binder and use a highlighter to study from the notes.

Clicks

Sometimes in the zeal to avoid scrolling issues, Web and online course designers will create too many hypertext links on their Web pages. Some of you may have already experienced the exasperating experience of trying to find information on the WWW and having to click on four or five links before finally reaching a Web page that gives you real information. Some designers have suggested the rule of "three": all essential information should be only three clicks away from the main Web page document. Though personally, I love the use of hypertext in an online "lecture" to allow students to explore background information behind concepts or have the opportunity to study them in more depth, some designers feel that too much hypertext can be distracting. Perhaps the balance is to provide hypertext links only to the most key information in a text lecture.

Screen Readability

The issue of screen readability encompasses such decisions as font type, size and color choices for text, background color and image choices, and the organization of content onscreen. At an online conference I "attended," I experienced the frustration of trying to read the black text of online documents against a marbled, dark gray background. The issue of screen readability goes even deeper when considering the ADA standards for Web page development that allows those with visual disabilities to access content online through screen readers. Images must be created with "alt tags," small written descriptions of images that pop up and allow the screen reader to describe images and the visually impaired to "see" them. Content must be organized in such a way that the screen reader can logically follow its progress. For more information on screen readability and accessibility, check out the Web Accessibility Initiative at (**http://www.w3.org**).

Navigation

Well-designed Web pages provide visitors with complete directions and cues on how to move through the website. It's easy to get "lost" as you click through multiple pages. They will contain links with directions on how to move and back and forth between pages; advice on how to move through the Web page, as well as headings and descriptions.

Visual Design

Content in an online course is not just text. As a matter of fact, "text online" is a standard you do not want to live up to. Visual content is as important as text. Online instructors will include graphics, images, photos, animations, and tables, colored backgrounds, charts and graphs. Visual design is effective when it enhances text, provides information, and draws the eye through the course.

Conducting a search online for "Web page design tutorials" will offer up a wealth of free advice. For example, *Bignose Bird*, boasting of the oddest name on the Internet, offers free materials and tutorials for webmasters (**http://bignosebird.com**). *Web Group Designs* offers HTML help and tips on Web design (**http://www.htmlhelp.com**). Additional tips are provided in Table 9.3.

Tips for Web Page Design in the Online Class

There are many books on how to create Web pages and how to best design them. Many of these tips will improve the "readability" and navigation of your online course for your students. The following tips are from *Creating Web Pages with HTML Simplified.* [3]

Tips For Web Page Design

Put Important Information First: People tend to scan through text online, hence making it important to highlight essential information. In the online class this tip translates into beginning your units of instruction with learning objectives and introductions.

Emphasize Important Information: This refers again to people's tendency to skip around when reading online. Long sections of text online can be daunting, even, unfortunately, for the online student. Creating online courses that contain series of small "chunks" of topic-focused discussions on external pages is one way of emphasizing important information.

Regulate Page Length: Strike a balance between too much and too little "text online." A few sentences on a Web page are probably not enough, while five or more screens of text are too much.

Use Headings: Headings allow readers to "skim" through a Web page and identify its important issues and ideas. Help your students navigate through your course by supplying them with clear headings that identify the topic focus for each particular section.

Research Copyright Permissions and Restrictions: Before copying and pasting text or images from another website into your course, be sure that these materials are "free" to the public. If copyright information is not available on the website, contact the owner and ask permission before making the materials a permanent part of your course. You might simply want to create a hypertext link in your course to the Web page and its content.

Consider Transfer Speed: Minimize file size for Web pages and images as much as possible. Some students may have older modems with slow connection speeds and /or poor phone connections that can make the downloading of a course excruciatingly long.

Plan for Variations in Browsers: A website in a Netscape Browser can look very different in a browser like Internet Explorer. Font appearance, image appearance, and placement of content can be altered from one browser to the next. In addition, the navigation tools in a browser can differ from each other, so be careful not to give explicit directions in your course on performing tasks such as book marking or navigating, by browser, through the Web pages of your course. Before opening your course to students, be sure and "QA" it in a few commonly used browsers.

Table 9.3.
Tips for Web page design for online classes

9.4 What Are the Best Online Course Design Practices?

So how do instructional design principles and Web page design mesh in the online classroom? Interestingly enough, the "limitations" that technology sets actually become opportunities for effective teaching strategies online. Below you will find listed a few of the "buzzwords" in online education and their descriptions. Each of these concepts addresses practices in designing an online course that have been found to be effective and essential.

Content Chunking

On a basic level, "chunking" content resolves the issue of scrolling in an online course. Content is split into shorter, focused units of material that are separated by headings or made into separate Web pages, or external pages. "Chunking" can also solve the problems of reading online: reading documents on a computer screen can be an eye strain. Recently on the DEOS listserv, the unsettling argument was made, based on the fact that reading online can be tiring, that text online should be limited to third grade level materials and consist of only a small number of words per sentence. Chunking can allow you to present more rigorous text online and still limit the eye strain to students.

But the concept of chunking has implications that go well beyond the easing of eye strain or too much scrolling. When content is chunked through the use of hypertext links to create what is called "hypermedia," opportunities for individual learning are created.[4] In other words, the organization of content through hypertext links can cause students to become actively involved in learning and to make choices based on individual need. This is a very "grass-roots" approach to providing the kinds of learning experiences that emerging technologies in adaptive learning will provide by using computers to assess individual student needs and acquired knowledge and then present to each student the content and activities necessary to fulfill the learning objectives of the course.

Redundancy

The online world is a new environment for your students. They may be dazzled and stumped by new ways of navigating a course, of reading text, and participating in discussions. Visually, there are so many new things for students to view in an online course that they may become "blinded" to some of the details of your course. Repetition in an online course of directions, important information, navigational information becomes particularly important. Each time you ask your students to use a new piece of technology in your course, you will want to supply them with brief directions on how to use it, even if you have these directions in your main syllabus. Assignment details should be repeated in your course as well even if you have used your syllabus to impart this information. Without redundancy in your course, you will suffer through an onslaught of email from confused and needy students. I realized after teaching my course a few times, that I had successfully made its navigation and use clear enough to my students when I no longer received emails from my students questioning every new and old move we were making.

Interaction

Web pages created for instruction can take the form of online resources, self-paced tutorials, or interactive courses that are instructor-facilitated. Kind, amount, and quality of interaction are key factors that distinguish the online class from the online resource.

Interaction in an online class is the ability, either asynchronously or synchronously, of students and teacher to respond to each other's questions and to encourage and support each other in directed and undirected tasks. Content presentation that encourages interaction can take the form of discussion questions and assignments that call for group collaboration and feedback. The actual interaction between students can be unmonitored by the instructor or facilitated, highly structured and evaluative, or "free." Online discussions are best generated by open-ended questions that ask students to analyze, synthesize, and critically evaluate issues. These kinds of questions do not allow for a simple "yes" or "no" answer. They revolve around "why"and "how." They ask for further explanations, for definition, for students to evaluate information to compare thought and idea between different text readings. Questions like these require critical thinking from your students and cannot be answered by fact or by mere personal opinion. Critical thinking skills are increasingly important in our complex world. For more information, check out one center for critical thinking, which is associated with Sonoma State University (**http://www.criti calthinking.org**). The site contains resources that define critical thinking; offers curriculum and assessment strategies for higher ed, primary, and secondary schools; and links to additional critical thinking communities of learning.

Content Interactivity

Making active involvement in an online course an integral part of the overall design structure is one of the keys to creating an effective course. Interaction through communication has been a key issue in creating a good online course from the beginning because the ability of students to collaborate in the learning process has been acknowledged from the start as a big determinant for any course's effectiveness. But simply scrolling through text online creates a passive learning situation. I have heard some instructional designers and online educators comment that for each Web page in an online course, students should be participating in some kind of activity with that content. Through the use of software programs such as JavaScript, Flash, Director, and many, many others, as well as by supplementing your online class with a CD-ROM, instructors can create some simple interactivity with content for their students. Mouse "roll-overs" allow additional information to appear on screen; Java "pop up" boxes can allow students to take self-assessments and be given immediate feedback; simple science experiments can be created where students can play with "filling" flasks; graphs and diagrams can be manipulated in mathematical problem solving; maps can be "clicked" on to discover further information (another form of "content chunking").

Multimodal Learning

Because one of the precepts of instructional design is individual learning, understanding how individuals learn and then designing your online course and how you will present its content will be major tasks. The classroom strategy of lecturing for forty-five minutes and then taking questions is not quite such a viable option online. Some instructors, looking for an easy solution to the challenges of creating an online course, hope that a videotape of their classroom lectures will suffice. Unfortunately, students taking your online course at home are not your captive audience and you and your lecture can easily be "clicked" off. Your students will be sitting in front of a box. It's your job to reach out and get them involved with your course materials, the other students, and you. Understanding that students are motivated to learn in different ways and then incorporating several different teaching strategies into your online course is a big step toward retaining your online students.

Learning styles have been classified as tactile, visual, and kinesthetic. Students can be reflective learners and active learners. You will find that some students learn online best through reading text, either online or hardbound, while others learn best when the concepts of the text are presented through graphs or charts, or are explained to them through audio lectures and slide shows. Some students may be "visual learners," who are excited by images and find concepts easier to learn when they are illustrated. Some students may learn best when they are actively involved with others in assignments that ask for group collaboration or synchronous chatroom discussions where there is instantaneous "give and take," while others may learn best when they are involved in individual activities and have time for solitary reflection before joining a discussion, such as a threaded discussion. Pushing your course past the basic "text online and email" course or a videotape posting will make it more effective. Designing for multimodal learning means incorporating audio and video, graphics and images, hypertext, asynchronous and synchronous communication. It is a course designed for the eye, the ear, and the brain.

Instructional Multimedia

Multimedia bring variety and interest to an online course and address differences in individual learning styles. Creating your own audio clips and short video clips for your online course can increase your "ownership" of the course and help to create personal bonds with your students. But superfluous and irrelevant use of multimedia can reduce the effectiveness of your course, hence the term "instructional multimedia." Remember also the issues with bandwidth and file downloading. Be careful of creating too large a file to download. Use audio to augment text lectures and PowerPoint to introduce units of instruction in your course, or to narrate the significance of diagrams and illustrations. Hearing your voice will help your students get to know you better and help you emphasize key information in your course. Short video clips are effective for introductions, short demonstrations of lab experiments, background information, and primary source materials. PowerPoint slide shows can display key concepts and summaries; graphic animations that allow for physical manipulations by your students can address the needs of your kinesthetic, "touchy feely" learner.

Portfolio Assessment

Presently, one of the most critical issues in online teaching is test security. Traditional classroom instructors trumpet the alarm for papers purchased online, while online instructors must ponder, even beyond that, the crisis of unproctored tests and student-substitutions for class "attendance." The anonymity of the online classroom and its "anywhere/anytime" nature make reliable student evaluation difficult at best. And the fact that browsers allow even online exams that are restricted by time and date to print only heightens the issue. Technologies are being tested now that would allow for more secured and reliable methods for student identification and for eliminating cheating in exams, but these are not commonly available as of yet. One solution for many universities with online programs is to set up test centers around a region so that proctored exams can take place, but the typical online student who has taken the course because it is "anywhere/anytime" can be quite disgruntled at the prospect of driving 60 or so miles to find a regional test center.

Unfortunately then, the common testing strategy of a midterm and final exam in the traditional classroom does not always translate effectively into the online classroom. You can email exams to proctors at your student sites. I have done this for students in England, on a Navaho reservation, and in a medical school in Worcester. You may not always wish to evaluate your students this way. Alternatively you can develop a collection of ways to assess your students in what we call a **portfolio**. Portfolio assessment simply means providing your students with many different ways to show you that they have mastered the content in your course. Testing is only one portion of that assessment and, often, the questions are subjective and qualifiable, rather than objective and quantifiable. To create a portfolio assessment strategy, consider including threaded discussions as a percentage of the grade; require short essays or journal writing; include group projects and presentations, participation in synchronous discussions, self-evaluation essays; include drafts for final papers in the grade. Let formal testing be only part of the grade. Requiring students to write and turn in drafts of papers is an excellent way for you to get to know each of your students' voice and style and can help you determine if a final paper is a purchased one or not. Because student retention is a problem and community building online is one solution to that problem, designate class participation as part of the portfolio assessment and decide on your standards for that. Portfolio assessment helps you address the problems of cheating, student retention, and multiple learning styles. It also can force your students into critical and evaluative thinking. Additional information on portfolio assessment can be found in teacher resources online, including The Access Indiana Teaching and Learning Center's Teacher Resource Guide, which may be viewed at the folowing location (**http://tlc.ai.org/portaidx.htm**).

9.5 Translating Your Content Online

The Online Syllabus

Principles, theories, and concepts can help you understand the larger picture behind developing an online course, but actually knowing what content to translate and the issues involved in translating it are essential practicalities. The content for an online course can be grouped into two large chunks: (1) the online syllabus and (2) the actual content for the course. Basically, the online syllabus can be the traditional classroom syllabus that you hand out on the first day of class, but with some changes that take into consideration the online environment (Table 9.4).

Course Policies and Procedures

While many of these will be similar to your traditional classroom policies, you do need to consider some new policies and procedures and some changes to the old because of the unique challenges and problems that can and will arise in the online classroom environment. For example, consider the following issues as you devise your course policies on attendance and participation (Table 9.5).

The "Disappearing Student" How will you deal with a student who simply does not "show up" for class (ie. post threads, reply to emails, participate in chatrooms for a week or two weeks or three weeks at a time), and then returns with all his/her assignments completed for the weeks missed?

The "Dog Ate My Homework" How will you deal with students who experience technical problems beyond their control, such as computers crashing, servers malfunctioning, "lost" papers? Or claim that emails were sent regularly and must have gotten "lost," which <u>can</u> happen in the Internet world?

The "Procrastinator" How will you deal with the student who never posts work on time, who never gets in touch with his/her group in time for collaborative work? And who does not respond to any of your inquiries?

Syllabus Item	Online Considerations
Instructor Bio: **Your standard bio**	Pretty self-explanatory, but don't forget that besides text, you can put up an audio/video introduction of yourself, a device that can help "humanize" the course and be helpful if you plan to meet your students face to face in a public setting such as an exhibit or reading. Your bio and welcome can be combined. You can also link to your personal Web page.
Instructor Welcome: **Your "greetings at the door"**	First of many ways to create a personal connection with your students. Especially important given the anonymous nature of the online environment. While a text welcome is certainly adequate, combining it with a photo, or delivering it through audio and/or video will help "humanize" your course and make that information accessible to those with visual or auditory impairments.
Instructor Office Hours	Because your students will be both on campus and at a distance, office hours should be a combination of formats—face to face on campus, through chatrooms, by telephone, by email, by asynchronous threaded discussion. Hint: keep in mind that your online students may inhabit different time zones. Split one long office "hour" into a couple of shorter ones and conduct them at different times during the day and the week.
Course Description	Not only given an overview of the course and course goals, describe how technology will play a part in the course.
Course Objectives	If applicable, include technology objectives with course objectives.
Course Policies	The online environment creates unexpected situations. You will run into conduct and performance problems in the online course that you have not had to deal with in the traditional classroom. Be very clear and exact in your course policies and very firm. Because the course policy section is a crucial component of an online course, please see **Table 9.5** on Course Policies for specific suggestions.

Table 9.4
Recommended items for the online syllabus and suggestions for adapting them to the online course

DEVELOPMENT

Table 9.4
Recommended items for the online syllabus and suggestions for adapting them to the online course

Syllabus Item	Online Considerations
Prerequisites for Course	Provide information on entrance exams and prior course requirements for your course, and technology requirements. Create an online self-assessment tool and review module to help students "bone-up" on basic information needed for your course. Include information on technology requirements for the course, including software and plug-in necessities. Along with technology prerequisites, you must also provide "help" sources and self-assessment opportunities to help students determine their own skill level with technology.
Required Materials for Course	For the online course, include not only text materials, but software, plug-ins, hardware information, browser specification, type of software needed for compatibility needs in group sharing and in turning in assignments, such as Microsoft Word as opposed to ClarisWorks or WordPerfect.
Grading Policies	If you want your students to interact and participate on a regular basis in the class, then make class participation a significant percentage of the grade. Define participation: responding to threaded discussions a certain number of times, participating in group work or chatroom sessions, etc. To deter cheating online, do not rely simply on a midterm and exam. Use a portfolio assessment approach for evaluating the achievement of your students.
Group Participation Policies	The online environment provides a wonderful opportunity for successful group collaborations because groups can "meet" both synchronously and asynchronously without having to physically travel anywhere. However, structuring and maintaining productive groups online is challenging. Be very clear in what your expectations are for the group work; assign groups and be ready to reassign groups when some groups fail to work well together. Appoint group leaders and make fulfillment of group assignments their responsibility. Give detailed instructions on how the groups will collaborate, in what form they will pass work to each other, on specific due dates and progress reports to you.

Syllabus Item	Online Considerations
Course Calendar	Create a course calendar that can be printed out by your students. List any readings, discussions, quizzes, etc., that will take place and the date "due." Consider assigning due dates that will help your class become a "learning cohort." You might consider some kind of weekly consistency: weekly readings, journal writings, discussions, and quizzes.
General Syllabus	This is the document that students will be able to preview for all your course assignments, topics covered, etc., and dates due. Many students print this portion of the syllabus off for a hard copy reference. A lot of this information you will be repeating in more detail in each of your course units since, in our experience, students often forget to "click" back to the syllabus for weekly information and, instead, shoot off an unnecessary email to you. Here you should hit the major assignments, readings, activities, and due dates. ***Note: If, normally, you organize a syllabus for a traditional classroom course into daily assignments/topics covered, you want to condense that material into weekly units or projects that span weeks. Remember, you are not making the most of the online environment if you require daily "check-in" for your student. Name and date by week (for example: Keats: Jan 4 – Jan 11). List reading assignments due for that week: text readings, Web links to outside material etc. List any assignments due for that week (for example, papers due, threaded discussions, journal entries). List any assessment strategies for that week (for example: exams, discussion questions, journal entries). List any audio/visual material to be viewed for the week.

Table 9.4
Recommended items for the online syllabus and suggestions for adapting them to the online course

DEVELOPMENT

The "Flamer" Imagine the disgruntled student who may, in the sanctuary of online anonymity, send you, particular students, or your entire class offensive email? Or the student who unwittingly sends objectionable email because he or she does not have the necessary skills to communicate well through text writing?

Course Polices and Procedures

Attendance: Decide how you will determine attendance. Instead of requiring daily attendance, which defeats the purpose of the online classroom for many of the non-traditional students in your class, require several assignments for a week's time or duration of a project. Require participation in the threaded discussion, weekly journal writing, participation in one of a few chatroom sessions. Make class participation part of your attendance criteria and give not only due dates, but due "times" such as Thursday midnight or Monday noon so that you can organize your grading time well.

Absenteeism: Make a firm stand on what you define as absenteeism and the accountability you will put on your students to adhere to that policy. Many first time online students come into the course expecting it to be self-paced and self-timed. If work or family matters interfere with the course, sometimes they will simply "take off," without explanation. If you are conducting your course as a successive progression from one unit of study to the next and you expect whole class participation, then you need to determine how you will deal with student family emergencies or work situations.

Also determine your policies on technology emergencies: student computers will crash; Internet connections will fail. Are there alternative methods for the student to notify you of these kinds of technical emergencies? Do you expect work to be turned in on a timely basis, no matter what the technological issue? One possibility is to acknowledge that technical problems do happen, but to put the responsibility on the student to contact you through emergency numbers etc.; to submit assignments via fax or postal mail or office mail. Also advise students to back up all their work as they are working on it in case their computer does crash. I created a "Worried Doctor" policy. If I did not hear from that student by toward the end of a week, I would send a "Worried Doctor" email inquiring if everything was okay and reminding the student that participation and assignments were due. If I did not hear from that student within that week, I would send another bit firmer email asking the student to contact me immediately. If there was no response by the end of the week, I had the choice of either calling that student by phone or of docking the student a percentage of his/her class participation grade.

Academic Dishonesty: The varied possibilities for student cheating online are one of the big impediments to many instructors wanting to teach online. Dealing with plagiarism and cheating in the traditional classroom is worry enough; adding a basically "faceless" environment in which examinations are un-proctored and student work in class is unobservable make online teaching overly daunting for some. Be aware that students online, and in the classroom, can find many websites that offer pre-written papers on topics in every subject area, and/or custom written papers on specific topics you may assign. Students may also pay others to take online examinations for them, or, if a group of online students are in the same area, congregate for group test taking. In order stave off these problems, have very firm consequences in place for any kind of cheating and design your course with "safeguards" implemented into it. For instance, create objective tests for self-testing, or create pools of questions that can then be distributed randomly across the students in your class.

DEVELOPMENT

Table 9.5
Course poli-
cies and pro-
cedures

Course Polices and Procedures

If you insist on objective tests, create timed tests and limit access to only a particular day for so many hours. Make the objective test strenuous by creating so many test question items that the student must rely on what he/she has learned and not an "open-book." Better yet, create questions that are open-ended, asking students "Why" and "How" so that they must provide answers of analysis, evaluation, and explanation. Use the writing process when assigning written projects—ask for early drafts and outlines and follow the progress of each of your students so that you will recognize personal writing style and understanding of content.

Courtesy Code: In order to combat bad behavior in the online classroom, create some standards for conduct and address issues in writing emails and responding to peer work in the threaded discussions or chatrooms. Give examples of appropriate responses. Determine ahead of time how you will deal with angry or belligerent students.

Email procedures: Unfortunately, email will be a big part of your course, even as you incorporate other ways to communicate with your students and receive assignments from them. If you are teaching more than one course online, you will need to establish some order as to how your students address their email to you and as to how they will sign their email. Many students are used to sending out personal emails with their user names only, such as "HotLips," or "MousieMan," and forget to put their names on their assignments or questions. You will also want to establish some way for both you and your students to know if email has been received. Because I was using EudoraPro and had established some "filters" in the program that would help me sort and respond to email automatically, I had some specific requirements. Here are examples of some of the email procedures I laid out for my students:

   Sending assignments: in the Subject header of your email, please put your last name, our course number, and the word "Assignment." (This way my email program was able to recognize to which student, class and assignment file this email was to be sorted, and then generate the appropriate "Your assignment has been received" email to be send automatically to the student next time I opened up the email program.)

   General email: when sending email other than assignments to me or the rest of the class, please identify yourself fully in the text of the email. Use the subject header to indicate if the email is a general comment, question for the entire class, question specifically for me.

   Attachment compatibility: not all word processing programs will produce documents readable by other word processing programs and not all attachment programs in email programs can create attachments readable by other programs. At the beginning of the course, we will "test" out each other's programs. Please be prepared to translate documents into RTF or Rich Text Format, or to paste documents into the body of your emails.

Table 9.5 Course policies and procedures

Course Polices and Procedures

Composing email: If you are sending assignments by email, please compose these assignments on a word program and copy and paste them into your emails. This will help you avoid "email disasters" and "wipeouts."

email Copies: please keep personal copies of all emails you send for this class.

Technical Help: instruct your students on how to receive technical support, whether that be by you or another "help desk" service. If you have the luxury of outside tech help and do not want to be overwhelmed by the number of technical issues your students may confront, clearly describe in your syllabus who they should contact and how and then create an "IT Help" email repeating this contact information that you can send out automatically to students who ask you for assistance. Also provide directions on how to contact you if they are unable to do so through email, either through an office phone number, administrative phone number, or student support service number. As in the traditional classroom, it is best not to provide home numbers. Also inform your students of how you will contact them if you experience technology problems.

Instructor Responsibility: Provide information on what the students can expect from you. Teaching an online course can be overwhelming. Conceivably, you can be "on call" 24 hours a day through email. You could provide endless written feedback on papers and threaded discussion responses. You could be responsible for "fixing" or providing information for all technology problems your students will confront. You must decide ahead of time what responsibility you will take in the course and provide it to your students in detail. For example, how often will you respond to email? On what days? At what times? Will you respond to every threaded discussion response by every student? Are you the "IT" person for the course, or are there alternative help resources for your students? How long will your office hours online last?

Help Hints: Provide students with any additional information they need in order to complete the course successfully. I provided my students with directions on how to navigate my course, reminding them to click on all "blue" words in order to access additional "pages" in my course; directions on how to use my email listserv; on how to post and respond to threaded discussions, etc. These "hints" I also placed throughout my course—the more directions I gave upfront on how to take my course, the less email I received from confused students.

Cyberspace and Writing

Already cyberspace "coinages" hint at problems in this faceless, electronic communication that are symptomatic of deeper issues inherent in poor writing skills.

In 1996, when my colleagues and I at the University of Colorado at Denver began teaching online, we had never heard of the word "Netiquette" (Newsgroup Netiquette) but we too soon faced the impetus for that later coining in the form of not only occasional "flames" from a malcontent (a poetry student of mine once "virtually" stood up on his "desk" and proclaimed: " I am great and you stink" to the entire class), but in subtle emails perilously close to the gray side of appropriate. We quickly wrote "Courtesy Clauses" into our course policies, wagging our heads in wonderment over these strange "solar flares." But we also asked ourselves this: could the online environment alone and its sanctuary of anonymity be responsible for such "shiftings" in student communication? The answer came for me in a phone call with a student who responded to my "interrogation" with true shock: "I didn't mean to sound like that. I just don't write too good."

Netiquette (Etiquette plus the Net). "Netiquette" may sound more like a matter for Emily Post than academicians, but we already know from our traditional classrooms how "not writing too good" often first translates itself as an ignorance of such basic writing considerations as audience and writer role. How can we expect these very same students in our online courses, who cannot control their writing enough to communicate to us in appropriate ways, to begin to formulate questions on a higher cognitive plane or to begin debate and analysis? For more information on Netiquette, try the following (**http://www.acs.appstate.edu/~krb/syllabus/netiquet2.txt**

Emoticons. The issue of student writing online does not end with "etiquette on the net." "Emoticons" is the coinage for graphic smiles and frowns (e.g. (-: and)-:) so prevalent in email messages now. They are used to "show" humor or disappointment or other "feelings" online. The question here is how can anyone, so mistrustful of his own abilities to communicate through words that he must resort to barely decipherable graphics, engage in thoughtful written exchanges with peers and instructors or collaborate fully in projects demanding critical analysis and feedback? Though emoticons are quick and easy ways to make sure your point gets across in the right way (it's amazing how difficult it is to express sarcasm or irony or just light-weight humor through email) and you and your students should use them at times, the emphasis should be on teaching by example how to express tone and feeling in writing.

Solutions for dealing with poor online writing can range from instructors providing links to web tutorials on writing, institutions providing online tutorial assistance, and "across the curriculum" teaching that pairs English instructors with other content experts to teach a course.

Content for the Unit/Week/Project Module

Now it's time to begin concentrating on what we consider to be the "meat" of your course development process: the content you will provide your students in individual units of study and the details of the work you expect your students to complete during your course. Before you begin designing your units, ponder the words an instructional designer once gave me: "If there's too much work in your course for your students, your students will complain. But if there's not enough, you'll never know until the final evaluation of your course."

Better, I think, to err on the side of too much, as long as it's not just busy work you are including. For my own courses, I wanted to make sure that each week my students were reading materials, discussing materials, and either critiquing or writing their own materials. I also wanted to make sure that there were a few deadlines during the week. The bigger assignments were always due at the end of the week, but during the week, I assigned due dates for threaded discussion participation and journal writing.

There are a couple of other issues you need to consider before designing your individual units.

Your Design Process: Does it make more sense to you to design each unit of your course in its totality before moving on to the next unit? Or do you want to treat the units as an extended group, creating, for example, a skeleton of common content and activities and then customizing each unit later? Part of your answer will probably depend upon your time constraints for finishing your course. If you only have a short time before your course is to be offered online, you may want to completely develop the first four or five weeks' worth of work and then continue developing the course as you teach it. (Not our first recommendation—teaching an online course for the first time can be extremely stressful and time consuming. Add continued design and development and you have the ingredients for a disaster.) If you have the time, begin developing the entire course at the same time and build all of your weeks' work consecutively. You might also want to completely develop one unit, learn from that experience, and then continue on with developing the rest of the units as a group.

Uniformity of Sections. Becoming comfortable with the technology of your course will be a major challenge for your online students. Creating a consistent schedule of activities can help them master that first sharp learning curve. How can you design your course so that there is some sort of consistency running throughout which will help your students know generally what to expect each week?

Could you design your course so that, in general, every section includes an introduction, objectives, readings, threaded discussions, journal work, a short assignment, etc., that are generally due on the same days of the week? For example, can "major" assignments for each section always be due on the same day of the week, such as papers, etc., always due by Sunday midnight? (And, yes, you want to include a time deadline too, not just a date deadline.)

If you want to create discussion, can you always assign first responses to threaded discussion questions due, for example, by Thursday midnight of that week, and then ask each student to read and respond to a set number of these responses by Sunday midnight? (An earlier due date during the week for threaded discussion responses helps ensure that the students will actually read peer responses. You can also make responding to a certain set number of peer responses by the week's end another part of the class participation grade.)

Beginnings and Endings

How can you arrange your course so that it takes into consideration the probable "lag-time" at the start and finish of it?

Beginnings: Unfortunately, despite all the cautionary preparation material that you and your institution will be feeding to your students before courses start, many students will experience all sorts of frustrating technical setbacks related to their equipment, servers, and inexperience with online technology. If you make the first unit of your course too "work-heavy," or assign collaborative exercises for your students right from the start, you may experience a great deal of frustration and risk jeopardizing your next section schedule. One suggestion (if you have the time in your course): let your first section focus on student introductions, introductory readings, and assignments that the timely completion of (or, better yet, the non-timely completion of!) will not interfere with the progress of section two.

Endings. You might want to devote the last unit of your course to the students' final work for the course—final papers, exams, portfolios, etc. Give them time to prepare and study for this week, eliminating threaded discussions and small assignments.

You

Online teaching can be more work-intensive and time-consuming than traditional classroom teaching, especially when you are teaching a course for the first time and are still developing and fine-tuning it. You need to consider your own "assignments" for each section:

DEVELOPMENT

Do you want to respond to every student's every threaded discussion response? How can you "participate" effectively and yet not overburden yourself? How can you engage in the threaded discussion and yet avoid "'Cause Teacher Says" syndrome? One suggestion: wait until all threaded discussion responses are posted by an assigned time and then put in your "two-cents." You could also send a general e-mail (to ensure that all students will get your "two-cents") and discuss general issues brought up in the threads and refer students to particularly well-written peer responses.

If your course includes journal writing, how are you going to respond to every journal entry? Or should you? Could you pair students and ask them to respond to each other's daily or weekly writing?

If the students are turning in other written assignments, such as papers, how much written feedback are you going to give back for each assignment? In the physical classroom with real paper, margins and the back of the last page give you "boundaries" for your commentary. If you're like we are, you can probably type as fast as you can think. How much feedback is adequate, whether it's for a paper assignment or a threaded discussion response?

Basically, you need to come up with your own "rules of thumb" for how much individual interaction you are going to have with each student. Keep in mind that while the most successful online courses do have lots of student/instructor interaction, not all of that interaction needs to be one on one. Give the students a chance to learn together. You do not want to burn yourself out.

A General Template for Designing Your Sections (Table 9.6)

These templates are guides to help you develop ideas for units or sections for your course. You should use whatever components seem appropriate. Good instructional design whether online or in the classroom demands that you give clear instructions to your students. It's helpful to give every unit an introduction that explains what to expect in that unit and how it may transition from the previous unit. Remember to give very specific instructions on how student work must be submitted.

Section Info	Content & Purpose	Format
Section Introduction	Title your unit. Simply give a brief overview of what material/issues, etc. will be covered. An audio introduction gives a nice "personal" touch to your course.	Text, Audio, Video, Powerpoint.
Section Objectives	Preview the learning objectives for your students to help them focus.	Text, Audio, Powerpoint.
Pre-assessment Quizzes	Help your students determine their own needs for mastering content materials in a section.	Flash, Java Popup Boxes (these methods allow your students to get immediate feedback to their responses).
Readings	List all readings, including textbook and journal readings, readings on the WWW, lectures, instructor notes.	Text. Make your WWW readings and "lecture" readings a hypertext link, which will send your student immediately to the Web document or external page when he or she clicks on it.
Lectures, Instructor Notes, Overviews	Though many advocates of the online course stress "student-centered" learning in which students guide themselves through the learning process under the helpful "prodding" of instructors, and much is said negatively about the "stand and deliver" lecture format, most students are taking the course because they want to know what you think. Short lectures based on your expertise and experience can be edifying and enlightening. The mistake is to simply base the entire course on your lectures.	Text lectures, which should be a challenge because you will be modeling good writing. But text online can be boring. Try PowerPoint slides with highlight information in combination with audio narration. Try short five-minute videos of lecture. Combine graphs and images with audio narration. Provide outlines of your notes.

Table 9.6
Recommended section information, content, and purpose format

Table 9.6
Recommended section information, content, and purpose format

Section Info	Content & Purpose	Format
Assignments/ Exercises	Papers, calculations, projects (group and individual), journal entries, threaded discussion participation, exams, quizzes, online chatroom participation.	Text; Hyperlinks to external pages. Be sure to include both the due date and time for each assignment/exercise, format requirements, and method of delivery (email, threaded discussion, postal mail, proctored real time exam).
Multimedia Materials	Graphics, Tables, Audio, Video, PowerPoint slide shows.	PowerPoint, .wav files, video clips. Some of you will have a lot of this material, some of you not. We do suggest that you employ multimedia in order to solve the "text online" taboo, engage your students, and spark your own creative juices. Have at least an introductory video recording of yourself because it is a nice "humanizing" element. Keep video clips short and sweet. Be sure to acquire any necessary copyright permissions. Keep the file size of your images small so that they will download quickly for your students..
Groups	Group names, names of students in each group.	Give group information in each section of your course, even if the information does not change. Provide forums for individual groups to meet, such as in separate threaded discussions or chatrooms, or email list serves.

Section Info	Content & Purpose	Format
Threaded Discussion Questions	Text questions provided for discussion through asynchronous tools.	Open-ended questions that ask for critical thinking, analysis, and evaluation can spark dynamic learning opportunities for your students. Create threaded discussions for your students that are both monitored and unmonitored by you. Model appropriate threaded discussion responses if thread participation is graded on quantity and quality. Use threaded discussion questions as a way to synthesize text readings. For example, ask how an author of an appropriateWeb article might respond to textbook materials.
Chatroom Assignments	Text instructions on using the chatroom when and where. Though the online course is best known as the "anytime/anywhere" medium and some students may resist the idea of having to report to the online course at a particular time, synchronous communication in an online course can help build community and ease student frustration at the "time-lapse" that can occur.	Thirty students in a chatroom can be harrowing. Consider breaking the class up into small chatroom groups. Assign small groups to separate chatrooms for group project work. Or, for a whole class experience, employ some strict managing techniques when conducting the chatroom and set up your expectations ahead of time. Be sure to consider time zone differences when you set up your chatroom sessions.

Table 9.6
Recommended section information, content, and purpose format

DEVELOPMENT

Table 9.6
Recommended section information, content, and purpose format

Section Info	Content & Purpose	Format
Assessments	Create timed and secured multiple choice, t/f, short answer, matching, fill in the blank, and essay exams which can include automatic feedback for the students and computerized scoring for objective questions. Evaluate students on their responses to discussion questions that you post on the threaded discussions. Ask students to post journal entries that you can read and comment on within the actual entries. Grade papers online or through email privately. Grade students on participation in the chat room.	Text, threaded discussion postings, papers, exams, JavaScript, quizzes, Flash, etc.
Technical and Navigational Informations	You can never give students enough directions in an online course. Repeat syllabus information throughout the course. Provide information or links to information on how to utilize any technology for a particular week, such as how to use a chatroom, etc. Remind students how to send materials to you; how to deal with formatting issues. Explain to students how to navigate through your course, how to go back to different pages. Tell them what they must do first, or better yet, time access to various content materials and tests so that they cannot "spring ahead" unprepared. Point out the links they must click on to obtain additional information. Providing this kind of information throughout a course may seem repetitive and silly, but you will save yourself from twenty or so emails a week just on directions.	Text, Web links, graphics, charts, tables.

9.6 Intellectual Property Rights and Copyright Issues

Before you begin the process of gathering up your content materials and translating them into your online course, you need to do two things. First, if you are affiliated with an academic institution, you need to find out its policy on intellectual property rights. Intellectual property rights has to do with your final ownership of your online course. Do you have the right to market and sell your course to other universities and colleges? Does your institution? Who would get the profit from that venture? Can your institution assign other instructors to teach your online course? These are questions that you need to have answered before going "online."

Second, you need to examine the content materials you are gathering for your online course and determine whether you need copyright permission to use them, and, even if you do have copyright permissions for using them in your traditional classroom, you need to determine if these permissions apply to your online course. Copyright has to do with the ownership of original materials and the right of the owner to distribute, sell, perform, and display these materials publicly. While you may have been using dog-eared copies of a favorite poem that you pass out to your class each semester and then collect again with no problem, can you "scan" that same poem, upload the file into your online course, and make it a permanent part of that course? Are you simply "broadcasting" the materials or creating copies that you are distributing to your students?

Intellectual Property Rights

Online technology and the opportunity it offers faculty members and administrators alike to suddenly "package" the classroom have put dollar signs in the eyes of many. While historically faculty members have transferred their knowledge and expertise into published textbooks, purchased by competing institutions, with little notice from administrators, the success of the dot com business has many believing that packaging online courses will be the next gold rush, and everyone wants in on the deal.[1]

Additionally, leaders in the college and university arena are suddenly fearful that faculty members offering their prepackaged courses online will ultimately affect the institution's stature and prestige, and their potential revenue from incoming students. And this fear extends to both the "canned" course purchased individually by another university, and the instructor-led course, created, offered, and taught by their faculty member. Imagine the ramifications for Harvard of a Harvard course, created by a Harvard professor, now "owned" and taught by an instructor from a small community college for a quarter of the cost?

The American Association of University Professors (AAUP) has flatly stated that all intellectual ownership of a course remains with the faculty member who independently created the course out of his/her own initiative. [2]

AAUP suggests that there are only three situations in which the faculty member's ownership could be called into question by the institution:

1. The college or university specifically directed the faculty member to create the course, or the creation of the course was a requirement for employment.
2. The faculty member gave contractual ownership of the course to the institution.
3. The college or university contributed significant resources to the development of the course, which extended well beyond the norm for traditional support in content development. [2]

A group of higher education leaders meeting in a symposium on the issue of course ownership described three general policy approaches presently taken by institutions:

1. The institution claims ownership of a course because of "work for hire" parameters.
2. The institution allows faculty to claim ownership, but asks for a percentage of the royalties for that course, or the right to run that course within the university as part of its normal offerings.
3. The institution contracts with the faculty member for the development of the course and then claims ownership because the copyright has been transferred to it by the course creator. [3]

Obviously, there is no black and white answer here. Interestingly, the group determined that the "promised gold" of the online course market is over-estimated, pointing to the revenue generated by faculty members who publish textbooks as an example. It also suggested that, as with textbook writing, only a small percentage of faculty members will have the know-how and gift for creating an online course that could achieve national and world acclaim and bring in any real revenue. The group also questioned whether packaged content is really a course at all, concluding that content becomes a course only through actions of an effective teacher.

The group recommended that the institution and the faculty work closely together and determine course ownership on an individual basis, reminding institutional leaders that maintaining an environment that encourages free thinking and creative initiatives on the part of its faculty is ultimately for its own good. Our suggestion is that you organize a faculty group and work with institutional administrators on crafting a fair policy on course and content ownership prior to creating the online courses.

Copyright Law and Fair Use

The problem with copyright law is that it was created long before the digital age and the sudden emergence of courses online that are trying to emulate and expand upon the learning experiences of the classroom. And it was written before the technology of the online world could allow content to be transmitted, copied, and made accessible so easily and on such a grand, worldwide scale.

Simply put, the Copyright Act of 1976 gives the creator of content ownership. The creator has the right to sell, distribute, reproduce and publicly display or perform the work exclusively. Two amendments to the Copyright Act addressed the issue of teachers using copyrighted materials in the classroom, allowing them in the face-to-face classroom to act out portions of a play, read a poem, or play a video. But these activities must be done face-to-face and cannot be broadcasted outside of the classroom. The first problem here then is the fact that online courses have to do with "transmission"— activities are not done face-to-face and are broadcasted via the Internet to online students.[4]

The concept of "fair use" was introduced by federal law and involves the use of copyright materials in the classroom without permission. "Fair use" of copyrighted materials is determined by four factors:

1. *Purpose:* Specifically, the use of copyright materials for non-profit purposes, i.e. teaching, for our focus. Simply not copying the work, but transforming it by incorporating it into other materials that create new ideas and vision, weighs heavily in determining if the fair use of copyright materials is actually being upheld. This factor also allows for teachers to make multiple copies of works for the classroom, even if the work has not been "transformed."

2. *Nature*: The nature of the individual copyrighted work can determine whether its usage complies with fair use. Creative work versus factual work; published versus unpublished—these characters weigh in differently. The use of factual, published work is looked upon more favorably than the use of creative, unpublished work.

3. *Amount:* This factor looks at both how much of the copyright material is being used and how much of its "essential essence" is being used. Copying of an entire work is not looked upon favorably, but what is considered an "entire" work, especially in qualitative terms—that "essential essence"—can be a changing variable.

4. *Effect:* What is the consequence for the creator of your using his work? Will its market value be lower? Will your use of his materials, no matter what form, undermine his potential sales? Obviously, any kind of commercial usage of another's original materials would hurt your chances of proving fair use. Using the materials for research makes this factor more difficult to determine.[4]

Copyright and adherence to fair use continue to be difficult issues in the online world. Some have suggested quantitative measures for the limited use of "multimedia projects" for educational purpose, for example, 3 minutes of a copyrighted motion media piece, 5,000 words of a copyrighted work, 250-word poems or less, 30 seconds for a music recording, and 5 images by an artist. [5]   Measures like these can be difficult to confirm. In May of 1999, a report put out from the U.S. Copyright Office, which was mandated by the Digital Millennium Copyright Act of 1998, did propose guidelines for educational fair use in distance learning. But it explicitly states that: "these guidelines do not cover asynchronous delivery of distance learning over a computer network, even one that is secure and capable of limiting access to students enrolled in the course."[6] Why? Because the technology is still evolving, educational institutes are still in the infancy of online course development, and the publishers and creators of copyrighted materials have yet to solidify their marketing strategies for distance learning materials.

For now, our suggestion is to obtain copyright permission for materials through the publishers, Web authors, and the like and to confirm with them the extent to which you are allowed to use their materials in your online course. Secure access to your online course, and, if possible, make it difficult for your students to copy and keep the copyrighted work in your course. Also, limit the amount of time your students have access to the work. We suggest making use of hyperlinks to websites that contain materials you want to include into your course. There is a mass of information on the Web that is only a "click" away for your students.

REFERENCES

1. **Guernsey, L. and Y. Jeffrey.** 1998. "Who Owns On-Line Courses?" *The Chronicle of Higher Education*, June 5.

2. **American Association of University Professors, Special Committee on Distance Education and Intellectual Property Issues.** 2000. "Suggestions and Guidelines for Institutional Policies and Contract Language on Ownership." <http://www.aaup.org/ipguide.htm>

3. **Twigg, C. A.** 1999. "Who Owns Online Courses and Course Materials?" *Intellectual Property Policies for a New Learning Environment.* The Pew Learning and Technology Program. (http://www.center.rpi.edu/Pewsym/mono2.html>.

4. **CETUS.** 2000. "Fair Use: Overview and Meaning for Higher Education." <http://www.cetus.org/fair5.html>.

5. **MacKnight, C. B.** 1999. "Copyright Law and Recent Changes: An Overview." *Newsletter of the Office of Information Technologies*, Vol. 5. Issue 1, pp. 12-16.

6. **U.S. Copyright Office.** "Report on Copyright and Digital Distance Education." May 1999. <http://www.loc.gov/copyr>.

DEVELOPMENT

The Mechanics of Putting Your Materials Online

Lesson 10

The Mechanics of Putting Your Materials Online

LESSON OUTLINE

WHAT YOU WILL LEARN FROM THIS LESSON

YOU WILL BE ABLE TO:

1. Identify resources for the development of online course materials.
2. Design and construct materials for online courses including text, graphs and charts, figures, audio, video, and animations.
3. Identify, obtain, and insert graphics and audio materials from the Web and CD-ROM collections into your website.

LESSON 10: THE MECHANICS OF PUTTING YOUR MATERIALS ONLINE

10.1 Getting Help

There you are with handfuls of transparencies written with a marker pen, notepads of scribbled lectures, page tearouts from numerous articles consisting of assorted graphs, charts, photos and figures, and maybe a collection of old 35 mm slides, and some videos. It's time to sit down and load your materials onto the Web or course delivery platform. Where do you start? What do you do? If you feel the least bit intimidated by the idea of scanning, digital photography, recording voice or music, or any of these adventures into the digital world, then you probably want to seek assistance. There are a number of sources you may be able to turn to for this assistance. The sources I have been able to use at the university have included IT personnel, library science personnel, faculty cohorts, and instructional designers.

IT Personnel

Many colleges and universities support an Information Technologies (**IT**) group on campus. The IT personnel often offer a wide variety of services including training courses on the use of selected Web course delivery systems, creating Web pages, and word processing. It's very likely that your school has an instructional computer laboratory where you may obtain hands-on experience in the use of computers, accessories such as scanners, and the variety of software useful in creating Web Based Training (**WBT**) courses. You should contact your IT office and find out what services are offered and how you may access them.

Library Science Personnel

The library personnel can provide a host of services useful to you in the venture. They can help to locate and supply images, text content, and multimedia files. They may be able to assist you with copyright issues. Our library at the university recently opened a multimedia room for faculty that houses all the computer equipment and accessories necessary for producing multimedia materials including flatbed scanners, 35 mm slide scanners, digital cameras, video capture equipment, voice recording equipment, and software, and both Macintosh and PC computers. They also provide personnel to instruct and assist the faculty in all of these operations.

Faculty Cohorts

There is usually one or more faculty near your office who has mastered much of the information that you are seeking. These "early adopters" have experienced the pain and the joy of learning the new technologies and are usually delighted to help others along this path. Take advantage of these people. They have invested a great deal of time and energy in this technology and pedagogy and can provide you with tremendous insight and save you loads of time. You might even suggest to your administrators to formalize a faculty cohort—one that meets periodically to exchange ideas and encouragement.

Instructional Designers

You may be fortunate to have instructional design people on campus. My university has a Center for Teaching that assists teachers in using technology to support a wide range of learning styles, facilitate active learning, familiarize students with technology, and use faculty time and expertise more effectively. This is an excellent place to learn more about pedagogy or the art and science of instruction. If your school has adopted a course delivery platform, then you may have access to these services outside the campus. The course development services of eCollege provide the technical support for converting materials to the Web. They support encoding audio and visual files, working with images, slideshows, and the translation of text to the Web. The instructional design team provides assistance in content delivery, unit layout, and perspectives on learning styles and basic pedagogy.

Videos and CDs

If you would like to learn how to use Web authoring tools such as Dreamweaver, create animations using Macromedia Fireworks, publish interactive Web materials using Macromedia Flash, become familiar with Microsoft Office, illustrate your own line art using CorelDraw, or use most of the software programs mentioned in this section, you can obtain excellent video and CD-ROM tutorials at (**http://www.pubtool.com**).

10.2 Doing It Yourself

Text (Lectures and Notes)

So you have the handwritten notes and the transparencies with magic marker written all over them. What do want to do with this stuff? The first decision you need to make is whether you want to make all of this material available for your students on the Web. You may decide it isn't necessary. I provide my students with class notes in the form of a detailed outline with full sentences. This is done unit by unit. The students really like this feature. They print out the notes, put them in a three ring binder, and bring them to class for following along with the lectures. They can write additional materials along the margins. They have access to the book for the comprehensive treatment. The figures are mentioned within the text and have a link to the actual picture in JPEG and GIF format that appears when the figure references are mouse clicked. If you would like to see how I arranged this, visit the instructor's gallery at (**http://www.mhhe.com/ucanteachonline**) and look for Moore in the course showcase. Once you decide what text is going online, then you have to input it into your computer. You can do this yourself, or you might be fortunate enough to have secretarial assistance or student help. In any of these cases, my suggestion is to enter the text directly into a word processor such as Microsoft Word for Office 97 or Office 2000. This will permit you to format the text, create paragraphs, indents, bulleted lists, and so forth. More importantly, these programs will allow you to spell check and identify grammatical errors. Most Web page editors don't support spell checking or grammatical checking. It's also a good idea to input the materials by unit or chapter. The completed unit should be saved as a Microsoft Word document and as a .txt document. The .txt files can be inserted or pasted into most any Web page creation (editing) tools such as Claris Homepage, Dreamweaver, Frontpage, and so forth. Use the *save as* feature in Word for this. Some course delivery platforms require you to input the text in a plain .txt format uncluttered with formatting. You can convert the Word document directly into a Web page by saving it as an HTML file (an option in the File menu). The HTML code is written into the background as it formats your .doc file for the Web. There is some HTML code that that may be confusing to some platforms and so doesn't translate well. Trial and error will tell you if can insert or paste a Word-created Web page into your platform without losing some formatting. Word also has a Web page template that is useful if you are starting from scratch. You choose *New* under the File menu, and from the Templates screen click on the *Web pages tab* and select *Blank Web page*. You have access to a variety of formatting tools and Wizards for creating standard pages, multiple columns, forms, and calendar designs for display on the Web page. If you have Netscape Communicator version 4.0 or above, then you also have Composer, that is useful for making Web pages. This Web page editor is free and when you connect to the Internet you have access to the Netscape Page Wizard. Go to the File menu and select *New* then *Page* from Wizard. You will be taken automatically through a series of steps to create a simple Web page.

Graphs and Charts

You probably have some graphs and charts in your collection of classroom materials that you would like to share on your website. There are two important issues here. The first is one of copyright. You must obtain permission from the author and or publisher to use that material. The second is one of quality reproduction. You may be starting with a second or third generation photocopy, newsprint, or a poor copy. None of these may be scanned to give you a sharp image. When you do have a good quality image from which to start, you will need to scan at very high resolution to maintain that quality image. The result will be a very large file that will take a long time for students to download. A faculty member in my school purchased a new scanner and was prepared to scan all the tables, graphs, charts, and page documents from assigned readings onto his computer. I suggested he do one page. It scanned in short order but required a file size of 1.5 megabytes to be readable. We made it Web-ready and uploaded to his site on the ISP computer. I asked him to open that one page using a 56 kbps modem connection. It took more than 10 minutes to see that one image. The particular assignment of 15 pages would have been quite an ordeal for most students. What's the solution? Here's what I do. I look at the graphs and charts carefully to see if I can substantially modify them while keeping the instructional purpose valid. This will allow me to reference the source and include the words "adapted from" in from the source. Copyright permissions are not normally required in this case. Further, I sometimes am able to use original numbers in a table to create new effective charts and graphs.

Once I have decided on the desired appearance and format of the chart and graph, I select the program I want to use for creating it. Ultimately, the chart or graph must be converted to a GIF, JPEG, or PNG file for inclusion into a Web page. I like to use Macromedia Freehand (now in version 9). This professional illustration program permits me to enter a table of values and automatically creates one of several styles of charts or graphs from templates that are provided. I can also create charts and graphs as an illustration or figure while drawing freehand using a wide variety of drawing tools. Once completed, I can save the file as a GIF file. I always save the file also as a native Freehand file in case I want to work on it some more. If you would like to see some examples of graphs and charts I have created this way visit my course at (**http://www.mhhe.com.ucanteachonline**). You might also consider creating your graphs and charts in Powerpoint. This program also comes with Microsoft Office and includes a powerful graph-generating component. You could generate a Web-ready version of the Powerpoint presentation using the wizard that comes with the program. Further, you could use the Excel program that comes with Microsoft Word to create graphs/charts by entering numbers into a table and selecting the desired chart/graph type from a variety of templates using a wizard. The chart/graph may be saved as a Web page.

Figures (Images)

Figures or images come in two varieties in the world of illustration. They are either **vector** or **bitmapped** images. Vector images are defined by mathematical equations that make up individual, scalable objects. The objects may be lines, curves, boxes, circles, other shapes, or fonts with editable attributes including line thickness, color, and fill. Skilled illustrators can form these elements into detailed images from a human heart to an Apollo spacecraft or a world map (Fig.10.1). These images are resolution independent and may be increased or decreased in size without losing their sharpness. You need to create these vector images in specialized illustration software such as Macromedia Freehand,

CorelDRAW, Adobe Illustrator or Deneba's Canvas. If you would like to see reviews of this software go to the About.com website at (**http://graphicssoft.about.com/com pute/graphicssoft/library/reviews/blr_illus.htm**). Most vector images have relatively small file sizes when compared to photographic images saved as bitmaps and are useful for creating animations and GIF files.

Illustrating or creating line drawings for scientific courseware is a relatively uncommon talent. You need to be able to master sophisticated illustration software, interpret the scientific principles behind the illustration, and then convert the ideas to a meaningful illustration that clearly demonstrates the principle to most who will read it. You may wish to seek out existing artwork. You can obtain detailed medical and health care vector images at (**http:www lifeart.com**). There is a charge for these images but they are very reasonable if you buy the CD-ROM collection. You can purchase a CD-ROM collection of environmental health and safety vector art at (**http://www.environ.com**). If you're looking for digital maps of the world, country, state, or county, then go to (**http://www/mapresources.com**). These companies all provide images that may be imported into vector-based illustration software such as Freehand and manipulated. There are many other companies producing vector art that you may locate on the Web. If you want a catalogue of artwork for a searchable database with multiple collections of clip art then try (**http://www.pubtool.com**). You may also obtain clip art at such sites as (**http://www.clipart.com**). However, these often are in GIF format and are no longer vector-based. Therefore they may not be freely manipulated.

You can also seek out experienced illustrators who can translate your work to a finished illustration that is Web ready. You should try your IT office on campus, the local newspaper, or the computer art department if you have one. There are likely to be talented students who could use a project.

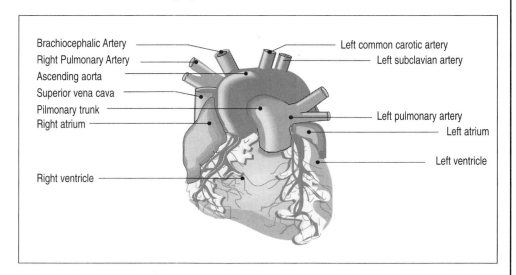

Figure 10.1
Illustration created as a vector graphic in Macromedia Freehand

DEVELOPMENT

Alternatively, if you want to jump in and try illustrating, many of the software programs mentioned above have 30 or 90 day free trials. You might contact Macromedia at (**http://www.Macromedia.com/**) and have them send you a trial CD-ROM that has fully functioning programs for Freehand, Fireworks, Flash, and Dreamweaver on it. These programs come with substantial help menus and tutorials. Once you open a particular program it will expire in 30 days. You have the option of activating the program by responding to the notice on your computer screen and purchasing the software.

Now let's look at bitmapped images. Vector images are not useful for creating the fine tones used in photographic images. A bitmapped image is normally used for this purpose. Bitmap images (often called   raster images) consist of dots (pixels) in a grid on your screen. Pixels are picture elements—tiny dots of individual color that make up what you see on your screen. All these tiny dots of color blend to form the images you see. Each dot consists of one or more bits of data. The more bits per dot, the more colors and shades of gray that may be represented by that dot. To demonstrate this, look at a magazine or colored newspaper with a magnifying glass. You will see that the picture is made of tiny colored dots. When combined, these tiny dots form an image. If you were to enlarge the picture each of the dots would become larger, and the picture fuzzier (Figure 10.2). The density of dots is known as the resolution and that determines the clarity or sharpness of the image on the screen or in print. Resolution is normally measured as dots per inch (dpi). The dpi is normally stated as the number of columns and rows of dots. A 600 x 1200 dpi scanner has 600 columns and 1200 rows of dots. If you see the word interpolated next to the resolution, then the manufacturer of the device (i.e., scanner) has included a formula in the system that adds extra dots to give the appearance of higher resolution. The typical computer monitor has 72 or 96 pixels per inch, depending on your monitor and screen settings. Therefore, most images to be used on the screen are set to 72 dpi while printed materials are set to 300 dpi.

To increase the picture size of a bitmap image while maintaining the sharpness, you would have to increase the number of pixels. Each pixel takes up computer memory. The

Figure 10.2
Bitmap images are composed of tiny dots that become larger as the picture is enlarged, making the image less clear.

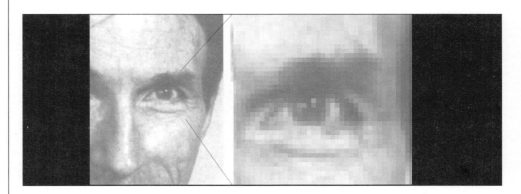

larger the number of pixels, the greater are the memory requirements. Further, color images normally require about three times the file size of the same picture in gray scale (shades of black and white). Because bitmaps are resolution dependent, it's difficult to increase or decrease their size without sacrificing a degree of image quality. When you reduce the size of a bitmap image through your software's resample or resize command, you must throw away pixels. When you increase the size of a bitmap image through resizing this creates new pixels by estimating the color values of the new pixels based on the surrounding pixels. This process is called **interpolation.** All scanned images and images from digital cameras are bitmaps.

There are at least three usual ways to obtain bitmapped images for your website. You may scan images, digitize your own photos, or obtain digital photos from a stock collection. Let's first talk about scanning. When you decide to scan an image for inclusion into your website it probably means that the artwork or picture belongs to somebody else. You need to obtain permission from them to use this material. Assuming you have permission, you are ready to scan. A scanner is a light sensing device that reads graphics and printed text and translates this information into dots called a bitmap. Most scanners available for use in the home today are 600 x 1200 dpi or better and are a flatbed scanner, meaning that they have a flat surface suitable for scanning 8.5 x 11 inch documents (Fig. 10.3). These are more than adequate for scanning images to be used on the Web. Larger scanners are available. Additionally, most scanners come bundled with software for running the scanner, and software for manipulating the images after they are scanned. Typically this would be Photoshop LE or another image editing software. The image editing software is necessary to manipulate the graphic image you have scanned or any bitmapped image that you have. This manipulation may include cropping the picture, increasing contrast, sharpening the detail, changing colors or intensities of color, and saving the file in the proper format for the Web. This usually means that you will want to save the file at a resolution of 72 dpi, a size that normally does not exceed 550 pixels wide (7.6 inches), and in a .JPG or JPEG format. If you want to

Figure 10.3
Typical flatbed scanner

become more specific and sophisticated in choosing these parameters then visit a website dedicated to the basics of scanning at (**http://www.scantips.com**). You should also save a master copy as a TIF file in order to preserve the original quality of the scan. The JPEGs are **lossy** in that each time they are manipulated and saved they will lose quality.

You will find that when you are ready to purchase a scanner there are lots of them out there. Perhaps the easiest way to decide what is best for you is to visit a site that provides evaluations of over 50 of the available scanners on the market, their process, and an option to purchase. That site is (**http://www.consumersearch.com**). Once at the site choose *Computers* and then the word *Other* until you see the word *Scanners*. As mentioned previously, many scanners come bundled with image editing software. I personally prefer Adobe Photoshop. There are many other image editing software packages available that you may purchase independently. You may see these reviewed at (**http://grapicssoft.about.com/compute/graphicssoft/library/reviews/blr_imged.htm**). Finally, maybe you don't want to do any scanning but have lots of materials to scan. You could send your materials to a professional scanning service and have them return with all of the documents scanned and saved as digital files on a CD-ROM. Try (**http://www.scandoc.com/**) for this service. You could hire a student to do the scanning using equipment normally available on campus.

You can also obtain images by taking photographs with a conventional camera or a digital camera. I have used both. My conventional camera is a Nikon with an array of interchangeable lenses and some years of my experience attached to it. I can take pictures at a distance or I can fill the screen with the words "one cent" on the penny. The pictures are usually sharp and bright because of the camera quality and my experience. I then bring my film over to the local camera store and have them send my film off to Kodak for digitizing the photos onto a CD-ROM. The process usually takes about two weeks so I plan ahead. Most image editing software can read the Photo CD format. Each CD can store up to 100 images saved in several sizes (from wallet size to tabloid) in color to a black and white image. I prefer this method because the digitized photos are usually of exceptional quality and are archived on the CD for retrieval at any time. There are a number of vendors now offering to digitize your film. If you want a tutorial on digital photos, want to know about Photo CD, would like to download Photo CD software, or locate a Photo CD service provider, then give the following URL a try (**http://www.kodak.com/US/en/dig ital/products/photoCD.shtm**). There are many other services now digitizing film and placing them on disk, on the Web, and offering prints or slides as well. If you have just a roll of film that doesn't require high resolution then most of these services will work just fine for Web applications since the resolution doesn't have to be very high. You might try Seattle Filmworks at (**http://www.filmworks.com**). They may be still offering free film processing for your first roll of film as a new customer. If you're really economical then try (**http://www.snapfish.com**) which will send you back your negatives, a full set of prints on Kodak paper, post your password protected photos on the Web, and notify you by email at no cost but the $1.69 for return shipping. Advertisers pay the rest. You can download the photos off the Web for use.

If you have a digital camera, then you can bypass all of this and immediately send your digitized photos to the computer where you may edit the images using one of the image editing software packages available. The digital cameras usually come with a cable or a specialized 3.5" diskette that permit you to transfer your pictures directly to the computer. Digital cameras are a relatively recent arrival in the technology field, and many of you probably haven't had the opportunity to use one. I find them very satisfactory for Web photos in a price range of $600 to $1200. You don't need to purchase $15,000 digital camera equipment for this type of application. However, there are a number of factors to consider. If you're planning to buy a digital camera, I suggest taking a short Web course in selecting a camera and another in using it at (**http://www.shortcourses.com/index.htm**). You can even download an electronic book on editing digital photos at this location. There are lots of digital cameras, but the most popular ones are reviewed at this location. If you want another source for digital camera reviews then try (**http://216.110.36.24/DIG CAM01.htm**).

Audio

The use of audio in your course can be very stimulating. I use mini-lectures attached to my figures in the chapter outlines. The students open up the outlines and see references to figures in the text. If they click on the figure number, that figure will appear on the screen. There is an option for them to listen to the streamed mini lecture associated with that figure. I like to make it their choice. The students really like this feature. You can use audio to introduce yourself, to introduce a unit, to feature a guest speaker, as a pep talk to keep students interested, as a side-link as I have done to describe an image, or as narrative associated with a slide show. If you want to add music to your online course then I recommend using short clips of 15 to 30 seconds. I use it very sparingly as an opener to the course. However, it can be very boring to listen to this music every time you enter the course, so give them the option at the site of turning off the music. Normally, you can do this by pointing to the audio clip and clicking on the right mouse button Because I don't want any copyright problems and I also want to make life easier by using properly formatted and digitized music that is keyword searchable, I buy a CD-ROM collection from Presentation Audio at (**http://www.networkmusic.com/webaudio/pres_frames.html**). Presentation Audio is a series of CD-ROMs that give you the ability to score your websites and other computer-based presentations with fully orchestrated and professionally recorded music, effects, and elements at an affordable price. Designed and formatted for use with presentation authoring programs such as Microsoft's FrontPage® and PowerPoint®, each CD-ROM contains 30 music beds, 100 sound effects and 100 production elements. It also comes with Trakfinder, an intuitive utility that allows you to select, audition, edit, and export the sound files in your choice of convenient formats. The CD-ROM collection includes a royalty-free license for non-broadcast, computer-based presentations. They normally give permission to use this in educational settings.

There are several ways to record your voice. You may record to an audiocassette and then have someone convert this to a digitized format such as a .wav file. I have found the application software "sound recorder" available as part of the Windows 98 operating system to be more than satisfactory.

Using Sound Recorder. You can use Sound Recorder to record, play, and edit sound files. To use Sound Recorder, you must have a sound card and speakers installed on your computer. If you want to record live sound, you also need a microphone. As noted in Lesson 6, if you are using a microphone, it may be a challenge to set it up and have it work perfectly the first time. You could obtain some help at the following URL (**http://www.mscomm.com/~twoton**/). If you are using Microsoft Netmeeting, the wizard will automatically guide you through the setup, testing, and use of the microphone.

You can also start Sound Recorder by clicking *Start*, pointing to *Programs*, pointing to *Accessories,* pointing to *Entertainment*, and then clicking *Sound Recorder*. For information about how to use Sound Recorder, click the *Help* menu in Sound Recorder.

To record a sound:

Make sure you have a microphone connected to your computer.

On the *File* menu, click *New.*

To begin recording, click on the red dot.

To stop recording, click on the black rectangle.

On the *File* menu, click *Save As.*

The *save as* menu will give you several options. Based on my experience you will have adequate quality and a reasonably small file size if you select 11,025 HZ at 8 bit mono for a 22KB /sec recording. This means that if you record for 60 seconds your file size will be about 1.2 megabytes or enough to nearly fill up a 3.5" diskette. If you record at much higher quality then your file sizes will double or quadruple easily.

When you are successfully recording the green line (Fig. 10.4) will produce significant waves. It only records 60 seconds at a time so you must keep your eye on the side bar as it moves across the field. When near the end click on the red dot. You may continue your recording from where you left off by depressing the red dot again. You can repeat this process several times to achieve recordings several minutes long. You can play your recording in Sound Recorder or in Media Player. You have many options in this program. You can delete part of a sound file. You can increase the volume or decrease the volume.

You can undo changes. You can decrease the volume on a sound file and then add it into another file. I do this with music and play the narrative over it.

There are some useful hints when recording. The first thing I do is to locate a quiet space and time in my home where I will not be disturbed by pets, chil-

Figure 10.4
A graphic of the sound recorder control (Microsoft Windows)

dren, or others. I write down what I am going to say so that I can read from a document. I try to add some interest in the form of a question or a little personal story, or even a bit of non-offensive humor. I practice one or two times and play it back to see if the volume is correct. I listen to see if I have spoken clearly and loudly enough for people to understand. I listen for annoying background noises (like the dog barking or the washing machine turning on, or constant electronic buzzing noise). I use a headset to keep my hands free. You can buy such a headset for about $25 or less.

Films—Electronic Archives, Digitizing

You can obtain digital video in three ways. You can purchase stock digital video clips, digitize clips from videotape, or take video with a digital camera. The stock video clips come from companies at the following URLs (**www.artbeats.com**), (**www.flixdisc.com**), or (**www.prismo.com**). Most of these motion graphics are designed to create artistic broadcast, corporate video, and multimedia productions. They include aerial landscapes, backgrounds, nature, animals, and special effects such as explosions. However, most of the time you will probably want to have course specific motion clips that may be used to introduce yourself, feature guest lecturers, give demonstrations, or show a difficult concept that can't be easily done another way. Video broadcast over the Internet is not broadcast quality, is usually limited to a small area of the screen, and can be choppy. Further, video consumes enormous memory on the computer that streams it. It doesn't have to be expensive to produce video with a digital camera if you do it yourself. However, if you engage a professional staff to do it, the costs will markedly escalate. If you are going to do it yourself, then you should view a four minute streamed video clip on the Web titled "How to Shoot Video for the Internet" presented by Steve Mack, the manager of the media lab at RealNetworks. You'll need RealplayerG2 or better to view the streamed video. Open your browser and type in the following URL to view the clip (**http://realmedia02.ecol lege.com/schools/ecollege/stevemack/home.htm**).

Generally you will want to keep the video clips short, probably less then two minutes each in most cases. Keep in mind that the encoding process reduces the clarity of the video as well as the viewing area. Therefore, you want to increase the contrast of the speaker against the background. This usually means the speaker should be wearing solid, dark colors against a light background. The light should be facing the speaker and not behind him/her. Avoid movement on the part of the speaker or camera (zooming in or out) since it will enhance the choppiness of the picture over the Internet. Avoid using titles on the video. They will be difficult or impossible to read unless they are *sans serif* (i.e., Helvetica, Arial, or similar) and more than 20 percent of the screen size. Just as with audio, write down the script in large letters, tape it behind the lens of the camera, and use it to remind you what you want to say. Once the video is completed, you must make it Web ready. Most of you will not want to tackle this step. Generally this means that the digital files have to be input onto the hard disk of a computer and then edited and encoded for use on the Web by a software program such as Adobe Premiere, made Web ready with a software program such as Realmedia that prepares the video for streaming, and then uploaded to a server that has a Realmedia application software to support the video streaming. My suggestion to most of you is to prepare the video on a digital camera, edit it if you have the equipment, save it to a CD-ROM using a rewritable CD, and then hand it off to experts who know how and where to load streaming media. If you would like some tips on basic to advanced video editing try the following location (**http://desk topvideo.about.com/compute/desktopvideo/cs/howtoeditvideo/index.htm**). Here you will also find information on shooting video, lighting, compression files such as AVI and MPEG, digital video camcorders, capture cards, and hardware requirements for the Mac and the PC.

Animations for the Web

What can you do with animations? The obvious answer is that you can give the appearance of motion to words and objects. If you open my website at (**http://www. unix.oit.umass.edu/~envhl565**), you will see a spinning globe because the title of my book that is the basis of the course is "Living With the Earth." As you travel through the site you will see a number of animations that are intended to add interest, provide humor, and direct attention to a particular action or section. I haven't added motion to illustrate a pedagogical concept, but that is an important part of animation. Animations could be used to illustrate principles of physics such as wave motion. It could be used to show the process of mitosis, or the separation of rocket stages. Whatever you choose to animate, you must realize that the process of animation is time-consuming and demanding. Also be sure that you don't overdue your animations. Too many and you end up with the "Christmas tree" effect.

There are several ways to animate for the Web. At the moment, Macromedia's

Shockwave Flash is the most widely used for creating vector-based Web animation, and most authors use the Macromedia Flash program when they want to create these animations. Flash also supports sound with animations. The viewing of Flash produced animations requires a Flash plug-in that is free from (**http://www.macromedia.com**). If you would like to see a variety of superior Flash animations then visit the following site (**http://animation.about.com/arts/animation/msubflashexemplars.htm**). This may give you some inspiration to try it out yourself. So we have discussed Flash animations where you may attach sound and create lengthy sequences such as a cartoon series, and animated GIFs that are without sound and usually a few seconds in length. Examples of GIF animations may be seen at (**http://animation.about.com/arts/animation/msub watchgif.htm**). GIF animations don't require a special plug-in and there are many free sites on the Web in addition to the one just given above where you may obtain the GIFs copyright free. Be sure to check on the site for permission to use them. You can also purchase from Xoom at (**http://www.xoom.com**) a collection of 6 CDs containing thousands of animated GIFs searchable by subject. This very inexpensive collection called the Web Clip Empire also comes with Web objects, photos, and video clips for use on the Web. Most of the animations on my site are animated GIFs and may be produced with Flash or Macromedia Fireworks. Fireworks doesn't support sound but is an excellent Web graphics tool that blends vector and bitmapped capabilities into one program. A partial listing of graphics animation and 3-D software for the Web is provided in Table 10.1. There are also Java animations, Quicktime animations, and Real Media animations.. You'll need Web graphics software to create animations. I have already mentioned that Macromedia Flash is the tool of choice for most who want to add sound and several sequences of motion. I use Macromedia Fireworks for creating animated GIFs that are rarely more then a few seconds of motion and do not have sound. There are several Web graphics software programs that you might wish to evaluate and that have been reviewed at (**http://graph icssoft.about.com/compute/graphicssoft/library/reviews/blr_web.htm**).

There are some general guidelines for working with Web pages that have been previously discussed. There are also some guidelines for creating and working with Web graphics.

- Make the graphic elements small in file size that so that they load easily. This is especially true for animations, since they are usually built from multiple images that play in a series. Try to keep your files under 150 K for animations and under 50 K for still graphics.
- Don't fill your page up with photos, illustrations, and animations. Every graphic takes more time to download. Try out your Web page on a 56K modem. If it takes 60 seconds to load you can be sure to lose most of your audience. I have hundreds of illustrations and photos associated with the chapter book guide (detailed

Grapics and 3-D Software	
Adobe Livemotion 1.0	Macromedia Fireworks 3.0Macromedia
Anark Interactive Media	Flash 4Metacreations
Animaniac	NetStudioSPG Web Tools
Cool 3D	Studio Bundle Pro 2
DeBabelizer 4.5	SwiSH
Emotion 3D	Web Razor
GIF animator	Webster
Headline Studio	Xara3D 4.0
Imageready	Ulead Systems
JavaCentro	XaraLtd.Xara Ltd

outline) online. Each figure is numbered in the text and linked to the GIF or JPEG image. It takes only seconds to load the entire chapter notes and then the students decide if they want to open the graphic files.

· It needs to make sense. If your animation or graphic doesn't have a purpose, then it doesn't belong there. The graphic should relate to the text in some way. I employ animations in my course materials that are humorous, but I also mention them in the text in some way. For instance, if I put a graphic of Odie the dog jumping up and down in the section starting the threaded discussion, I might say *"Odie and I are excited about the topic today. Let's find out why."*

· I try to avoid backgrounds that are too busy. This is especially true for areas that require a lot of text such as the class notes. White is good with black text because it can easily be printed and is easy to read on screen. Please don't use colored text on a colored background if you want your students to study from it or print it.

Here are some suggestions to follow when creating animations.

· Start with an idea of what you want to do. Ask yourself, "What's the purpose of the animation?" Is it important enough to spend the time and energy on it? Does it add to the instructional strength?

· Go buy a stack of blank paper that's letter size. Buy a clip that you clip all these sheets together at the top. This way you have a pad on which you can draw a series of actions and remove any sketches you don't like.

· Starting with the last scene of your little plot, sketch out the figure and any background you might want. Work forward one drawing at a time and flip through the chart to see the action unfold. This process can actually be repeated in the animation software when you finally move your concept to the computer.

· Make it very simple. The more lines and detail, the more complicated will be the final rendition. Remember, *Homer* and the *Smiley Face* make someone a lot of money but they are artistically very simple.

· Animate only things in the scene that have purpose to the storyline or plot. If someone's speaking, then make mouth movements and possibly eye movements. It's probably not necessary to have feet and hands moving or background scenes changing unless necessary for the story. If you're simulating a physics or chemistry experiment, then move only what's needed to convey the important concept.

· Avoid gradations or textures in your drawings. Use solid fills only.

· If you plan to add narrative, sketch in the dialog with each action sequence.

· Try it out. Rehearse it. Make changes if necessary.

· Begin the process of entering the scenes into the computer and frequently reviewing and saving the efforts.

· Be patient. Experiment. It's actually fun to create motion on the screen and to provide something educational or entertaining at the same time.

10.3 Prepared Course Materials from Publishers

Pearson-Prentice Hall

Pearson Distributed Learning provides a showcase of technology solutions grouped into four major categories that include: Book Specific Websites, Discipline Specific Websites, Courses Management Systems, and Other Technology Solutions. These technology solutions may be viewed at (**http://www.pearsoned.com**). The book-specific websites complement individual textbooks published by Pearson-Prentice Hall and offer online learning environments for instructors and students. There are text-specific websites, custom companion websites, and premium websites. Pearson Education will customize an existing companion website for professors teaching courses that enroll 250 students or more with a course syllabus, assignments, handouts, lecture outlines, line drawings, and Web links. The premium websites extend beyond the scope of the textbook and provide students and instructors with a comprehensive and interactive teaching and learning resource. Students must purchase an access code either as a stand alone or as a package with their textbook. Pearson also offers Discipline SuperSites that provide students and faculty with the tools and resources to enhance an entire discipline from introductory to upper level courses with Web links, demonstrations, activities, and discipline-specific information. Pearson Education's online content may be combined with a number of course delivery platforms including WebCT, BlackBoard, eCollege.com, and Pearsons' own course management system. Pearson also offers a variety of stand alone CD-ROMs, Web/CD-ROM combinations, and videos.

DEVELOPMENT

McGraw-Hill

McGraw-Hill offers online learning centers that are pre-formed digital supplements in each of 38 subject areas (previously shown in Table 7.4). The digital supplements include lecture materials, self-grading quizzes, interactive exercises, Powerpoint slides, and other key supplements. These digital supplements give you complete ownership in the way digital content is presented to the class and are compatible with multiple online course delivery platforms. This means that you can place your course online with very little development time since all that upfront work has been done for you. You just have to select the right textbook and publisher. Since more publishers are entering this digital arena continuously, there's a good chance that your subject matter is adequately covered by one of these publishers. To learn more about digital solutions from McGraw-Hill visit (**http://www.mhhe.com**).

Houghton-Mifflin

The publisher Houghton-Mifflin offers a wide variety of electronic resources to faculty that may be accessed by keyword and subject searches at (**http://www.hmco.com**). Some of the services listed at this site are shown in Table 10.2.

Cogito

Cogito Learning Media, Inc. recruits leading educators as authors to produce course content that is accurate and up-to-date with engaging interactive lessons and exercises designed to provide instant feedback. You may obtain more information and see demos at (**http://www.cogitomedia.com**). The multimedia and online learning materials review key ideas and provide self-assessment tools for high enrollment courses in science, mathematics, statistics, business, and economics. The materials are delivered on the Internet or CD-ROM and may include animations, film clips, interactive diagrams, and self-tests.

Each of the Electronic Companion courses incorporates a wide variety of problems, solutions, and summary material of key ideas that may be printed or downloaded. The Electronic Companion materials are available in CD-ROM formatted for the Windows or Mac environment and include the following subject areas (Table 10.3).

10.4 Are You Ready?

Before teaching your course, you need to do some "QA" on it. Online, you must not only worry about the "rightness" of your content and assignments, but the functionality of the technology behind it all. Despite your very best intentions and the most thorough work on your part, you are going to find small annoying errors in your text, content gaps that you overlooked, hyperlinks that don't work, URLs that suddenly lead to Web resources that no longer exist, and links to images that are "broken."

Topic	Service
Instructor Websites	Provide resources designed to help instructors teach the course, such as teaching guides, lecture outlines, suggested activities for the classroom, Instructor's Resource Manuals, answers to quizzes, and PowerPoint Slides. Instructor websites and ancillaries are sometimes password-protected—please contact the Faculty Services Center at 800/733-1717 for your password
Student Websites	Offer study materials that help students master course concepts, such as chapter summaries, chapter links, terms definitions, Internet exercises, practice tests, and video clips.
ACE Self-Tests	Short for "A Cyber Evaluation," ACE is a free self-testing program that allows students to test their knowledge of topics covered in each chapter and have answers scored immediately. Questions can be multiple-choice or true/false. Students can also email quiz results to professors.
PowerPoint Slides / Transparencies	Many instructor websites offer downloadable PowerPoint Slides or generic transparencies for use in class. Alternatively, some Houghton Mifflin textbooks offer the slides on an Instructor CD-ROM.
Instructor CD-ROM	May include PowerPoint slides, key book assets, and a classroom management system.
Student CD-ROM	May include PowerPoint slides, key book assets, and a classroom management system.
Blackboard	Houghton-Mifflin offers content online delivered in Blackboard's distributed learning system. Blackboard's Course Cartridges, similar to study guides, allow an instructor to create and manage an online course or an online supplement to a traditional course. The Course Cartridges contain collections of Houghton-Mifflin course materials that professors can purchase and download into their online course, including customizable quizzes, reviews, exercises, outlines, and summaries.

Table 10.2
Some of the electronic online services listed at the Houghton-Mifflin website (**http://www. hmco.com**)

DEVELOPMENT

Table 10.2
Some of the electronic online services listed at the Houghton-Mifflin website (**http://www. hmco.com**)

Topic	Service
WebCT	Houghton Mifflin also offers content online delivered in WebCT's electronic framework. WebCT's WebCourselets, similar to study guides, allow an instructor to create and manage an online course or an online supplement to a traditional course. The WebCourselets contain collections of Houghton Mifflin course materials that professors can purchase and download into their online course, including customizable quizzes, reviews, exercises, outlines, and summaries.
I-Guides	I-Guides, written by instructors who are using the textbook and online materials, feature a wealth of teaching strategies, ideas, exercises, and examples that help instructors get the most from a wide array of technology components.
Test Banks	Computerized test banks allow instructors to create customized tests for their class. Instructors can select, edit, and add questions, or generate randomly selected questions to produce a test master for easy duplication.
Video	Clips, case scenarios, or real world examples tied to the text.
Other	This category includes additional websites and software affiliated with Houghton-Mifflin textbooks, including cassettes, disks, and instructor training programs.

Some General Checks:

· Material completeness: Bio? Course description? Course policies? Grading Scale? Syllabus? Text requirements? All units complete or at least the upcoming few? Lectures? Multimedia? Threads? Slide shows? Clear instructions on how to navigate through the class, to submit assignments, to use the technology you have provided your students for learning?

· Material placement: Are materials where you want them to be? Right section?

· Right lecture link? Headings clear and well marked? Do your images show up properly?

Subject Areas	
Business and Economics Business statistics Principles of macroeconomics Intermediate macroeconomics Operations management Principles of Microeconomics	**Health Sciences** Essential nutrition Complete nutrition
Biological Sciences and Chemistry Genetics Molecular cell biology Microbiology Biostatistics Biochemistry General chemistry	**Mathematics and Statistics** Pre-calculus College algebra Statistics

Table 10.3
Subject areas of Cogito Companion materials available on CD-ROM formatted for Windows or Mac operating systems

DEVELOPMENT

- Material correctness: Correct page numbers on assignments? Correct groups? Correct spelling/grammar/punctuation? Correct directions on assignment submissions? If you used background colors, can you read the text easily?

- Hypertext link function: Are all links to external pages, URLs and multimedia functioning properly? Are the websites you are linking to still functioning and there? Video/ audio working? Slides working?

- Dates/times correctness: View dates correct for each unit? View dates and time duration for exams and quizzes correct?

Other Considerations:

- Have you created an active, multimedia course for your students that will keep them engaged and motivated to learn online?

- Do students have enough opportunities for interaction in your course through threaded discussions, email, chatrooms, and document exchange?

- More importantly: are <u>you</u> going to have fun? Have you thought out ways to have a full, engaging course for your students without overburdening yourself!? How are you handling the assessment of threaded discussion participation? Assessments in general? Journal entry feedback? Feedback in general? Email? Assignment submission? Repetitive questions?   Gabby students in the chatroom or the threaded discussions?

You may find that reviewing and editing your courses becomes a continuous process. I made course review a weekly part of my online teaching schedule, checking content and technology a few days before I opened up each section of the course to my students for these reasons:

- This is a <u>new medium</u> for many of you. You are dealing with a load of work and the visualization of a new format for your materials. It's easy to overlook small annoying errors. This becomes especially true every additional time you teach the course. It's easy to forget specific due dates you may have put into the course, or specific directions or comments to a particular class. You'll have to remember to "clear out" your threaded discussions, clean out your chatroom logs if you archived your chats.

- An online course has inherent and instantaneous <u>flexibility</u>. Initially, designing an online course can seem restricting because you are asking yourself to deter-mine all of your content and your activities upfront for a five-, ten-, sixteen-week course. This can be daunting, especially if you are a teacher who thrives on "to the moment" teaching and student participation and direction. What happens if a student says something brilliant or brings up an issue that opens up an oppor-tunity for unexpected exploration if you've already laid out all of your units of study? But just as in the traditional classroom, an online course does not have to be static phenomena. Make changes to your course as you are teaching it. Create new content for your course and new assignments based on those sudden oppor-tunities. While changing videos and audios can be difficult to do quickly, you can easily make changes to text, add new hypertext links, and create new assign-ments and discussion questions "on the fly."

- As you become more comfortable with teaching online and the technology that enables you to teach, you'll begin to see new and inventive ways to present your content and to interact with your students. You might want to make changes immediately or simply take notes, waiting until the end of the semester to (<u>should I even say this</u>!) revamp the whole course for the next time you teach it.

Last Words

I'll be absolutely honest: some instructors never stop designing their courses. It's addictive and, the more you learn, exhilarating. In the online classroom, you are not limited by the number of texts and supplementary materials your students are able to buy, or that you are able to copy off without violating copyright laws. There is a vast amount of good and useable materials out there on the Web that you can bring into your classroom with a simple click of a mouse! Suddenly, in the online classroom, you realize how perfect a medium online technology is for leading students into in-depth, full-participation, critical thinking learning and how far the classroom wall can extend!

DEVELOPMENT

:

Design Issues	Check Complete
Scrolling	
Clicks	
Screen readability	
Navigation	
Visual design	
Content chunking	
Redundancy	
Interaction	
Multimodal learning styles	
Instructional multimedia	
Portfolio assessment	

Syllabus Item	Check Complete
Instructor bio	
Instructor welcome: Your "greetings at the door."	
Instructor office hours	
Course description	
Course objectives	
Course polices	
Attendance	
Absenteeism	

Syllabus Item	Check Complete
Academic dishonesty	
Courtesy code	
Email procedures	
Technical help	
Instructor responsibility	
Prerequisites for course	
Required materials for course	
Grading policies	
Group participation policies	
Course calendar	
General syllabus	

DEVELOPMENT

Unit 3

Implemention/
Evaluation

The most daunting tasks should be behind you. You may have already taken the first unnerving steps toward treaching online by organizing your materials, creating the course infrastructure, posting materials to the Web, and checking over all the elements to make certain that you are ready. Now it's time to start the exciting part of your journey. Contact! You are actually ready to meet your student body online. How do you actually implement and teach the courses? How will you manage your class and conduct the interactive components? How will you measure success? What steps will you use to refine your course to better meet the needs of your students and your own expectations? Those elements are covered in these next two lessons. Good luck on your continuing adventure.

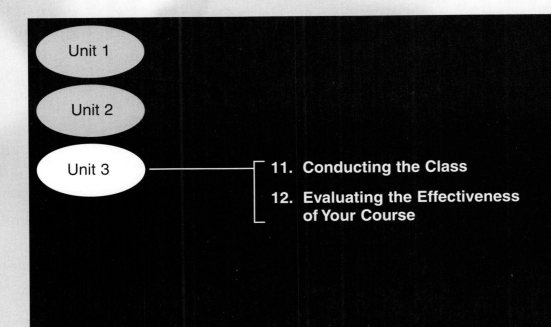

Unit 1

Unit 2

Unit 3 ———— 11. **Conducting the Class**

12. **Evaluating the Effectiveness of Your Course**

Lesson 11

Conducting the Class

LESSON OUTLINE

WHAT YOU WILL LEARN FROM THIS LESSON

YOU WILL BE ABLE TO:

1. List and explain the components of good practice in the classroom.
2. Compare and differentiate the online class with the Web-enhanced class.
3. List the major elements of management and conducting online interactive classes using threaded discussion, chatrooms, and email.
4. Appraise technology failures and choose alternatives to conducting class.
5. Identify the non-traditional student and formulate methods of instruction online.
6. Design methods for teaching large classes online.
7. Describe and compare various types of online courses.

LESSON 11: CONDUCTING THE CLASS

11.1 Introduction

Let's begin this way: imagine you have been asked to teach in a new kind of classroom. You are led to an open doorway. Beyond the doorway, there is darkness. Before entering, you are given a pair of earplugs so that you can no longer hear anything around you. You are led to a small desk where a single light shines down on the surface of it. You are told that, periodically, your students are present, but you can neither see nor hear them. Occasionally, a piece of paper appears on your desk beneath the light. It is a message from one of your students written a few minutes ago or an hour ago or days ago. To respond, you write your own message on a piece of paper, place it under the light, and watch it disappear—to where, you do not know. Besides these messages, you have been given only one other tool to teach with: a large screen upon which you may place anything.

It's a daunting prospect, isn't it? Recently, one faculty member who had only just finished her first course online said it was like diving into a great chasm, blindfolded. There will be many issues for you to face. For example, how will the traditional protocols of teaching, which the physical layout of a classroom reinforces, translate into this new environment? Or, even, should they? Think of the cues that the traditional classroom gives to both students and instructors alike. An orderly row of desks asks the students to sit down quietly and become part of a group there for instruction. The lectern and blackboard at the head of the classroom direct the instructor to stand in front of his or her "audience" and to begin the business of instruction—of delivering explanation, exploration, and evaluation. The instructor takes attendance, makes announcements, introduces the issues of the day, and then directs the students to open the prescribed textbooks already chosen by the instructor and to begin following along. In some ways, there is already closure—what is to be learned is already contained within those four walls, those books, that instructor; authority is established; the regiment of learning is begun. But in the online classroom, there is no place to stand in front of an audience; the voices of the students become as essential as the instructor's voice in establishing the presence of a class; the tools of technology offer the opportunity to open the doors and the windows of the classroom and let the world in. But you have to become comfortable teaching there in that "virtual" room.

This past year, an unpublished case study on students taking a particular online course was picked up on the Internet, and, finally, by *The New York Times*. The case study professed itself to expose student frustration in the online classroom, a topic previously "taboo," pinpointing three specific sources for the frustration: the teacher didn't give prompt feedback, the teacher didn't give clear instructions, and the teacher didn't properly prepare the students for the skills and equipment needs necessary to be successful in this particular class. The study concluded by asserting the "need to develop new pedagogies online." [1] Granted, online technology offers us opportunities to learn new ways of teaching that can solve some of the problems we have experienced in the classroom and, more importantly, offers us and our students as of yet unimagined learning experiences, but the three problems outlined in this study serve first to remind us that good practice in the traditional classroom makes for good practice in the online classroom. And that can be a comfort.

Good Practice in the Classroom

Prompt Feedback

Students want to hear from you, whether that's in the classroom or online. Not responding to the emails of students who ask questions or make requests for additional information is like ignoring the flailing arms of your regular classroom students. Not critiquing their work or commenting on their responses to a threaded discussion in a consistent, timely manner will indeed cause frustration. If email fast becomes a loathsome burden in your online course (and it will, if you aren't careful), and keeps you from responding swiftly to your students, it's your responsibility to find another means of communication, whether that be the threaded discussion, a publicly posted announcement, or synchronous communication.

Detailed Instructions

Whether online or in the classroom, instructions need to be clear and detailed and correct. As many online instructors often discover, there seems to be a causal relationship between too much email and not enough instructions provided to your students throughout the duration of your course. Online you will have to repeat yourself more times than you think necessary, but is that really so different from the regular classroom? And you have to specify the "hows," "whys," "wheres," and "whats" for any assignment. How will the student accomplish this assignment? What are the objectives? What are the steps involved? How will the student submit this assignment to you and when? Don't just put this information in the online syllabus. Repeat it often in numerous places throughout your course. Post announcements; send out reminders. Explain, repeat, explain. And, above all, remember to update your online course or your instructional Web page every time you teach. The remedy here isn't new pedagogy, simply common sense and foresight.

Prerequisites

Be prepared. Prepare your students. Provide detailed prerequisites for your course. Give hardware and software requirements. Give students resources that will teach them how to use technology before they need to use it in your class. And be sure that the technology resources you are using for your online class best suit your needs. For instance, does an outside commercial chatroom for synchronous discussions that allows anyone to enter into the discussion, whether student or not, really make sense for an online course? Keeping students on track in a chatroom is difficult enough without having to deal with the passing peanut gallery. Be sure that you have familiarized yourself thoroughly on all the technology options out there on the Internet before making your choices.

Conclusion

Prompt feedback. Quality instruction. Preparedness. The "P's and Q's" of good teaching. These concepts we learned within the brick and mortar of the little red schoolhouse. If there is any difference in how these concepts should guide us in our virtual rooms, it's that we need to remember them even harder and to be even more diligent in their applications. In this unit, we will help you learn how to use online technology to enhance your classroom teaching and provide your students with new ways to communicate, collaborate and learn outside of the classroom. In addition, we'll help you to translate your good teaching skills into the classroom of the virtual world and give you some hard-won tips on how to use this technology most effectively for your students and yourself. But before we get into the specifics, we want to share with you some more basics of good teaching that are the cornerstones for both the traditional classroom and the online.

Implementing the Seven Principles: Technology as Lever

In 1987, Chickering and Gamson translated raw data from decades of research on the "undergraduate experience" into a document they called the "Seven Principles of Good Practice in Undergraduate Education." Their goal was to give instructors an overall guideline to make their teaching more effective in the classroom, with suggested practices ranging from the establishment of frequent teacher/student contact to the recognition of different learning styles.

In response to the emerging role of technology in education, Chickering and Ehrmann (1996) revisited these principles and discussed the role that technology could play in advancing these principles. This essay, "Implementing the Seven Principles: Technology as Lever," holds some of the keys that can help us, once more, to translate good teaching from the classroom of the "real" to the classroom of the "virtual."[2]

> **Good Practice Encourages Contact between Student and Faculty**: Frequent student-faculty contact in and out of class is a most important factor in student

motivation and involvement. Technologies for online communication such as email and threads encourage swifter communication, more open communication and more reflective communication. Use them.

- **Good Practice Develops Reciprocity and Cooperation among Students:** Learning is enhanced when it is more like a team effort than a solo race. The same technologies that enhance student and faculty communication allow for greater collaboration, problem solving, and community building among students. Make the students responsible for their learning.

- **Good Practice Uses Active Learning Techniques:** Learning is not a spectator sport . . [Students] must make what they learn part of themselves. Computer and online software allow the creation of simulations that students can actively manipulate in the learning process and tools that allow the student to directly engage in scholarly research online. Create your courses so that your students must do something, not just read.

- **Good Practice Gives Prompt Feedback**: Knowing what you know and don't know focuses your learning. Technology offers immediate and reflective feedback opportunities, as well as opportunities for presenting and archiving student performance for comparative evaluation in portfolio assessment strategies. Let your students know when and how you'll reply and then do it.

- **Good Practice Emphasizes Time on Task**: Learning to use one's time well is critical for students and professionals alike. Online courses and their technologies offer strategies for time-saving, whether because of their anywhere/anytime nature that can eliminate commutes to class, or because of the wealth of information resources they can offer at the touch of a mouse within the conveniences of a student's home. If you want community and cohort learning, define for your students what is self-paced in your course, and what is not.

- **Good Practice Communicates High Expectations**: Expecting students to perform well becomes a self-fulfilling prophecy. Communication tools and archiving capabilities offers instructors many opportunities to display criteria to students, to model and exemplify expectations for quality work. "Publishing" student work in an online course can create new incentives for excellence. Expect and demand as much online as you do in the classroom.

- **Good Practice Respects Diverse Talents and Ways of Learning**: Many roads lead to learning. Different students bring different talents and styles to college. Text, multimedia presentations such as video and audio, asynchronous and synchronous communication tools, and the use of images and hypertext links allow instructors to present content in multiple ways, to accommodate both immediate and reflective discussion, and to establish core competencies for students by pro-

viding background and supplemental resources. Don't create text online courses. Experiment with alternative ways of presenting content.

Good practices in the traditional classroom translate into good practices in the online
classroom. The technology you use to teach your online course will allow you to emulate
much of what you did in the classroom, but, more importantly, as you become experienced
with online teaching, will allow you to experiment with new teaching methodologies that
may not even be realized yet.

11.2 The Online Class vs. the Web-Enhanced Class

It has been predicted that "in a few years, high-performance computing and communications will make knowledge utilities, virtual communities, shared synthetic environments, and sensory immersion as routine a part of everyday existence as the telephone,
television, radio, and newspapers are today." [3] How can technology then not become a
vital part of education, <u>and</u> a catalyst for its change?

Yet, debate still rages over the effectiveness or non-effectiveness of online learning
when compared with learning in the traditional classroom. "What's the difference?" has
become a rallying cry for researchers on both sides of the online learning debate. Each
side has compiled a compelling array of research studies supporting either the "no
significant difference" phenomena (**http://distancelearn.about.com/education/dis
tancelearn/library/blpages/blnsd.htm**) or the "significant difference" camp
(**http://cuda.teleeducation.nb.ca/significantdifference.htm**). Other researchers have
been quick to pull the trigger on either side, criticizing sloppy research techniques and
non-credible research sponsorship. The most recent finger pointing has come from the
Institute for Higher Education Policy in its "What's the Difference" review of research on
distance learning and online learning (**http://www.ihep.com/difference.pdf**).

What's becoming interesting is that, for many who have taught online, the thought of
ever going back to the regular classroom and not using Internet technology seems impossible. They have learned that the Internet offers extensive, readily-available resources,
alternative ways to present those resources so that as many learning styles as possible can
be accommodated, new ways to communicate with students, to manage a class, and gives
students new ways to become more active and directly involved in their own education, to
become those life-long "self-learners."

But for instructors unfamiliar with online teaching, that ongoing debate and the unease
many have at the thought of learning a technology foreign to them and then depending
upon it totally for the operations of their class make the alternative of simply incorporating technology into portions of their traditional classroom good sense. The Web-enhanced
class versus the online class is not so much a competition, as a gradual progression for
some instructors as they become more and more comfortable with technology in their reg-

ular classroom and begin to use more and more of it in their instruction. Often, many end up teaching the totally online course.

Clicks in the Bricks

What can a new "clicks in bricks" classroom offer students? Right now, we have interdisciplinary teaching in the traditional classroom, but with clicks in bricks, interdisciplinary teaching can cut across geographic boundaries, so that the expert in political science in the East can combine forces with the history expert or the social studies expert of the Midwest and South. These same experts can be available to any course and spotlight as guest lectures in live Webcasts or discussion facilitators in asynchronous discussions. The experiential learning from probing a formaldehyde frog occurs in labs everywhere now, but there will be increasing opportunities for experiential learning through Internet technology, online animation, and simulation. Right now there are teams of educators who bike through the Andes or hike through rain forests with a laptop and teach K-12 students about these places through updated websites that contain video, audio, digital photos, and text that anyone can access. This is only a first baby step: imagine the live Webcast from *The Duomo* in Florence as the roving professor teaches on site, interviews experts and the locals, facilitates discussion with these people through expanded chatrooms. Preparation for classes will be repetitive for neither the instructor nor the student: standard information will always be available, and the instructor and the student can concern themselves with keeping the course updated and dynamic by providing each other with live and experiential learning. Students of these courses can join life-long cohorts of self-learners, create academic communities that will keep them in touch with peers who share their same passions. Internet technology could be the vehicle norm for research, presentation, class interaction, and life-long learning. The classroom becomes dynamic, exciting, a portal to a field of study that suddenly is a viable and intrinsic part of the world outside. But expanding the traditional classroom through the Internet doesn't happen overnight for most instructors. It's a step-by-step process.

Managing Information Outside the Traditional Classroom

Using the Internet can be as simple as creating an online "bulletin board" that provides students with class information outside of class. This provides students with information 24 hours a day, 7 days a week, and can assist you in keeping your students on track.

The first day your students walk through the door into your classroom, you hand them your syllabus, you give a personal introduction, and you discuss the parameters of your course. In the online world of education, you will "virtually" carry out the same tasks by:

1.   Putting your syllabus, along with your introductions to the course, on a Web page in simple HTML form.

2. Posting your syllabus so that students can never again "lose" their syllabi.

3. Posting announcements to students with changes in schedules, updates, and reminders.

4. Keeping students up-to-date with every class period, even those students who miss a class.

5. Letting students know ahead of time if there are any emergency cancellations of class.

6. Reminding students to bring materials to class.

7. Posting assignments and reminding students of upcoming assignment due dates and specifics.

8. Posting student grades and, if possible, including commentary on grades and providing some one-on-one feedback.

Using the Internet this way gives your students access outside of the classroom to some very important information, mainly the syllabus (so seldom held onto in paper form). It allows you to try your hand at building a Web page with HTML documents. It's a handy supplement to your course, and if for some reason the server connection to your Web page "goes down," your ability to teach your class will not be affected. Students especially like the opportunity to access their grades online. This helps them keep up to date with their progress in the course. You will want to make sure, of course, that whatever "grade book" you use online is secured and will only let each student see his or her own individual grades.

Creating Instructor Packs

Once instructors have become accustomed to this first step in using Internet technology in their course, they will often start to include lectures and instructor's notes to complement the readings they assign in textbooks, creating an archive for students to refer to throughout the course. They may also upload other documents outside of the texts that students can read and/or link out to important resources on the WWW. These sources can be background materials to the text information, journal articles, resource information sites on proper documentation and writing strategies, tutorials on math and science. The savvy classroom instructor can create an entire instructor pack online that will cost the students nothing to obtain. In order to combat the services online that now offer lecture notes to students for a fee, instructors will post their own lecture notes either before or after the class for their students. Instructors may also begin adding images to their websites to enhance the text materials of the course. Often, in preparation for a classroom discussion, instructors will:

1. Post the discussion questions prior to the class and ask students to come in to class prepared for some comprehensive discussion. Or ask small groups of students to come to class prepared to lead the discussion.

2. Post lecture notes: Give students either review notes of your lectures or preparatory notes before your lecture to help them prepare questions ahead of time.

3. Post upcoming discussion topics: Have students come to class prepared to discuss specific issues and reading assignments and as small groups present their answers to a discussion topic.

4. Post review criteria for tests: Provide students with extra resources for study sessions.

5. Post exemplary work of students: provide after-test examples of successful question responses and/or successful essays or short answers.

6. Post links to primary and secondary resources both on the WWW and external pages: supplement primary text.

7. Post small group information: List individual group members and specific assignments for each group.

Online Communication beyond the Traditional Classroom Wall

Along with posting more and more extensive resources on the Web page, instructors will begin to experiment with email, listservs, and commercial chatrooms and threaded discussions. One of my colleagues refers to this as "breaking the fourth wall," as in theatre, where the playwright and the actors attempt to draw the audience more and more into the activities of the play. In this case, it's the learning activities of the classroom. If one of the acknowledged good practices of teaching is frequent interaction between students and instructor, adding online communication to the classroom can only enhance the learning experience of the student. How often in the traditional classroom have you noticed that some students continuously take the "center stage," asking questions and responding to questions, while others "lurk" shyly in the back of the class? Communicating with you online gives some of those students alternative ways to approach you that may be more comfortable for them. The more instructors experiment with the opportunities that online resource allocation, course management, and communication give them, the more instructors begin to create that hybrid class that balances the best of the face-to-face classroom with the best of the online classroom. Sometimes the number of face-to-face sessions will be cut because of the work that can be done online. What becomes important is finding the "mix" that makes both the online and in the classroom portion of the course equally essential. Classroom functions and corresponding online tools are shown in Table 11-1.

Function	Online Tools
Office hours: Instructor/student counseling and advising.	Threaded discussion, email, online chatroom
Discussion preparation: Students prepare for discussions in class.	Threaded discussion, email, online chatroom
Group work: Groups work together anywhere/anytime.	Threaded discussion, email, online chatroom
FAQs: Provide all students with answers to FAQs and to grades.	Online answers to FAQs and online tool for grade book
Guest visitor: Allow guest lectures to visit online	Threaded discussion, email, online chatroom
Tutorial services: Provide online resources, either school-sponsored online tutorial services or use of teaching assistant for designated hours.	Threaded discussion, email, online chatroom
Website tours: Create learning opportunities on effective WWW research.	Threaded discussion, email, online chatroom
Online documentation, presentation, and discussion of in class lab activities.	

Table 11.1
Classroom functions and online tools

Teaching in the Bricks with Clicks

Don't forget that part of using technology in the traditional classroom is using online technology in the classroom. Along with providing students with resources and communication outside of the classroom, use the classroom for high-level, intense face-to-face activities. For some subject areas, such as lab-orientated science courses, language courses, and speech courses, having a face-to-face component in addition to the online component is especially important. And don't forget that any resources you have online for your students you can use for your classroom, saving you from hauling a lot of AV equipment and photocopied materials around for in-class presentations (Table 11.2).

Table 11.2
The online and classroom experience

In the Classroom (Bricks)	Online (Clicks)
Traditional testing.	Deliver proctored or online exams.
Class discussions.	Expect informed, reflective, and prepared discussion contributions from your students using threaded discussion tools.
Peer critiques and workshops: Require individual review of peer work outside of the classroom. Expect prepared and detailed group discussion in the classroom.	Expect the same using document sharing features, email, or threaded discussion.
Student presentations may provide face-to-face experience in presentation.	Less intimidating, students may use threaded discussion or chatrooms.
Lectures: Deliver necessary lectures.	Lectures may be delivered online in text or by graphically rich presentations supported with audio narrative.
Student speeches: Monitor in-class speech presentations.	Have students prepare 3-5 minute audio presentations and submit them for uploading to a server supporting streaming media.
Lab activities: Conduct hands-on labs.	Use animations, video, or live experiences at-a-distance in proctored settings.

The Internet and the Arts: Classroom Style (A Case Study)

For an article in *itpe,* (*information technology in postsecondary education*), I discussed how I would change a class I had taught many times in the traditional classroom by adding an online component to the class. Below is an excerpt of that article:

It would be easy to spout out generalities on how the Internet could serve even the "geographically-bound"—through time management, content delivery, communication tools, self-assessment opportunities—but it doesn't seem enough. Theory is often easy. The practical application of it, hardly ever. So the question becomes: "how can the Internet be used in a particular course so that it becomes an integral and necessary part of the class instruction and not just some 'cool' factor?"

In the summer of '98, I taught a five-week course on Modernism in Poetry and Painting for a graduate liberal arts program. My objective for this class was to provide these students with both the academic and creative means to understand the literary and artistic movements within what has been called "Modernism." And I wanted them to understand how the ideas and methodologies within these particular movements could be windows toward understanding contemporary painting and poetry. On top of that, I wanted them to have a little fun creating their own works of poetry and art.

Needless to say, this five week, three and a half hour class had some inherent problems. I not only needed general readings on modernism, but specific readings on both the poetry and art movements within modernism as well as poems exemplifying those movements and reproductions of paintings from the modernist age. I also needed the very words of the poets and painters who had so deeply influenced each other so that my students could begin to understand how ideas are shared and translated between mediums. Finding the right texts proved difficult, and besides the two books I asked my students to buy—one being an exorbitantly expensive art history book with reproductions—I was forced to create an instructor packet, which because of copyright laws, was quite expensive for my students. I also had to raid the art history department for slides, which I was permitted to borrow only under terms of financial ruin should one be lost—a threat so unnerving, I consistently put the slides into the projector upside down and backwards. Because I was no painter myself, I also needed to bring in artists to present their works and the influences on their work to my students and inspire them to do their own experimentation.

Time was a big issue from the start: with only five class meetings, the first night had to be more than simple introduction. My students needed to have already done the first readings and be ready to discuss them. They also needed to bring in their first poems, so that as we were discussing, say, symbolism, we could consider their poems in that light. Though I knew covering all the materials we needed to cover each class would be quite a challenge, I hadn't factored in the extra time needed for happy artists talking in front of a captive audience.

The students, as always in this particular liberal arts program, were wonderful, high-achieving adults, passionately interested in studying the world around them. The class, despite the one moment I panicked and contemplated hara-kiri via paper cutter, went beautifully, and the work the students ended up doing, both creative and academic, far surpassed what I had hoped for. But it could have been better for the students and me because of what the Internet has to offer.

Next time, with what is on the WWW, I can eliminate texts, the instructor packet, and the borrowed slides. For the purposes of this class, the art history books were actually too in-depth and caused some confusion. I only wanted to introduce them to ideas and concepts of modernism and the artistic movements within it. Expressionism, Symbolism, Cubism, Surrealism, Abstract Expressionism—all these are on the Web. The artists and

IMPLEMENTATION/EVALUATION

their most famous paintings from each of these movements are on the Web too. While poetry anthologies tend to be "one-notes," omitting the influential poets outside of America and Great Britain, the Web is multicultural with full-text poems available and sometimes audio recordings. I only have to link my students to these sites and create a "virtual" instructor packet at no fee to them. As for the first night problems, I have only to put my syllabus online, to create discussion questions online for my students to consider before they come to class, and create a place where my students can post their poems before class so that the other students and I have time to read and critique each one carefully ahead of time.

The one complaint I received about the course was that it was too short; the students wanted more. By using the Internet, I can make it "more" without changing the number of hours or weeks we meet. The students wanted to continue our discussions outside of the class; they wanted to share more of their work with each other and with me. And the happy artists obviously wanted more time to share with the students. Unfortunately, the artists were never able to see the art projects they instigated in class since each week I had to move forward with a new artist. The students missed out on some professional feedback. With the Internet, not only will I be able to set up discussions both asynchronous and synchronous for students and artists to continue their conversations, but also more importantly, I can ask these motivated students and artists for digital copies of their work that I can put online. The students can either get their work scanned or take a regular snapshot of it and then have a photo shop put that picture on disk for them.

And, as it turns out, with sites like (**http://www.virtualchautauqua.org**), where the performing arts have been put online in video, audio, and text, and the artists are available via synchronous and asynchronous discussion, there are no longer geographic boundaries. We can now go out into the world and invite any artist anywhere to make virtual visits through the chatroom and threads. Even the gabby ones. The Internet is a nice way to keep them "virtually" hanging around. [5]

11.3 Teaching the Online Class

Once instructors use online technology as an integral part of their traditional course, often they will consider taking the next step—the pure online course. Why? Some do it for reasons of pure curiosity. Some, like the instructor who informed me that he would be teaching next semester from a condo in Hawaii, because they realize that the anytime/anywhere advantages of the online course applies to them as well as to their students. Some because they want to attract students outside the geographic boundaries of their schools or because their school wants to put up an online degree program and the course they teach is part of that program. This next step is easy because they already have the framework and the content for the course online and they are familiar with using the tools. And they'll use many of the tools they used for the traditional classroom in the same way for the online classroom. But now they need to learn how to teach effectively totally online to students they may never see face to face. What becomes important? How do you teach and interact with your students online, especially students often described as "non-traditional?" For that reason, we are going to explore a term that keeps cropping up in online teaching quite often, "facilitation," and discuss what its practical application really means in the online classroom. We are also going to look in depth at both asynchronous communication, especially in the threaded discussion, because it can be such a powerful teaching tool, and synchronous communication in the form of the chatroom because it is such an exciting technology to so many students.

Facilitation and the Adult Learner

"Facilitation" is the word heard most often in conjunction with online education. But what does it really mean to "facilitate" an online course? Simply to "make it easier?" The assumptions that underlie adult learning are the key to understanding the usage of this term in the online classroom.

What Is Adult Learning?

Basically, it's the recognition that the adult student has different needs and expectations from the child student because of the experiences and maturity that the adult student brings to the classroom. Not only historically (though a short "history" indeed) has the adult nontraditional student been the one to predominately populate the online classroom, but the characteristics of the online classroom demand that students have the traits—maturity, self-motivation, a tendency toward self-directed learning—of the adult student in order to succeed in the online classroom. "Andragogy" is a word that is ousting, in online education particularly, the still not quite familiar term for many of "pedagogy." While "pedagogy" has to do with the practice of teaching children, "andragogy" is about teaching adults.[4]

Malcolm Knowles, one of the most prominent voices in adult education, interprets learning as "not the discovery of an independent, existing world outside" of the self, but the "construction of meaning through experience." [1] In other words, knowledge is actively "constructed" by the student, not passively received from the environment, and learning is "an interactive process of interpretation, integration, and transformation of one's experiential world." [4] Knowles saw the adult student characterized by individuality, by the history of prior knowledge and experience he or she brought into the classroom, by his or her capacity for self-directed learning, and by his or her uniqueness that demanded respect and nurturing from the instructor or "facilitator." [4] These assumptions are why so much emphasis is put on "active" learning, rather than "passive" learning, and why online teaching is about facilitating self-directed and individual learning. Not only do we have a large number of adult students that pass through our classrooms, but the circumstances in which we teach online demand that we allocate a large percentage of the responsibility for learning to our students, adult or otherwise.

What Is Facilitation?

But this still doesn't explain what we do when we facilitate a class. In some ways, we give up control, though I have heard the extreme of this—one online instructor presented his online class with an empty course shell and told them to "fill" it. There is a balance between presenting your online students with content, with ideas, and instruction, and asking your students to discover content and ideas on their own and then instruct each other. Here are a couple of examples of how a facilitated online course might be conducted.

What Is Problem-Based Learning?

Problem-based learning comes from the assumption that learning takes place in "fields of social interaction." [2] The ultimate goal of problem based learning in, say, the language classroom is to have students actively using language in various ways in order to solve the problem. Students are given real-world problems and asked as groups to investigate and solve these problems. It is in the group communication that language learning takes place.

For real-world problems to work effectively as teaching tools in any kind of classroom they must have these characteristics. [5]

- They are complex, with no one right or wrong answer associated with them.
- They are relevant to the students.
- They require students to research multiple kinds of resources beyond the teacher and the materials he/she has provided.

What's important here is that the instructor is not the source of ultimate knowledge. Instead of answering "right" or "wrong," the instructor asks questions such as "Why?" "What do you mean?" and "How do you know that is true"[2] The students must begin reasoning for themselves, using the materials that they collect as proof or not proof of the validity of their solutions. To begin the exercise, the instructor presents the problem, describing the situation and the possible consequences of the situation that could become problematic if a certain decision is made or not made. The students are then asked to join their small groups and work collaboratively. Working collaboratively may involve the following exercises. [2]

- Generate working ideas or possible solutions.
- Identify available information related to the problem.
- Identify learning issues (what they need to know before deciding on the best solution).

- · Identify resources to look up or consult.
- · Assign tasks to various group members.
- · Gather information.
- · Propose solution.

The students take over the responsibility for the learning process and begin to teach themselves. The facilitator's role is then to listen, redirect if necessary, question, and probe. Exercises like this can easily and effectively be done in a threaded discussion, and final presentations to the entire class from each small group can be done through a chatroom or a well-written piece of documentation that all groups will evaluate and give feedback on.

What Is the Case Study Method of Teaching?

Teaching the case study method in business is quite popular in the traditional classroom and a practice that the Harvard Business School advocates. The "core of case teaching" has been called the "facilitation of student learning." [6] The Harvard Business School Publishing now offers case studies online as well as course templates centered on these case studies (**http://www.hbsp.harvard.edu**).[7] Like the problems presented in problem-based learning, case studies are real-world examples of situations in the business world that are complex and have no right or wrong answer. At a seminar I attended, called "The Art and Craft of Discussion Leadership," the facilitator, Dr. Louis B. Barnes, described case study teaching as being about discussion, about teaching students how to ask good questions, to look at actual experiences and analyze and understand the higher issues and implications involved in these scenarios so that they might be able to face their own problematic situations with reason and foresight.

In facilitating our group, Dr. Barnes engaged in these kinds of activities:

- · He asked open-ended questions and diagnostic questions (What do you think? What do you think the meaning is?)
- · He challenged and probed (Why do you say that? Do you disagree? Give me an example of what you're saying.)
- · He asked priority questions and questions that forced students to begin thinking about action (Which issue do you think is the most important? What would you do? Shouldn't do?)
- · He asked students to summarize and generalize (Let's step back for a moment; Let's look at the larger issues.)

I noticed that Dr. Barnes never disagreed with what we said, but he refocused and redirected us when he felt it was necessary. And he, consciously, was never the center of discussion, physically removing himself from the center of the classroom, prodding students

IMPLEMENTATION/EVALUATION

to direct questions and challenges directly to each other. This model of teaching is something that can be directly applied to how the online instructor facilitates the threaded discussion. When the students, who were all college professors, were asked to describe their own methods for teaching the case study in class, they outlined these activities that all centered around the case study:

· Written assignments
· Peer critiques
· Group presentations
· Group work
· Role-playing
· Quizzes
· Peer evaluations
· Individual projects

Note that all of these activities can make up the portfolio assessment for the online class, which we mentioned earlier in the book. The best online courses are built to accommodate all of these different kinds of learning activities. When an online course is facilitated, rather than "instructed," and the students enrolled have the capabilities to engage in adult learning, two things happen: first, responsibility for learning is handed back over to the students, and claimed by them, and, second, students begin to engage in those higher levels of cognitive learning—analysis, synthesis, evaluation.   Dr. Barnes left our class on teaching the case study method with these words, which I think illuminate the balancing act that we must engage in online: though we as instructors and facilitators must have a standard in our own minds of what constitutes good learning from our students of our subject material, the meeting of that standard should not be our ultimate goal for our class. The purpose of a standard is to accomplish something else—to educate, to create a space for learning.

Teaching with Threads

Certainly creating a sense of community in an online course with its firewall of technology and its "invisible" student body is a major challenge for the online instructor. Though mutual computer video and sound could add the "human" touch, the costs at this time of such tools are beyond the pockets of many students, and teachers too. Real-time chatrooms are another alternative where students directly "talk" to each other, but most students who take online courses take them because they are nontraditional students who cannot commit to an outside regimented schedule, while others inhabit different time zones. The threaded discussion then, which can ensure thoughtful reflective participation from all students enrolled—a cornerstone for community—becomes one of the best tools for engendering that empathetic, affirming spirit of the best classrooms.

The threaded discussion can serve as a learning tool that fosters in-depth, academic discussion, a workshop arena in which your students work collaboratively or conduct peer analysis, a non-threatening "hang-out" for your online students, or simply a place where students submit assignments. Most instructors I have worked with have had real qualms over the prospect of giving up face-to-face discussions that can be so powerful in the traditional classroom. And yet, over and over again, these same instructors express astonishment and happiness over the quality and quantity of discussion that occurs asynchronously in their online classroom through the threads. But threaded discussions will be successful for you and your class only if you understand how best to use them and how best to facilitate them. Let's visit briefly the pros and cons of the threaded discussion and then look at how best to use them.

The Pros of Threaded Discussion

Anytime/Anywhere/Anyone: The most obvious, and well known, argument for using an asynchronous communication tool like the threaded discussion is that it can make learning accessible to virtually everyone. It can also give a new sense of security for those who may have experienced gender or race bias in the classroom or bias because of physical disabilities.

Freedom and Reflection: Threaded discussions can create a sense of freedom for students in giving honest, direct peer feedback during collaborative learning activities. The threaded discussion also allows students the opportunities for reflection and organization in their responses and can be a tool to encourage higher skills in writing and critical analysis.

Practical Alternative to Email: Initially, you may well think of email as the primary mode for asynchronous communication. But you may soon realize that the threaded discussion offers solutions to "email headaches" like overabundance and the practical management problems that overabundance can create and the problems of "missing" emails (or the "ISP ate my homework" syndrome). By using threaded discussions, you need only answer the same questions that keep coming up once and everyone will see your answer. And you and your students do not need to send each other emails confirming whether an assignment or responses have been received because everything on the threaded discussion becomes public record in the course. This public posting is conducive to peer learning.

Community Building: Beyond the solution to email problems, the threaded discussion allows you to create peer communities in the online classroom and to "publish" work that can serve as an incentive toward excellence for many students, motivating them to do their best work and to emulate the strong work of their peers. It can make any of these kinds of group "in the classroom" learning activities possible online:

> Informal and formal small discussion
> Project collaboration
> Peer editing
> Brainstorming
> Small group work
> Instructor/student consultation

But despite all the wonders of the threaded discussion, there are some possible drawbacks to using threaded discussions that you need to consider before creating your threads.

The Cons of the Threaded Discussion

Because there is little or no face-to-face contact, a perpetually disconnected, non-communal class is usually the first "con" on anyone's list. But asynchronous communication can also share some of the "pitfalls" of "real time" communication in the classroom, especially from the student's point of view.

Fear of Public Speaking: Though the online classroom is heralded for its encouragement of "reflection and preparation," this same advantage is a disadvantage to some. The fear of "public" speaking in the traditional classroom becomes the fear of "public" writing in the online classroom. The very fact that there is time for reflection, organization, and rewriting can intensify that fear for the student because suddenly there's "no excuse" for a poor answer. These fearful students may either not "attend" the threaded discussion or try to "make do" with quick and simple responses, like "I agree with Bill." This attitude can create problems for the entire class. Students who <u>do</u> respond consistently and well to the threads will end up feeling "cheated" by those who do not.

Thread Monopoly: At the opposite end of the "problem" spectrum can be the literate students who dominate the "threads" and intimidate everyone else from participating. How does the instructor easily "step in" to bring equilibrium to the discussion without quelling the enthusiasm of these "heavy-threaders?" (One solution I've used is to privately contact the students, thank them for their good work, and then express concern that he or she will "burn" himself out responding to the threads so zealously. The students tend to respond positively to my concerns and will pull back a bit.)

Informality vs. Formality: The underlying purpose of the threaded discussion is another issue. Some instructors feel that the threaded discussion by its very nature must be kept informal in order to facilitate the give and take of students. To impose standards or expectations is to stem the kind of learning that can occur between students informally discussing issues at hand. These instructors believe in entirely open threads that have no restrictions placed on them whatsoever. (One instructor once reported that he purposely responded to the threads with spelling and grammatical errors in order to enforce the informality of the thread.) The students write as they want and participate when and how they want to. Participation in these threads and the quality of that participation are not a part of the grading policy for the course. This, of course, brings up the problem of responsible students feeling frustrated when their peers do not contribute to the threads as often or as well as they do.

Technology Inequalities: Last, but not least, the same technical inequalities that can plague synchronous communication online, especially inequalities in the ability to access the Internet, can plague asynchronous communication.

Managing (Facilitating) the Threaded Discussion

Certainly, you as the instructor must use the threads in ways that best contribute to your course. Using threaded discussions informally can be one way to give students the opportunity for online discussion but spare you the work involved in managing the threads. But the threaded discussion used well can be an effective learning tool that encourages students to engage in higher cognitive thought. Experts such as Lev Vygotsky, A. R. Luria, and Jerome Bruner have concluded, "that high cognitive functions, such as analysis and synthesis, seem to develop most fully only with the support system of verbal language—particularly, it seems, of written language." [8] The key is to learn how to facilitate the threads so that they become a source of student-centered learning with just a little bit of "pushing" from you.

Staying focused: In a survey study on the management of asynchronous discussion, 13 techniques for managing successful threaded discussions were rated by a number of online instructors (Table 11.3). The first four techniques were rated as especially important for the effective facilitation of a threaded discussion. Success was defined as the ability of the students to stay focused in the threaded discussion on a particular topic. [9]

Because designing effective questions for the threaded discussion question and providing students with information on how to craft a good response are such important points, let's look at them in more depth.

IMPLEMENTATION/EVALUATION

Creating Well-Designed Questions: Creating good questions was deemed the overall most important factor for the success of student discussions online, questions specifically that either "promote active participation of the learner by stimulating various levels of thinking, and/or by creating cognitive dissonance." [9] Open-ended questions are the key to

Table 11.3
Keeping online asynchronous dIscussion on topic

Keeping Online Asynchronous Discussion on Topic[2]

1. **Well-designed questions that keep students topic-focused**: Creating the open-ended question that fosters on-target discussion is a matter of experience. See Bloom's Taxonomy for some guidance.

2. **Provision of guidelines for students on preparing acceptable responses**: A few times I have heard new online instructors express surprise that their class's threaded discussions did not pan out even though they had heard that threaded discussion is such an effective learning tool online. Usually, these same instructors simply created a space for discussion to happen with no parameters or guidelines. See our section on guidelines for creating the free thread, the moderately informal thread, and the formal thread.

3. **Revision of original threaded discussion question when responses are off-target**: Online courses offer the instructor flexibility. If a particular question is not working well and students are confused, change it immediately and send out an email to your students regarding the change or post a thread in the threaded discussion.

4. **Consistent summaries of discussion**: Usually the entire class will answer a threaded discussion question by the time the discussion is over. But the class does not always realize this. Send an email to your students summing up the issues presented and resolved in a discussion; pinpoint especially interesting and informative responses by your students. You can also do this by posting a "my two-cents" response after the conclusion of the threaded discussion. Waiting until the discussion is over (if you have placed a date due on it) will help you avoid any "teacher says" syndrome.

5. **State the expectation that online discussion stays on topic**: Give clear detailed directions to your students on what you want in their responses at the beginning of each thread.

6. **Provide café or informal threaded discussion elsewhere in the course**: Have more than one threaded discussion in your course. You might have a permanent "water cooler" thread at the very start of your course which students can access as they come and go. A colleague made the suggestion that the "Café" thread or "Student Lounge" thread can be used as a place to get your students to decide on the parameters of threaded discussions in the course—let them jointly decide how structured the thread should be or how often class members should participate.

7. **Include a reminder that students stay on topic**: Don't ignore the threaded discussion if you want it to be effective. If students begin to stray from the topic, send out an email pushing everyone back in the right direction, or, better yet, if the direction the students have strayed is a good one, reinforce it and allow the discussion to focus on the new topic.

Keeping Online Asynchronous Discussion on Topic²

8. **Present the rules of conduct to eliminate off-topic discussion**: From the start, detail the "p's and q's" of the thread. Or use the informal thread as a place for your students to determine the "p's and q's."

9. **Provide a reward**: Offer extra credit for excellence in thread participation.

10. **Privately reprimand and give constructive feedback to students with off-topic conversations**: Don't be afraid to shoot off an email to a student who is doing a poor job in the threaded discussion. If the problem is chronic and quite disruptive, call the student and make sure he/she understands the protocol of the threads.

11. **Provide a grade for keeping on topic**: Make both participation and quality of response a part of your grading policy.

12. **Screen postings and route off-topic posting to alternative locations with explanation to submitter:** Model your threads after the DEOS listserv. Ask all your students to email to you their threaded discussion responses and post them yourself on the threads. Notify those students whose responses are not adequate.

13. **Expel offenders after a certain number of off-topic submissions**.: Delete threaded discussion postings by those students who refuse to play by the rules and then deny them access into the threads and dock their class participation grade. You also might include threaded discussion responses in an overall Courtesy Code for your course.

Table 11.3
Keeping online asynchronous dIscussion on topic

IMPLEMENTATION/EVALUATION

encouraging thoughtful discussion for your students, and the more you can encourage your students toward higher-level cognitive thinking, the more useful the threaded discussion will become to them.

Cognitive learning is "demonstrated through the acquisition and use of knowledge." [9] Bloom's Taxonomy is a well-known classification of " intellectual behaviors important to learning." [11]   It ranks cognitive learning from the lowest level to the highest level (Table 11.4).   We can use his definitions and levels to help us create questions that demand higher level thinking from our students and that create the best kinds of questions for threaded discussions.

In looking at Bloom's Taxonomy, it's clear that discussion can be created around any of the levels, though those levels that ask for analysis, synthesis, and evaluation can invite the most interesting debates that can allow you to determine if your students have moved from "fact-finding" and "knowledge-gathering" to true assimilation of the content. In creating your threaded discussion questions use the verbs that are associated with a particular level of cognitive learning. For example, ask your students to analyze, evaluate, distinguish, and create.

Table 11.4

Bloom's taxonomy of "intellectual behaviors important to learning." [10]

Keeping Online Asynchronous Discussion on Topic[2]

1. **Knowledge**: remembering previously learned material.
   a. **Examples of learning objectives**: Know common terms, know specific facts, know basic concepts.
   b. **Associated verbs**: Arrange, define, duplicate, label, list, memorize, name, order, recognize, relate, recall, repeat, reproduce, state.
2. **Comprehension**: ability to grasp the meaning of material.
   a. **Examples of learning objective**: Understand facts and principles, interpret verbal material and charts and graphs, justify methods and procedures.
   b. **Associated verbs**: Classify, describe, discuss, explain, express, identify, indicate, locate, recognize, report, restate, review, select, translate.
3. **Application**: ability to use learned material in new and concrete situations.
   a. **Example of learning objective**: Apply concepts and principles to new situations, apply laws and theories to practical situations, solve mathematical problems, demonstrate the correct usage of a method or procedure.
   b. **Associated verbs**: Apply, choose, demonstrate, dramatize, employ, illustrate, interpret, operate, practice, schedule, sketch, solve, use, and write.
4. **Analysis**: ability to break down material into its component parts so that its organizational structure may be understood.
   a. **Examples of learning objective**: Recognize unstated assumptions, recognize logical fallacies in reasoning, distinguish between facts and inferences.
   b. **Associated verbs**: analyze, appraise, calculate, categorize, compare, contrast, criticize, differentiate, discriminate, distinguish, examine, experiment, question, test.
5. **Synthesis**: refers to the ability to put parts together to form a new whole.
   a. **Examples of learning objective**: Write a well-organized theme, propose a plan for an experiment, and integrate learning from different areas into a plan for solving a problem.
   b. **Associated verbs**: arrange, assemble, collect, compose, construct, create, design, develop, formulate, manage, organize, plan, prepare, propose, set up, write.
6. **Evaluation**: ability to judge the value of material for a given purpose. Judgments based on definite criteria.
   a. **Examples of learning objective**: Judge the logical consistency of written material; judge the adequacy with which conclusions are supported by data.
   b. **Associated verbs**: Analyze, appraise, calculate, categorize, compare, contrast, criticize, differentiate, discriminate, distinguish, examine, experiment, question, test.[10, 11]

Some Question Possibilities

·   **The open-ended question:** Ask for the how's and the why's instead of the what's.

·   **The controversial question:** Take the unpopular stand and get your students riled up.

·   **The "naiveté" question:** Ask the "dumb" question to get your students riled up.

·   **The "synthesizer" question:** Draw from related reading materials, asking your students to determine what "Dr. A" would have to say about "Dr. B" because of "C."

Provision of Guidelines for Students on Preparing Acceptable Responses

Whether you choose an informal structure over a formal structure for your threaded discussions, or choose to use both kinds in your online course, you do need to give your students some guidelines on how to contribute to these threads.

The Informal Threaded Discussion: The informal thread can be as informal as a place made available for students to participate in discussions at will. Many instructors will label these threads with names like "Water Cooler," or "Coffee Klatch." The idea is that students now have the opportunity to "shoot the breeze" as they might in the hallway or cafeteria. No grades are attached to the amount of their participation or the quality of their participation. Sometimes instructors may join in; sometimes they may leave the thread completely alone.

The "Write to Learn" Thread: But the informal thread can be used in a little more struc-tured manner that can still give students the freedom to brainstorm together unselfcon-sciously. And it can be a non-threatening prospect for the instructor who is used to the lecture and exam style of teaching in the traditional classroom but looking for a way to incorporate student discussion into the online course, without feeling overwhelmed with the responsibilities of feedback and critique. Perhaps the first painless step might simply be to use what Writing Across the Curriculum advocates call "write to learn assign-ments,"—frequent, informal writings that become the "germs" for formal academic dis-course.[12]

A study of a pilot program to integrate asynchronous learning networks into a writing across the curriculum program, concluded that those faculty who were happiest in using asynchronous communication "prepare[d] a context for each assignment...ask[ed] stu-dents to write about what they know...use[d] peer[s] to motivate and educate each other" and made writing a regular activity.[13]

Notice that none of these suggestions absolutely requires formal grading on the part of the instructor, but instead reinforces the simple concept that " To learn to write, students must write." The study notes that: ". . . students sometimes need to be encouraged explicitly—given "permission" as it were—to use forms of discourse that go beyond the relatively narrow and confining conventions of academic prose."[13]

In cyber language, "written talk" is a term coined for writing that has an "informal conversational tone quite different from that of traditional academic prose . . . and is considered "evidence of students' critical reasoning, intellectual growth and thoughtful contribution to a type of discussion."[14] "Written talk" is the "expressive writing" of the WAC movement—"the means by which the new is tentatively explored, thoughts may be half-uttered, attitudes half-expressed."[15] It is the writing of the best "write to learn" assignments. It represents the first formation of thought on paper and is the "fodder" for what WAC calls "public" or "transactional" writing, [15] that formal prose with its academic conventions toward which we ultimately encourage our students. In other words, it is the "germ" of learning.

The best "germs" of learning can show evidence of the students' thought processes, how they synthesized readings, formulated questions. The informality of the threads invites them to ruminate on "paper," while awareness of the public audience pushes them toward more academic conventions in writing, such as direct examples from text and references to outside sources. Many times, students will begin to emulate this style in their own responses, and you can step back and allow your students to instruct each other. In order to avoid the cryptic generalities that totally unstructured threads can sometimes produce, you need to take another conclusion of the study to heart: "modeling [what would be] appropriate online responses...[is] a strategy to which students [respond well]."[13] Students want to "talk" with each other and certainly there are open-ended questions that any instructor can devise to get the conversation and learning to begin. If you need to encourage your students to respond in a little more thoughtful way, you could make the thread a certain percentage of a class participation grade—the student either does or does not adhere to a model of response and, accordingly, does or does not receive credit.

The Formal Threaded Discussion: I tend to find writing such an extremely important extension to thinking, and the threaded discussions to be such an opportunity for pushing students toward more coherent and developed writing, that I place a lot of structure on my threaded discussions for my online students. Sometimes my threaded discussions ask my students to submit an assigned paper to the threads. The rest of the class, or a small group, can then critique the paper in the threaded discussion. My general feeling is that because the online classroom, as of yet, is primarily a text-based medium of instruction, it is my responsibility to coach my students as much as possible in good writing and in good reasoning and critical analysis. In general, I set up my formal threaded discussions this way:

Example of informal "write to learn" student thread

The biography on Rita Dove finally gave me some insight into what it means to be a lyrical poet. Besides putting that term in contrast to confessional poet, it made me look the word up. So now I have a little more understanding of what different types of poetry are, and that poems are actually classified by these angles. . . I found myself paying a lot of attention to her titles because I was having particular trouble with the title of my poem and I'm thinking I like how she uses one-word titles. They're very simple but they say enough about their respective poems. The Biography mentioned how she doesn't borrow myth, that she actually creates her own myth. With this in mind I couldn't help but notice the line "light hairs/ on a wrist lying down in sweat." Is this a reference to Theodore Roethke's "the premonition" a coincidence?

- **Explain expectations for threaded discussion responses:** I let my students know immediately if this particular threaded discussion will count for a grade and how that grade will be determined. Usually, I simply make the grade a percentage for class participation. I clearly outline for my students how to access the threads and post responses, even if I have these directions elsewhere.

- **Assign a specific <u>time</u> and date due:** I post clearly in several places the dates and times that responses are due. I tend to make the day and time consistent across the weeks, for example, Thursday midnight. Due dates for threaded discussion threads are always in the late middle of the week because otherwise students often move onto the next unit's work and do not look over the threaded discussion contributions of their peers. Since I depend upon the entire class to finally answer the threaded discussion question in the threads, it is most important that students read each other's responses and understand how the question has been answered.

- **Model acceptable thread response:** I give my students examples of what I consider to be suitable thread responses. Either I make up my own, stressing the need to support any assertions or arguments they may make with reasons and examples, or get permission from excellent students to use their threaded discussion responses as permanent examples for each rendition of my online course. Most students are thrilled and flattered.

- **Motivate with "class participation" grade:** Good participation in threaded discussions may account for 15% of their final grade.

IMPLEMENTATION/EVALUATION

Require more than one posting: To get real discussion going, I generally ask my students to respond to my initial question (or the student leader's) once by a particular day and time and to then post two or three responses by the end of the week to the rest of the class's postings. This way I know that they are in fact learning from each other.

I am always surprised at the thoughtful, in-depth responses I get from all of my students on my formal threaded discussion questions rather than the silence at the back of the traditional class room or the bashful staccato of a few. There is a rigor to professional writing, a rigor of form, a rigor of thinking and we must not forget this in our online classes. But perhaps this rigor and formality work best when combined with the more informal threads that allow students first to learn how to fully "speak" to us and to each other online.

The Instructor as Facilitator in the Threaded Discussion

Threaded discussions will not be successful in your course if you do not learn how to "facilitate" them—in other words, learn how to make your students do most of the work in the threaded discussion. Let's say you have a class of 20 in your online course and you have asked each one of your students to respond to a threaded discussion and to then post responses to at least two other classmate's responses. You have now given yourself 60 assignments to critique and give feedback above and beyond all the other assignments you may have assigned for that week. You will notice two things immediately—one, that by the end of the threaded discussion, with or without you, your question has most likely been answered collectively by the class. And, two, that not every threaded discussion response needs a response from you. To ease your workload and to make the threaded discussion an effective learning tool for your students, you need to do the following things:

Give up the "center ring": Hardest is perhaps stepping back and giving up center ring of the discussion for your students. If teaching online teaches the teacher one important lesson it is how to give up control and still teach effectively. You can keep your students on track with some pointed inquiries or point out an especially interesting and/or well-done response while the discussion is ensuing. But refrain from answering your own questions until after the discussion. You'll find that you don't have to anyway.

Respond selectively: Respond to every thread and you will overwhelm yourself. This is an opportunity for a student learning community. It's the small discussion groups of your traditional classroom. Let this be the opportunity for students to work through a problem. You might simply record participation and respond in the threads selectively to two or three that catch your eye. Just let your students know up front what your responsibilities are in the threaded discussion.

·   **Assign student leaders:** Choose thread leaders for each week and ask these students to take over the responsibility of monitoring the threaded discussion and then wrapping up the discussion.

·   **"Wrap up" major issues:** Again, either add your two cents at the end of the threaded discussion or send out a general email outlining the threaded discussion and highlighting some of the major issues or answers that came out of the discussion.

·   **Direct toward particular responses:** Prompt your students to return to the threads to read particularly interesting student responses.

Creating Small Group Workshops on the Threads

The traditional classroom workshop is conducted this way: Students are given a written assignment to bring into class. Each student is placed in a small group. Ideally, the students in each group receive their peers' written assignments prior to coming to class for discussion. Students are asked to write critiques of each other's work. Students bring their critiques to class, the small groups gather together, and the students discuss each other's work.

The threaded discussion is a perfect tool for accommodating this kind of workshop activity. It provides an advantage over the classroom because students can exchange work easily and meet online easily. The thread also provides a permanent record of each small group workshop that you can make available to everyone in your course. The same technology can allow you to create many threads and to secure access into those threads only to each small group. Using the threads as a workshop format is one of the best ways to create student-centered learning and community.

But, don't be fooled into thinking that managing small group work in an online course is easy. Unfortunately, despite all the precautions you might take, some students in a small group will do the work, some will not. All may even do it, but some will always excel while others simply try to get by. This can cause frustration for your active students who feel like they are giving away valuable feedback but getting nothing in return from their fellow students. For group work to be successful it depends upon all students to participate on time and to participate fully. Try these tips:

- Make groups fluid—be prepared to change group members around several times during the duration of your course. Experiment with grouping active students together and less active students together. And then switch and see if any of the leaders of a group can motivate others in the group to participate fully.
- Be firm on deadlines and on expectations. Make group work a part of the class participation grade.
- Reach out privately to group members who are not participating well. Often you can help them feel more comfortable participating in a group, if the reluctance is based on low confidence and experience.

Creating the Group Work on the Threads

Your threaded discussion "question" will ask each group member to post his or her work on the threads by a certain date. (Try and create groups with five or six members each.) Be sure and identify group members clearly in several places in your course and send out reminder emails. The rest of the group is asked to read the work and post critiques in the threads as "responses" under each particular work. For peer critique work particularly it is important to give your students guidelines. I made these general suggestions and then wrote part of a "lecture" on the art of critiquing and why they had the abilities already to critique each other's work in a writing course I taught.

1. Discuss what is successful in the work using detailed examples from the paper/story itself to support what you said. Don't just say, "I really like this." Say: "The reasoning behind this analysis is exceptional because . . . For example, . . ."
2. Discuss what is not as successful in this work. Don't just say "I didn't like it"; It was confusing"; etc. Give examples; be specific in explaining what you had problems with in reading the piece.

In creating peer group workshops, the first response you may get from many is "I don't know anything. How can I critique my fellow students' work?" I would write "mini lectures" on the art of critiquing, reminding students of what they already knew and could do.

> *Critiquing the Story: No one is asking you to be an expert in fiction writing to do a critique of a story. You know how you felt as you read these stories: awe, confusion, boredom, excitement. You know if you felt that you really knew the characters in the stories or if something is missing. You know*

if you were reading summaries of action rather than scenes.
You know if the story led up to a moment of epiphany, no mat-
ter how small, and you were right there to share that moment.
You know if the story started in the middle or was too slow or
tried to explain too many things at once that probably didn't
need to be explained and would come clear as the characters
reacted to the world around them. You know if the story has
concrete, sensory language in it. You know if the story
seemed to lead inevitably to that final moment because the
writer had paid attention to dominant impressions. You know
if the story has that chain of promises in it. You know if the
story is about a problem that the character must resolve in
some way. You know if the ending clunks or finally sings. You
know if the writer got nervous and thought everything had to
be neatly tied together at the story's end, so the writer did
you the favor of telling what the meaning of the story was
finally.   What information would you want to know if
this were your story? How would you like to be told this
information? You don't want to just sing the praises of some-
thing that you think needs some work, do you? Wouldn't you
want to know, if you were the writer, what was not working?
Isn't doing that then an indication of your respect for
this writer that you believe this writer can make the story bet-
ter finally?

Conclusion

The threaded discussion is one of the most important teaching tools in an online
course. Online instructors have learned to utilize it in many ways. The threaded discussion encourages active participation by all your students and can serve to push students
toward analysis, synthesis, and evaluation, some of the higher levels of cognitive thinking.
For it to be successful, whether you use it for group discussions or peer group workshops,
you must anticipate your students' needs, prepare to be flexible, and communicate your
expectations to your students. A summary of the threaded discussion section is provided
in Table 11.5.

Facilitating Chatrooms
Experiences

I've tried using chatrooms for online instruction with less than remarkable enthusiasm

Table 11.5
Summary of the
threaded discus-
sion section

Summary of Threaded Discussion Section

Why threaded discussions over email discussions?
- Lost correspondence
- Less work to manage
- More control over students meeting deadlines
- Peer learning
- Establishment of different writing forums

What kinds of threads can an instructor create?
- Informal and formal discussions
- Request for assignments/exercises
- Student-led discussion forums
- Workshop areas for collaborative work/peer review

What are some kinds of discussion questions good for the thread?
- The open-ended question: The how's and the why's
- The controversial question
- The "naiveté" question
- The "synthesizer" question
- Bloom's taxonomy

How can I organize the formal threaded discussion?
- Explain how to do threads
- Assign a specific <u>time</u> and date due
- Model acceptable thread response (show example)
- Motivate with "class participation" grade
- Require more than one posting
- For adult students, ask them to determine parameters

How can I facilitate the threads?
- Give up the "center ring"
- Respond selectively
- Assign student leaders
- "Wrap up" major issues
- Direct toward particular responses

Threads as workshops
- Post request for materials
- Specify standards for critiques
- Model acceptable responses
- Enforce due dates

on the part of the students. Let me explain why I think this has been a problem. The reason most students come to online courses is because they are unable to make the commitment to a structured time or a place. They lead busy lives and/or live very distant from available instructional opportunities. Text-based or voice-based chatrooms require the students to be present at a particular time. This is synchronous communication and has been discussed in earlier lessons. Even with a small class it is difficult to achieve complete attendance at a session. There is also the problem of time zones. Have you tried a conference call across three time zones with three people in the United States? I have, and we still became confused about when we were supposed to be online. This problem becomes more difficult across international time zones. As long as I am whining a little, let me also say that there is a reasonable limit to the number of people that can successfully interact on a chatroom. I think that number is around five or six. There are likely to be some in the group who do not actively participate because English is second language, or because the idea of going "live" on the Web is intimidating, or because they are ordinarily shy students. This problem is made worse when students are asked to "talk" on the Web using a microphone. It's equivalent, I think, to pushing a mike in front of a person on stage. Finally, there is the technology problem. Most students will have the technology to type in responses and questions on a text-type chatroom. However, many students do not have the equipment or technical knowledge to use a voice chatroom. I experience this problem with my online class of very sophisticated medical professionals. Several of them tried many times to use a microphone and speak over the computer during a "live chat" session. Less than half of the group was finally successful in mastering this technology on a regular basis.

Whether voice or text, there has to be management of the chatroom. This management should include a valid reason for using this medium in instruction. Some of the reasons may include:

1. Experience students discussing issues "live" and able to reason with facts in real-time.
2. Use it for student group discussion by breaking the class into smaller groups to work on projects or exercises. This is a way to encourage collaboration and negotiation among students.
3. Take students on a virtual field trip by typing in a URL that they can all see and leading them "live" through the Amazon Jungle or the Metropolitan Museum of Art.
4. Use it to hold office hours where you can answer questions or talk informally with those who attend.

Strategies: You will be more successful implementing your chatroom if you adopt the following strategies.

1. Inform your students at the beginning, before they take the online class, that they will be required to spend some scheduled time online.
2. Establish rules of etiquette. No one is to use vulgar language, type or talk incessantly, or humiliate others.
3. Students raise hands in the classroom to talk. You may devise ways to do this

online. One professor has each student type in an asterisk to indicate they wish to talk.

4.   Be prepared to lead the discussion with open-ended questions that are provocative. Much of the previous section on threaded discussions and keeping on topic is appropriate for this section as well.

Tips for Online Teaching Practices
First Day Tips

1.   *Getting Students to Class*—you may experience the surprise I did when none of my students "showed up" for the first day of my online class or even for the first week for that matter!   Some students will think your course is self-paced; some won't realize they were supposed to check in for the first week; some will have lost their password to your course; some will be experiencing technical difficulties. To prevent this from happening to you:

   a.   Send a welcome email to everyone in your class on the first day, inviting/reminding each one that class has now started. Be sure to provide a phone contact number, preferably an office number rather than a home number.

   b.   Telephone those students who still have not entered the class by the end of the first week. These students may not be receiving email because of technical problems, changes in ISP providers, etc.

   c.   In case your students can and have entered your course already, put up a welcome message informing your students that a welcome email has been sent out to the entire class and that they must contact you if they did not receive that email.

2.   *Creating Reasonable First Week Work Expectations*—Because you will most certainly have students who do not show up for class the first week, do not create work assignments that ask for any group collaboration or that serve as a basis for the second week's assignment. Otherwise, your class will quickly fall behind. Better to use the first week for basic preparatory work and communication:

   a.   Keep assignments low key. Ask students to introduce themselves on the threaded discussion. For the introductory thread, it is important that you respond to every one of these. Make your students feel at home. Provide your own introduction in the threads, as well as a welcome video or audio. Assign introductory reading assignments and ask a general question on that material to be turned in by the end of the week.

   b.   Help students be prepared to take your online course. Provide them with a self-test on the use of the technology in your course. Ask them to send you and the rest of the class a file attachment to their email so that you can determine software compatibility within your class. Have them check out any video or audio clips you may have or to check out your chatroom. If these tools are not working, advise them to contact your technical help or to go to the appropriate URL for more information.

3. *Using Timed Access in Your Course*: Create your course so that units of instruction have timed access, if this is appropriate to your teaching style. This will enable you to make necessary changes to your course before your students can begin working in a particular unit. It also ensures that your students are progressing through the course so that one section builds upon the other.

4. *Creating Your Work Schedule*: Teaching online can be all consuming the first time. Create a realistic weekly schedule for yourself and stick with it:

   a. Determine your work week and course week. For example, you might establish Sunday midnight to Sunday midnight as the work week. This will give your working students a chance to catch up on assignments during the weekend.

   b. Choose a day each week for QA. Text errors online happen. URLs disappear. Images break. Information from a prior class taught can be overlooked. Plan on spending time each week going over the materials for the following week, before your students are able to access the work. This will save you emails and confused students in the long run.

   c. Post "office hours" and stick with them. Also define them for your students. Are your office hours a combination of face-to-face office hours, chatroom office hours, and email responses? If you choose to offer chatroom office hours, establish two half hour sessions for the entire week, at different times of the day to account for differences in time zone among your students. I've heard horror stories of online instructors stuck to empty chatrooms for an hour at a time, so make chatroom availability short and sweet. Email is all consuming. Determine to only answer email inquiries twice or so a week and stick with the schedule. (Though you probably won't, but if you have the time restrictions in your syllabus, your students can't complain if you don't answer them within an hour's, even a day's time.)

   d. Decide on a grading schedule. Conceivably, each week you may have written assignments turned in to you by email, threaded discussion assignments, journal writing assignments, and tests. Decide when you will grade each and when you will turn each back to your students. Instead of grading each as they come, you might want to block off large portions of your week to do the entire grading in one session. Or you might divide your grading time into email assignments, threaded discussion responses, and tests. Decide whether you are going to turn back assignments as soon as you are done grading each one, or if you are going to wait for a particular day to turn these back. I tended to grade several times during the week, save my work, and then return it to my students on Monday morning.

5. *Establishing Regular Communication with All of Your Students:* Keep your online course interactive. You don't have to have regular individual communication with each and every one of your students all the time, but communicate with the class as a whole on a regular basis:

   a. Update the coming week's work: The night before the next week's work opens, send the entire class a friendly email informing them of what will be taking place. Reinforce learning objectives and goals for the week. Remind them of group changes, important assignments that are due.

   b. Review the work's week: In the same email, or another, summarize what took place during the week, high points and low points, interesting issues that were raised. You might send the class an electronic greeting card for fun, congratulating your students on a week well done.

   c. If something newsworthy happens during the week and is relevant to your class, send them the news. The important thing is simply to let your students know that you are there and available to them.

Grading Papers Online

Don't do what some first-time online instructors do and print off all of your students' assignments; grade them in pencil and then type in your responses online. Too much work. Learn to grade papers online.

1. *Grading Papers through Email:*

   a. Create mailboxes for each of your students and set up filters so that their assignments go into their individual mailboxes.

   b. Create and then save an email reply to each assignment. This will allow you to write textual commentary within their text. Or plan on opening their attachment, using a grading program that will hide your text comments in their text, saving the attachment and then reattaching it to an email with some general comments about their work

   c. Create a form email that will automatically let your students know when an assignment has been received by you.

d. Distinguish your comments from their text through different color or size font, asterisks, highlights, etc.

e. Queue your graded work. Instead of sending assignments back piecemeal to your students, use your email program to assign a "send" date. Your email program will then automatically send out all of your queued emails on that specified date.

f. Be sure to save all copies of your communication with your students. Ultimately, the record is useful for your final evaluation of the students' progress in the class. More immediately, you will be saved the hassle of re-grading assignments when your students "lose" your email.

2. *Grading Papers through the Threads*: you may choose to have students post assignments to you through the threaded discussion format. This way you and the student have a public record of when an assignment has been turned in.

   a. If you are not compromising privacy, you could comment on the paper in the thread as a response, and then email the grade to your student. You will not be able to comment within the text of their assignment.

   b. Copy and paste the assignment into an email for your student. Grade the assignment and then return it to your student via email. Be sure to save a copy of your work.

3. *Grading Work with Symbols and Figures*: I saw an innovative way to deal with the problem of grading homework involved with math calculations.

   a. Create a multiple-choice quiz with possible final answers to the math calculation. Advise students to round their answers to the closest multiple choice and select. Then ask students to send paper proof of their calculations to you through the mail.

Dealing with Technology Failures

It just happened to me yesterday. I invited a small group of new online students into the Continuing Education office to show them how to access the online site. I wanted to demonstrate its features. The site was down and wouldn't allow me access. Now what? Do I just sit around and stare at them? They were hoping I didn't. I anticipated technological chaos. I prepared and printed out the class syllabus and some of the main Web pages. I then asked the DL coordinator to call the company delivering the course platform to check on the source of the system failure. The class had the materials in front of them, and we discussed all the major points that I wanted to cover. This could have just as readily been done on email to distant students since that part of the system was still operational. Before I finished, the system was back online and we were able to view the actual materials online.

The good news is that Web-based courses are mostly asynchronous, and students may access their materials around network failures while still meeting the scheduled course requirements. You just need to be flexible. The real problems arise when students are expected to be online at specific times. This is normally during scheduled chatrooms or when electronic examinations are being given. My solution is to not require participation in chatrooms but use them for casual meetings or office hours. You may specify a particular day and time for an electronic exam, but you should not put electronic limits on the time the exam must be completed since network problems often arise causing needless frustration and anxiety to the student. My recommendation is to instruct the student to try to complete the exam within a specific time but that they may reenter and complete the exam should there be technical failures.

Students will frequently experience problems that are difficult for them to identify as occurring on their own computer or on the network. This makes it difficult to resolve the problem. One answer is to give them access to a help desk. Some companies that provide course delivery platforms also provide a 24/7/365 student help desk that assists students in overcoming technical problems. Many universities and colleges will provide some level of computer assistance to students whether online or though a telephone. You should inform students of where such assistance may be obtained. If you are unsure, then your students will be in for a frustrating experience when things don't go their way on the computer. This problem is almost assured within your class. Deal with it ahead of time and anticipate the problem. Provide a mechanism for student technical help that removes you from the loop if you don't want to go loopy.

Teaching Large Classes Online

The issues about teaching a large class in the classroom are very similar to teaching a course of any size online. One of the major challenges is overcoming the distance and lack of personal interaction that can exist between the student and teacher. Just as in the large classroom, the online student must feel actively involved and feel engaged in the process of learning. Students want more than to simply receive information and spout it back. Managing a large class online, or anywhere, demands that you provide opportunities for discussion, feedback, and learning in an active environment that recognizes the efforts of the individual. The following recommendations have been derived from several sources.[16, 17, 18]

1. *Personalize the Class.*
    a. Let students know who you are: I introduce myself at the beginning of the

class and share with them some aspects of my more personal interests such as hobbies and sporting events. I try to interject acceptable humor. I invite them to do the same. I ask them for a "hook" to remember their name. This tells my students that I care about who they are.

b. Send out a greeting: I send out an email at the beginning of class and welcome everybody. I make sure that I recognize participation in class activities by sending out electronic postcards complete with music and graphics.

c. Be accessible: My students know that if they contact me by email or phone I am ready and willing to respond to their inquiries.

d. Encourage students to share experiences about a particular question you are posing, and then move on to the abstract: When I ask a question about water pollution, overpopulation, or environmental disease, I ask the student to share any personal experiences with this issue before moving on to answer the question in a more academic form.

2. *Provide Opportunities for Feedback.*

a. The "60 second" response: " It's a good idea to periodically find out how your class is doing. Ask them to evaluate how the class is going every 3 or 4 weeks. Encourage them to comment on positive and negative aspects of the class, and then respond in a positive way to the comments. Show them you care and are willing to make adjustments that make sense. Ask them to take 60 seconds and jot down these comments and/or questions in the form of an email.

b. You might also create small focus groups that can interact with each other via chatrooms or email and have them make recommendations regarding making the class more interactive or interesting from their perspective. This gives them some ownership in the class.

3. *Make It an Active Learning Experience.*

a. Create small groups of 5–6 students: It's so much easier working with small groups, so divide up your large class. Give each group an assignment and have them select a group leader who will report back electronically about the progress of the project they are working on.

b. Rotate the responsibility of leading the threaded discussion each week to a different student. Let them organize, respond, and cajole the class on the threaded discussion topic of the week.

4. *Using TAs.*

a. Choose a teaching assistant (TA) who is has demonstrated a positive experience in the classroom and who has good computer skills.

b. Make sure the TA is part of the teaching team and let him/her introduce themselves electronically to the class at the outset.

    c.   Meet weekly with the TA and provide guidance as they assist you in refining the syllabus, writing exams, grading portfolios, supervising class projects, and responding to threaded discussions. This will give some ownership of the class to the TA and ensure him/her that they are part of the team. It will also help to establish uniformity in evaluating student performance.

    d.   Spend time together developing unity and cohesion in a socially acceptable way. This might involve having a lunch together in a public restaurant as an example.

Many of the recommendations that I would make for conserving energy or time have been made in the previous sections. Provide detailed instructions to your students. Clearly define your expectations. Use filters on your email to organize responses. There are several excellent websites that address the issues of teaching large classes and/or using TAs. I suggest the following:

- **http://virtual.park.uga.edu/cdesmet/231stud.htm**
- **http://ubli.buffalo.edu/libraries/projects/tlr/large.html**
- **http://www.inform.umd.edu/CTE/lcn/index.html**

Teaching Students to Use the WWW as a Research Tool

The WWW is both a gold mine of rich academic material and a mine field of wannabe bombs. Because students are already online, they will want to research online. There are some clues you can pass onto your students which will help them recognize when a website is legit or not.

11.4 Real-Life Stories about Teaching Online

A Core Course in Environmental Health (Gary Moore)

I teach a course in the School of Public Health and Health Sciences at the University of Massachusetts titled "Environmental Health Practices: EnvHl 565" This is a core course for the school and therefore required of all students seeking graduate degrees in our CEPH accredited school. I began this journey into online education about four years ago when I first began writing the book for this topic. It covers all the major environmental issues dealing with population, environmental degradation, toxins, emerging diseases, food-borne diseases, hazardous and solid wastes, air pollution, water pollution, risk management, and environmental law. The field is so rapidly changing that I thought it would be useful to create a website available for my on-campus class that would provide useful Web-links for each subject category. This website soon evolved into much more. I used it to provide class notes, course syllabus, class policies, practice exams, associated websites, searchable databases, opportunities for students to show class projects or assignments, and

Excerpts from "It Must Be True—I Found It On the Web"[19]

As an instructor, how can you guide your students through the vagaries of the Web? After all, though it has some faults, it is the largest compendium of information ever created, and it will only grow in size and importance.

There are two parts to the answer. First, remember that the Web is a source of information, not necessarily knowledge. Equipping students with the critical thinking to turn information into knowledge is the essential guidance that teachers bring to all computer-mediated learning. Second, the information itself almost always provides clues to its veracity that are visible to the critical eye.

When the Web is used as an academic resource, students need to know that there are—and that they are expected to use—some basic guidelines when evaluating information on a website. The tips that follow are both a survival kit for wired scholars and a proactive attempt to define the field by demanding quality:

- **Does the website have a date?** This most basic piece of information is not negotiable. Without a date (minimally the date of writing or copyright; preferably the date of the most recent update as well), the online material simply cannot be considered a resource worthy of the name.
- **Are the author's name and contact information clearly displayed?** This is another non-negotiable demand. No matter how brilliant the argument, if it's not attributable, it's not a resource.
- **Do accepted scientific methods and clear citations support the author's argument?** Scholarship is a craft with tested and time-honored standards. Online scholarly works must adhere to the same rigorous academic criteria as printed materials, or they do not constitute scholarship and should not be used. Rather than excusing the shortcomings of a resource because it's online, just refuse to use it. You will do a great service both to online scholarship—and to the author..
- **Is the text clearly and carefully written, with proper grammar and punctuation?** Given the plethora of spelling and grammar checking software available today, what reputable scholar would permit any work bearing their name to see the light of day with mistakes in it? Shoddy work is not only offensive, it is suspicious.
- **Are differing opinions or positions presented? Are they treated respectfully?** While this point may not be immediately obvious to students, it cannot be overemphasized. No online resource that makes its case by attack or disparagement can be considered reputable.
- **Does the website support a product for sale?** If so, you may want to evaluate the motives of the site and its advertisements.
- **Is the website associated with a political, social, or religious movement?** While a site of this type may contain gems, it's important—as with print material—to be able to identify whether or not the site has a certain slant.
- **Does the website use garish or obtrusive graphics?** Like corrupt politicians who wrap themselves in the flag, less-than-credible online materials often hide behind bright colors and twirling icons. If something other than solid, well-substantiated information catches your eye, chances are it's no accident.

IMPLEMENTATION/EVALUATION

Excerpts from "It Must Be True—I Found It On the Web"[19]

· **Does the website *feel* right? Is it the kind of work you would expect of a scholar?** At the end of the day, you are the audience and consumer of the online resource. If anything about a website leaves you feeling uncomfortable, just click out of it and find another one. Your academic peace of mind really is worth more than the illusion of convenience— even at 2 AM.

Evaluating websites is a learned skill, the same as evaluating print resources, and one that is sharpened with practice. Fortunately, the Web itself offers countless examples, both good and bad, on which to practice. (As an instructor, you can place a variety of URLs in your course and have students analyze them in a journal assignment or threaded discussion. A few obvious examples for analysis might be a well-written scientific study proving the harmlessness of nicotine on a tobacco company's website, or a first-hand account of the ethnic cleansing written in broken English on an Albanian website. The exercise in critical thinking will provide an opportunity for your students to challenge their patterns of media usage, and for you to hone their skills on the ultimate goal of all education: turning information into knowledge.)

The following websites contain useful tools and additional links for evaluating web sites:
Modern Language Association (MLA) Style website at:
http://www.mla.org/main_stl.htm

American Psychological Association (APA) Style websites at: **http://www.beadsland.com/weapas/**

more. You can visit the site at (**http://www-unix.oit.umass.edu/~envhl565**). This site has become a component of my class and a useful ancillary for the book I wrote titled "*Living with the Earth – A Web-Enhanced Resource*" published by CRC. The site became so useful that many of our graduate students who live off campus and have full-time jobs asked if they could take my course primarily through the website since they were unable too attend class. I reluctantly gave permission at first, but found that it was a positive experience for them. I used proctors to give them exams the same time as the class and used email to communicate and accept their class assignments. I even created a "live" chatroom for them that they could visit at specified times. Some of our students do internships at very distant places and still needed this core course. I had one student in England and another on a Navaho reservation in the United States. They were able to satisfy the requirements of the course quite nicely. You can see that once I became comfortable with this arrangement, it wasn't much of a leap to putting a course fully online. I added a few things to increase interest and interactivity.

One of the important components of the course includes detailed sets of notes for each unit that the students may print out. The on-campus students print them out and come to class with them in a 3-ring binder. Within each of the sets of notes are references to figures that are linked to JPEG or GIF files. The student has the choice of wanting to view/print these or not. It also saves time in downloading the notes because the images are pasted in the note section. The online class differs in that I have also included streaming audio files with each figure. Here again, the student has the option of listening to the audio file or not by clicking on a link. If they choose to do so, the audio file streams to their computer so that download time is brief in most cases. My online students seem to really like these mini lectures associated with each of the figures, and they provide a useful way of learning for those who need audio stimulation. The students also get to hear a little of my voice in the process and that helps with the personal touch. You can visit a unit of my online course at (**http://www.mhhe.com.ucanteachonline**).

I use threaded discussions as the major mechanism for involving the students interactively. I will say that it is important to grade the students on this activity since there is little incentive or raw entertainment power in this exercise. However, my experience has been positive. I am fortunate to have students with medical and public health backgrounds from many areas of the world. It is very "eye-opening" to have students from Russia, India, China, and countries in Africa share discussions of population problems, food scarcity, and environmental degradation and disease in their respective countries. All of my students benefit heavily from these observations. I will often include a graphic, a table, or a document for the students to examine and comment on with focused responses regarding the unit of the week. It helps to drive the thread. I find that the students comment on the other students' responses and provide additional insight or experience. They often cite studies or personal accounts.

The online and in-class students really like the practice exams. I don't test my students with online exams. I send exams via email to proctors for them to print out and give to the students. I have a practice exam for each unit that the students may print out and take. They may then print out an exact duplicate of the exam with the answers in place and the page numbers where the answers may be found. I believe nearly every student finds this of great use.

I have also provided on both the online and on-campus sites numerous useful Web links categorized by unit or chapter. The students find these sites very useful for class projects, and often use them for their other classes as well.

Just a final thought. Since I instruct the same class online and in the classroom during the same semester, use the same text, and provide the same exams, it was of some interest to me if they would perform differently. The classes were both diverse in country of origin, included many medical doctors and persons in the public health field, and were mostly in the 20–40 years of age range. There were a few outliers. Although not statistically evaluated, the online class performed slightly better overall on the proctored exams than did my on-campus class, and both classes very much enjoyed the experience.

Cyberspace and a Piece of the Soul: Teaching Poetry Online (Kathy Winograd)

In 1996, I entered into the realm of online education blindly confident not only of my teaching but of my computer skills, despite the fact that I was a self-taught hacker, a spastic blasphemer of computers since the first moment the Apple fell onto my desktop. I prided myself on already knowing how to handle email and the Internet, but I was in no way prepared for managing the 60-70 email messages I began to get daily once I started teaching online, or the labyrinth of technology I had to master in order to successfully navigate my own course. But none of that mattered in comparison with what became my biggest challenge, creating a poetry workshop online.

Poetry workshops are about community. The best workshops vibrate with that powerful sexiness of the truly intimate. I have had students come to me with poems in hand and say, "Here are the pieces of my soul." How do I make contact with these same students through a modem and a computer screen? How do we pass our human hearts through a "virtual" reality we cannot imagine—the words we type are not even ink anchored to the fibers of paper, but an electronic stream you can delete with a button tap?

I picked my texts. I assigned readings, exercises, peer critiques, formal and free verse poem forms to follow, all neatly packaged into a 15-week unit that could be translated into Web pages and links. I sent "Gaecela of Unforeseen Love," Lorca's passionate reverie, over the invisible steel of the Internet, and waited nervously at the keyboard for the first student "transmission."

And then I made the ugly realization that there was nothing of me in this course. Here were the black and white bones of it, but not my skin and flesh, not the quiet, but constant, stream of talk and banter that had propelled my previous classes along, forged community. I began to write "lectures," to try to capture what for years poured out in spontaneous give and take between students and me. But now words that might have simply "floated in the wind" of the traditional classroom were suddenly permanent and public record. And this was a creative writing course, a course of crafted words. I could no longer hide behind a professor's robe and lectern. Here was the blank computer screen. How could I fill it with words—disembodied, wired—and create my living voice? How could I reach through that screen and cajole, ignite, love my students into speaking out loud secrets even they had not yet guessed?

No one responded for the first whole week of the course. I felt bereft. And then responses came: joy, excitement, fear. My work week became almost impossible as I continued to refine my course, to respond to the constant upheaval with this technology so new to all of us, to read my students' work and respond to it, and, at the same time, to write complete "papers," what I hoped to be "poetry in prose," that revealed me, who I was, that might unstall this teaching from the cold instructional static of technology into something viable and human.

My endeavors at this task extended into every dimension of this course. The subject headings of my emails became "hooks" designed to lure students in. "Worried Doctor," I wrote. "Housekeeping." In the threads, those asynchronous records of public discourse, I tailed my comments to their posted work to begin with what I hoped was eye-catching: "Ugh," "Wow," "Beautiful," "Dead Chickens." The students began to respond in the same way. The subject headings of their email messages began to categorize their feelings for the day: "Frustrated," "Aaaargghh," "Thank you." They gave me the happy faces and the unhappy faces of virtual reality, as sign-offs to their messages.

In cyberspace, you know your students first only by the user names they give themselves in their email messages: "MousieMan," "attilathehoney," "Rage." But what is astonishing to me in virtual reality is how we crave real reality. Though cyberspace is genderless, raceless, though I cannot tell if my students are rich or poor, green-haired or bow-tied, though the very blessing of cyberspace is the fact that we can send our words into the world unfettered by our physical selves, I could not help but see the "mouse" or the buxom, helmeted "Attila" or "justdana."

The other blessings of an online course are apparent in the email I get from my students: "Deare Dr. Winograd: Sorry if my poem is a couple of days late. I just gave birth to a baby boy." "Dear Dr. Winograd: I'm now on business in Taiwan. Hope my poem gets through okay." "Dear Dr. Winograd: sorry if I'm a bit touchy. Once, in a classroom, a teacher thought I could not be as smart as I am because of the color of my skin."

I want to conclude by saying that I was wildly successful in my endeavors. I want to conclude by saying that my course became a "nursery" for "warm fuzzies," a New Age oasis within the light years of cyberspace. But I can't. Though I gratefully received some glowing student reviews, though my university considered my courses successful, though I was excited by the truly in-depth responses I got on discussion questions, and though my students celebrated in writing critiques of each other's work that they say were more honest and straightforward because there was not the awkwardness of encounter, it is difficult to forget that one student who firebombed the entire class, standing up in virtual reality and making his astonishing announcement: "I am great and you stink." Or the student I inadvertently sent into a spasm of fury with a single stupid typo in an email message.

My online courses were not without their meteoric collisions, despite my best intentions. Online we face being victims of our own advanced technology for immediate gratification. Our mice click "Send" and our words spin out into space with no chance for retrieval. For many, a "courtesy clause" becomes a permanent part of syllabi in anticipation of the disgruntled student sitting alone in the dark at his desk, his finger hovering over the mouse, fevered by the twin powers of autonomy and anonymity.

Perhaps for those who are already computer and Internet literate, the design of an online course is a simple, onetime deal. But for those of us who are not particularly technological, who only learned by our flawed selves to pick out what we needed to do on those first primitive boxes, the online course is a continuing challenge of trial and error. The course becomes an object outside the self, an artistic, creative, almost palpable work you cannot keep your hands off, an entity in itself that arises out of your pride and love for the art of it. In cyberspace, there are only words, written words where typos can lead to disaster and where, in a classroom of pure writing, we learn to infuse our words with voice, the essence of ourselves—what, finally, poetry is all about.[20]

Teaching Computer Science in the Synchronous Online Classroom (Art Blevins)

When Art Blevins, ABD in Computer Science, won a two million dollar grant on new technologies for adaptive learning, funded by the National Institution of Standards and Technology, he left his fulltime teaching position at Carson Newman College to direct the NIST grant project at eCollege.com. In doing so, he left a full-time hole in the Carson Newman computer science program that he is now filling part-time.

As the fall semester of 2000 rolled around and still no one was to be found to fill Art's old position, Art offered to teach at a distance the fall offering of a Java programming course. Carson Newman quickly took him up on his offer. Art assumed that he would be teaching a typical online course for Carson Newman that relied, predominantly, on asynchronous technology. But Carson Newman had other ideas. What it wanted was a synchronous class experience for its students, meaning that the Newman students would gather together in a classroom three times a week in Tennessee while Art, their instructor, would conduct the class the same three times a week from his office in Denver, Colorado.

"I would have preferred not to do the synchronous, but the school wanted it. The question," Art says, "was how do you go about doing that with current software and with the limitations of bandwidth which were primarily on their end? I didn't feel like synchronous video would be the right solution, but we also needed a high degree of reliability in uptime from our course system during class time." What Art and Carson Newman agreed to try was a relatively low-tech, but highly reliable system of using eCourse (an online course platform), conference calling, and an inexpensive Web camera bought from CompUSA.

Three times a week, students meet for 50 minutes in a regular campus classroom equipped with ten computers, a screen set up in front of the class, and a projector hooked up to one of the computers. There is no TA or aide in the classroom, simply a couple of student "drivers." In the middle of the classroom is a speakerphone. At class time, the students sit down and look toward the screen.

What they see is the "teacher" divided into three Web pages: the eCourse, the Web camera which is pointed at the whiteboard in Art's Denver office so that anything he writes can be viewed onscreen, and a live "notepad" that Art designed which is basically a Web page he can type into and then send immediately to his students through this third Web page. "It made sense to have this third window I could type into," says Art, " since it is a programming course and typing out examples of code would be clearer than trying to write them out by hand on the whiteboard."

During class time, students and instructor converse with each other, just as in a conference call. "Sometimes, I'll stick my face in front of the office cam just so my students know it's a live person here." Typically the students ask a lot of questions, waiting for Art to pause before posing their question. But to facilitate the discussion over the speakerphone, Art made class participation 15 percent of their grade, including participation in class questions and threaded discussions.

"I understand on their end that it is working out well. If you lecture in person you can tell if something doesn't quite make sense because of facial expressions, etc. I miss that but I compensate by stopping a lot and asking questions just so I know they are understanding the material."

The course also consists of two non-proctored exams, which for some instructors might seem risky in such a nontraditional class. "Last time I taught the class in the traditional classroom, the exam was 'open book.' Obviously that doesn't require a proctor as long as I can grade their work and know it is their work and that they haven't copied their classmates'." To get to know their individual working styles, Art requires writing assignments across the semester mostly on how Java might fit in with the newest technologies, as well as numerous programming assignments because, as Art puts it, "Programming styles are very individualistic."

In the eCourse, Art has lecture notes and links to the office cam and the live "notepad" at the top of every lecture page. The lecture notes will explain the new material in general, and then Art will give an example of code with links to each line in the code that pop up a new Web page and describe what that single line of code is accomplishing in that particular program. "The best way to show students how to program is to show them example programs" Art says. Most examples he finds on the Web. He then asks his students to go off and create their own websites. According to Art, there are tons of businesses that provide free Web page postings so all students have to do is sign up and during the course create their own website and do Java coding there. Art will then check their websites once a week, asking them to redo a site if necessary. Grades for this portion of the course will be based on the programs that are up on the student's site.

The class structure was a surprise to the students, who were only told that the instructor was not going to be physically in the class. Though the class is not for everyone, Art has gotten some positive feedback from some of the professors on campus who have heard the students talking. "Students like two aspects of the course—that the guy teaching it is working at an Internet company and in touch with the real world. And they like the technology. They can access course materials from dorm rooms, from home. They can have instant access to grades. They particularly like the fact that the course itself is actually using the Java programs they are learning."

Ultimately this kind of teaching strategy cooked up by Carson Newman College and Art Bevins could be used to get adjunct teaching faculty from the industry to pitch in more regularly with the training of college kids on computer programming. "If I had to jump in a car in the middle of the day and go drive to a college campus to teach this course, I wouldn't do it. But to simply put my work aside for an hour at a time and teach from my office makes it easy."

Teaching Spanish Online (Judy Hubble, Rogers State University)

"I can't teach Spanish online!" I screamed.

Well, that's what I felt like doing when my department head proposed it. Instead, I mumbled that I would think about it, hoping that it would go into that *Crazy Ideas* folder I was sure she kept buried beneath all the other books and files on her desk. But, of course, it didn't. Ideas about online education just won't go away!

So I did think about it. And think about it. I looked at other online courses and became engaged by the challenges presented by this new learning environment. Still, I was not convinced it was possible to teach a *language* online. However, the next time my department head asked me to develop a Beginning Spanish I course, I reluctantly agreed.

Much of what I did at first was very familiar. I divided the material I wanted to cover into weekly units. Objectives for each unit were planned, along with textbook and workbook assignments. Then I decided to use the online journal for reading and writing assignments. Next, I added four unit exams. My basic structure was complete.

The course needed a little tweaking, though, I decided. I added introductions to each unit and sprinkled reminders and encouragements throughout the course. There, that was better, but it was still far too serious a class for me. I like to play in my language classes. Having fun helps students accept the always-present frustration that accompanies the acquisition of a new language. I could find no fun in the class I had designed for my online students.

I decided to use the threaded discussion area for a chat zone, a kind of safe haven from the rigors of grammar and punctuation, a place in which students don't have to be "correct"—they just have to communicate! Hey, wouldn't some role-playing be fun in here? What if we were abducted by aliens and . . . well, sometimes I did get a little "carried away"!!

Then the elephant stood up.

You know the one I mean—the same one that is whispering in your ear right now, saying, *You know there is no way to learn to SPEAK Spanish online!* Yes, *that* elephant.

I lived with that elephant for several months, and it made me a better teacher. I learned to find new ways of doing and being. I added lots of audios—pronunciation, vocabulary, text review—and planned for my students to send me cassette tapes, voice mail and .wav files. I added slide presentations, lecture notes, and Webliography projects. I revised my evaluation plan to include as many elements as possible. I was very busy. And then one day I noticed that the elephant was gone. I had a class that would work. As a bonus, I also had lots of new material and new tools I could use to improve my on-campus classes!

I was a happy teacher—happy, but not satisfied. I know there are better ways of doing some things, and there are lots of new tools I can use. This summer I learned HTML and JavaScript. I'm adding interactive quizzes and working on some games, and I'm looking at a way to do "voice" threads and video conferencing and—hey, I'm having a good time! Maybe this wasn't such a crazy idea after all.

IMPLEMENTATION/EVALUATION

REFERENCES

1. **Hara, N. and R. Kling**, 1999. "Students' Frustration with a Web-based Distance Education Course: A Taboo Topic in the Discourse." *CSI Working Paper.*

2. **Chickering, A. & S. Ehrmann.** 1996. "Implementing the Seven Principles: Technology as Lever." *The AAHE Bulletin at American Association for Higher Education,* October.

3. **Dede, C.** 1997. "Distance Learning to Distributed Learning: Making the Transition." *NLII Viewpoint,* Fall/Winter.

4. **Pratt, D.** 1993. "Andragogy After Twenty-Five Years." *New Directions for Adult and Continuing Education,* 57, Spring, p. 15.

5. **Winograd, K.** 2000. "The Internet and the Arts: Classroom Style", *itpe (information technology in postsecondary education),* 3 (10), June, pp. 6-7.

6. **Abdullah, M.** 1999. "Problem-Based Learning in Learning Instruction: A Constructivist Method." *ERIC Clearinghouse on Reading, English, and Communication*, p. 132.

7. **Shapiro, B.** 1984. "Hints for Case Teaching." *Harvard Business School of Publishing*, p. 1.

8. **Emig, J**. 1994. "Writing as a Mode of Learning." *Landmark Essays on Writing Across the Curriculum.* Ed. Charles Bazerman and David Russell, Davis, CA., Hermagoras Press, 1994, pp. 89-96.

9. **Beaudin, B.P.** 1999. "Keeping Online Asynchronous Discussion on Topic." *Journal of Asynchronous Learning Networks*, November.

10. **Carneson, J., G. Delpierre, and K. Masters** "Designing and Managing MCQs: Appendix C: MCQs and Bloom's Taxonomy." *Designing and Managing Multiple Choice Questions—Handbook Aimed to the Staff of the University of Cape Town,* South Africa. <http://www.aln.org/alnweb/journal/jaln-vol3issue2.htm>.

11. **Lane, C.** "Distance Learning Resource Network." *DLRN's Technology Resource Guide, US Dept of Education Star Schools Program,* <http://www.dlrn.org/library/dl/guide.html>.

12. **McLeod, S.** 1992. "Writing Across the Curriculum: An Introduction." *Writing Across the Curriculum: A Guide to Developing Programs*. Eds. Susan Mc Leod and Margot Soven. Thousand Oaks, CA. SAGE Publications, 1992. pp. 1-12.

13. **Hawisher, G. E. and M.A. Pemberton.** 1997. "Writing Across the Curriculum Encounters Asynchronous Learning Networks or WAC Meets Up with ALN."

Journal of Asynchronous Learning Networks, Vol. 1, no. 1 (1997), pp. 1-19, March 16, 1999.

14. **Abdullah, M.H**, 1999. "Electronic Discourse: Evolving Conventions in Academic Environments." *ERIC Clearinghouse on Reading, English, and Communication Digest*, March 10, 1999.

15. **Martin, N., et al**. 1994. "The Development of Writing Abilities." *Landmark Essays on Writing Across the Curriculum*. Ed. Charles Bazerman and David Russell, Davis, CA, Hermagoras Press, pp. 33-49.

16. **Well, M. 2000.** "Teaching Large Classes**.**" *Teaching and Learning Resources*, State University of Buffalo, 2000.
    <http://ubli.buffalo.edu/libraries/projects/tlr/large.html>.

17. **Desmet, C.** 1997. "Teaching Large Classes with the Web."*Office of Instructional Development*, <http://virtual.park.uga.edu/cdesmet/231stud.htm>.

18. **Center for Teaching Excellence**, 2000. "Teaching Large Classes." *Large Classes: Resources*, Univ. of Maryland. <http://www.inform.umd.edu/CTE/lcn/index.html>.

19. **Margolis, P**. 2000. *Handbook for eTeaching Solutions.* Version 4.2. eCollege.com.

20. **Winograd, K.** 1998. "Cyberspace and a Piece of the Soul: Teaching Poetry Online." *The Bloomsbury Review*, p.16.

IMPLEMENTATION/EVALUATION

Evaluating the Effectiveness of Your Course

Lesson 12

Evaluating the Effectiveness of Your Course

LESSON OUTLINE

12.1 WHAT MAKES AN ONLINE COURSE EFFECTIVE?
12.2 CREATING EVALUATION STRATEGIES
12.3 ACCREDITATION AND BEST PRACTICES

WHAT YOU WILL LEARN FROM THIS LESSON

YOU WILL BE ABLE TO:

1. List and explain the components of an effective online course.
2. Summarize the major benchmarks associated with effective online courses.
3. Create and administer effective course evaluations using portfolio assessments,
4. Distinguish the criteria being developed for distance learning courses.

LESSON 12: EVALUATING THE EFFECTIVENESS OF YOUR COURSE

12.1 What Makes an Online Course Effective?

Introduction

In lesson 9 we discussed three basic stages to instructional design. These included: (1) determination of needs and goals, (2) planning instructional events, and (3) assessing your students and the effectiveness of your course. Because online course design and teaching are so new, evaluating the effectiveness of your course and then refining it based on the results of that evaluation become imperative. If you have already been through the process of teaching your online course for the first time, you have probably already realized what works well in your class and what does not and begun to make a list of changes for your course for the next time you teach it. You also have probably begun to feel more comfortable in the online teaching environment and begun to envision how you might change your course to use the technology available to you in new, effective ways for your students.

Regardless, you will need feedback from your students, whether that comes from a direct request from you for feedback or indirectly in how your students achieved the goals you had set for your class. This information will help you decide on directions for modifying your course. Or, if you're lucky, it may point out to you that your course is already successful and you have hit upon that "magic" formula.

Before you begin determining how you will evaluate your course, let's take a moment to look at what makes an online course effective. On one hand, what makes a course effective is very individualistic. What works for a geometry course may not work well for a literature course. But aren't there some overriding general goals we have for all students who enter our educational system? Would any of us want to say that the purpose of education, higher education or K-12, is simply about "job-training"? Or is it about giving people the passion and skills to make cognitive and analytical sense of this dynamic, information-laden world on their own? Some have accused educators of producing dependents, who lack initiative on their own: "we do not teach them to become self-learners. I am continually amazed at the number of adults who assume that, if they are to learn anything new, they must "take a class."[1] Are we guilty, as some accuse us, of not teaching our students how to become "self-learners"? How do we teach them this? Isn't it through the material resources we help our students to find that engage them, that we guide them into understanding and critically assessing? Isn't it through reflective and dynamic academic discourse? Isn't this what Internet technology can make available to us and our students: a wealth of content easily accessible, a way to make content instructionally engaging to our students no matter what their natural learning styles may be, the opportunities for our students to interact with that content on many different levels, a way to create community and peer mentorship outside the time and geographical boundaries of the classroom, a way to easily assess our students beyond standardized, quantifiable means?

Benchmarks

General parameters for effective online courses do emerge. The Institute for Higher Education Policy was charged with examining traditional quality assurance benchmarks for distance education specifically in how they applied to Internet-based distance education[2] and, even more importantly, how valued they were to the administrators, faculty, and students who were involved in this kind of Internet-based instruction.

Here is a summary of some of the significant benchmarks, for the purposes of this book, which were considered "Essential for Quality Internet-based Distance Education."[2]

Course Development Benchmarks

1. *Use of guidelines and standards for developing online courses.* These standards ultimately use learning outcomes in decisions made for creating the course, rather than the "latest and greatest" technology. This benchmark harkens back to the mandate that good teaching is about good teaching, not technology.

2. *Design of courses that ask students to engage in higher cognitive level thinking.* Once more, analysis, critical thinking, synthesis, problem-based learning, and evaluation are pushed to the forefront.

Teaching/Learning Benchmarks

3. *Creation of multiple opportunities for interaction in multiple formats.* Interaction remains the core of teaching, whether online or in the classroom, and that interaction is both real time and asynchronous.

4. *Provision of effective and timely feedback to students.* Being responsive to students remains essential, and this responsiveness needs to be structured and acknowledged ahead of time by student and instructor alike.

5. *Instruction on proper research methodologies.* Right now, the WWW is about information. Students need to be taught what information can be used to create good knowledge.

Course Structure Benchmarks

6. *Prior to taking the courses, students are given all necessary course information that will facilitate their success in the course.* Students have to be prepared for learning. They need to understand the expectations, goals, and requirements of the course before they begin taking it.

7. *Creation of a "contract" between student and instructor regarding nature, amount, and regularity of contact and feedback.* This goes back to the "p's" and "q's" of good teaching.

Student Support Benchmarks:

8. *Students are provided with training on the use of technology both prior to and during the course.* It should not be the technology that students have to struggle to learn and use in order to meet the learning goals of a course.

Evaluation and Assessment Benchmarks

9. *Assessment and evaluation of the course through a variety of methods.*
10. *Continued reassessment of learning objectives for the course based on clarity and applicability.*

There are twenty-four benchmarks considered essential to quality of Internet-based education that deal with all levels of support and involvement in the success of an online learning program and teaching experience. You should familiarize yourself with all of these in more detail. The study focusing on this issue can be found through the Institute for Higher Education Policy website (**http://www.ihep.com**). For our purposes, the benchmarks listed above serve to reinforce the points that have been made throughout this book, hopefully points that you have taken into consideration as you developed your online course.

Technology Standards

The International Society for Technology in Education has recommended its own National Educational Technology Standards for K-12 educators (**http:// cnets. iste.org /teachstand.html**). These standards are the results of survey and consensus.[3] Given what the Society sees as the importance of technology in education, these standards in general ask that teachers learn the technology themselves, continue to educate themselves on the changing scope of technology as part of their professional development, and plan for the effective use of technology in their teaching as part of their curriculum development. Some highlights that reiterate a gathering consensus on overall general standards for online teaching are: [3]

1. The use of technology to support learner-centered teaching strategies that recognize the diversity of students' skills and needs.
2. The use of technology in creating a variety of student assessments.
3. The use of technology to encourage higher-level cognitive thinking skills and creativity.
4. The use of technology to enhance interaction and community building.
5. The use of technology to encourage equal access to education.

Again and again, what comes shining out is the need for interaction and community in the online classroom, for teaching methodologies that encourage higher-level thinking skills in our students, and for the continual practice of good teaching that outweighs any innovation in technology.

But how do you get the feedback you need in the online environment to know if what you have created is successful according to any standard? Course evaluations, standard and non-standard, portfolio assessments and reflective students essays, and the assessment of learning outcomes are just a few of the ways.

12.2 Creating Evaluation Strategies

Course Evaluation

The student evaluation at the end of the course has been the standard answer. But, surprisingly, an overwhelming majority of education institutions still conduct pencil and paper evaluations at the end of an online course, despite the fact that the entire rest of the course may have been online. In one survey, 81.4 percent of 200 colleges contacted indicated that they used paper and pencil evaluation methodologies for their online course.[3] Even though this is an historical approach in the academic institution to course evaluation, the process is not without its problems, problems which some suggest may be solved by an online solution.[4] For instance, end of course evaluations have been called the "autopsy approach," the course dead and no longer able to be revived for those particular students no matter what the responses to the evaluation may indicate. Yes, the course can be changed for the next incoming wave of students, but only if the instructor receives the feedback well enough in advance. In fact in this survey, 90 percent of schools indicated that results of course evaluations were released somewhere within two months of the end of the course.[3] Only between the spring and fall semester could instructors realistically complete substantial changes to their courses based on these evaluations, and could administrators have any kind of tool that would help them to evaluate whether a particular course and/or instructor should be offered again.

Creating the right Web-based evaluation process is one way to shorten the time it takes for a student to respond to the evaluation and the instructor to receive that response.

A three-step "feedback-and-refinement" online process for evaluation has been one recent recommendation: [4]

1. Conversion of paper-based evaluation to online evaluation.
2. Frequent student feedback evaluations throughout the duration of a course.
3. Organization and analysis of student feedback for ease of "just in time" course change.

Some immediate consequences to consider in converting to this methodology are the opportunity for the instructor to make changes to a course still in process that seems to be going "off-kilter" and the increased interest in students to provide instructors with valuable, thoughtful feedback since the process of their learning in the course could be directly affected by that feedback.

Your institution may have standard evaluation forms and processes which you must abide by, but creating even a couple of simple surveys that you could send out by email to your students during your course could give you valuable feedback to help make your course even more effective. This process could also have the added value of reinforcing a sense of community and shared responsibility for learning in your students.

Portfolio Assessment and the Self-Reflective Essay

Another method of evaluation used by online instructors is the portfolio assessment approach. There are many types of portfolios, but basically, a portfolio is a collection of student work that exemplifies his or her learning process throughout the course and his or her achievement of learning goals. The portfolio can be used for instructional purposes, giving students a chance to review and reflect upon their progress in a course, or for assessment purposes—the portfolio becoming an integral part of the overall evaluation strategy of the course. This method of evaluation can be valuable to the online class because it can help an instructor determine the mastery of learning goals that are perhaps not assessable quantitatively. It can also give the instructor a chance to create a record of learning and have a broader view of a particular student's participation in a course. For an excellent overview of what portfolios are and the many types of portfolios that can be used in the classroom, including the online classroom, check out the Association for Supervision and Curriculum Development's (ASCD) website (**http://www.ascd.org /readingroom/books/danielson97book.html**).

Generally speaking, one main characteristic of a portfolio is that it must be more than simply "stuff"" thrown together by the student. It should be a systematic and formalized collection of work recognized by the teacher and the student to represent the student's growth in a class. For an online class, given its preponderance of non-traditional students and the need to instill the characteristics of self-direction and self-motivation in all students online, often the instructor will ask the students to determine on their own what work best represents their cumulative knowledge during the course. Others will outline specific assignments that must be turned in at the end of the course in a portfolio format. To inhibit cheating, online instructors may ask students to turn in multiple drafts of particular writing assignments along with the final draft.

For the dual purpose of using the portfolio as a way to evaluate the course as a whole, as well as an individual student's achievements in that course, some online instructors will ask students to write a self-reflective essay and ask the students to include in their essays responses to specific questions regarding the structure, process, and content of that course. As a final assignment for the course, the portfolio assessment with its self-reflective essay can give instructors valuable feedback on the course itself and give instructors the time to make changes to the course before it runs again. Of course there is the real possibility that students will not feel comfortable giving negative feedback in a self-reflective essay that they know is not anonymous and is in fact part of an overall grade. But if you have established a real community with your students and shown them respect for their contributions to the course and indicated to them that you want genuine feedback on the course and their progress in the course, you'll be surprised at how honest and helpful their responses will be. You also may easily be able to read "between the lines" of many of your students' writing and get a sense of the real picture for them. The portfolio assessment at the end of a course acts as both an assessment tool and an instructional tool. Beyond giving students a chance to give you immediate evaluative feedback on your course, you have given them a chance to see their own progress in a course and evaluate themselves.

Be sure to treat the portfolio and the self-reflective essay as a formal assignment. Give specific guidelines for what is to be included in the portfolio; ask for a thesis format for the self-reflective essay. Create specific criteria. I usually suggested a two-page essay, asked for specific references to work and assignments, etc. Stress that this assignment not only documents their achievement in a course, but represents it.

Learning Outcomes Assessment: Pretesting and Post-testing

A third kind of evaluation you can do in your online class to help you determine student achievement and changes to your course necessary to enhance the achievement of future students is a learning outcomes assessment. Instructors will construct pretests taken by their students at the beginning of a class and post-tests taken at the end of the course. These tests can contain the exact questions and the achievement of the student determined by how much the student improved in responding to the test questions. Other instructors will also make use of standard exit exams that may apply to the same courses taught institution-wide.

12.3 Accreditation and Best Practices

Ultimately, evaluation is tied to accreditation, both at the course level and the insitutional level. It has been recommended that "new models for college and university accreditation are needed," given the dramatic changes in how education is delivered because of technological advances. [5] Some believe that accreditation standards must change across the board, away from focusing on the procedures colleges use to evaluate students toward what students actually learn. [6] The American Federation of Teachers seeks changes in standards that would require control of distance education courses and programs passing into the hands of academic faculty. The Federation recommends that advanced information regarding course requirements, equipment needs, and skills in using technology be given to students prior to the start of the course. And they suggest that degree programs be both online and in the classroom.[7] The Council for Higher Education Accreditation made these recommendations: [8]

1. Institutions set guidelines for measuring student performance in distance-education courses.
2. When judging institutions, accreditors should consider contact between students and professors, and the use of distance-teaching techniques that have proven effective.
3. Institutions should make distance education a consideration when hiring and training faculty members, to ensure that professors are prepared to use the new teaching technologies.
4. Institutions should keep up to do date with technology to ensure that students don't have difficulty "attending" classes.

The Council of Regional Accrediting Commissions make up the eight bodies that grant accreditation to colleges and universities in the United States.

The remarkable increase in the use of the Internet for on-campus and distance instruction has forced higher education officials to consider difficult leadership questions. The major focus has become the problems of managing technological change, organizational change, and operational change. Many institutions, accrediting agencies, and associations have directed their attention towards this rapidly escalating phenomenon of online education. A growing body of educators now recognizes a number of **"best practices"** that are necessary for the successful use of the Internet in instruction. The ability of higher education to attract online students can only succeed for those who can combine sound educational principles in an interactive and motivating pedagogy. The educational system must adopt an approach to online education that uses "best practices" recognized by the regional accrediting commissions. Failure to do so puts the entire higher education system

IMPLEMENTATION/EVALUATION

at risk. Where do "best practices" come from? What are these "best practices"? Why are "best practices" and evaluative guidelines important to us?

Where Do "Best Practices" Come From?

There are eight regional commissions that accredit higher education institutions throughout the United States. The Regional Accrediting Commissions recognize that the online course delivery systems are increasing in use and popularity with institutions that are developing national and international student populations with little or no on-campus residence time. The commissions are seeking to establish cross-regional consistency among the programs. The commissions are seeking to assure that "technologically mediated instruction offered at a distance by whatever institution in whatever region meets the same high standards for quality through the application of effective evaluative methodologies." Each commission adopted and implemented a common statement of *Principles of Good Practice in Electronically Offered Academic Degree and Certificate Programs* developed originally by the Western Cooperative for Educational Telecommunications (WCET) (**http://www.wiche.edu/telecom/Projects/balancing/principles.htm**). These guidelines cover curriculum and instruction, evaluation and assessment, library and learning resources, student services, and facilities and finances.

Additionally, the accrediting commissions developed a draft document on *Guidelines for the Evaluation of Electronically Offered Degree and Certificate Programs.* These evaluative guidelines may be found at (**http://www.wiche.edu/Telecom Guidelines.htm**). [9] The intent of the Council is to standardize guidelines for the evaluation of distance-education programs so that similar standards will be applied across the country. The guidelines focus on student learning and the personalization of curricula to students' needs. The attention will be directed to the learner and on interactivity and support services. The standards being set for distance education appear to be at a higher level than for traditional education. [9] Courses that are simply passive messages would have to be changed to incorporate more interactivity. It is expected that universities will be able to use the guidelines to help maintain high quality in their own distance education programs. This may become apparent to the universities when they come up for accreditation, since their distance learning programs will be reviewed at the same time.

Why Are "Best Practices" and "Evaluative Guidelines" Important to Us?

The commissions will apply these guidelines using a peer review system common to all the regions within the framework in "Draft: Statement of the Regional Accrediting Commissions on the Evaluation of Electronically Offered Degree and Certificate Programs." [10] The following words are taken from the guidelines. [10]

A. The first-time development of distance education programming leading to a degree designated for students off-campus will be subject to careful prior review;

B. Institutional effectiveness in providing education at-a-distance will be as explicitly and rigorously appraised as a part of the regular evaluation of colleges and universities such as the comprehensive visit and the fifth-year interim report;

C. An essential element in all evaluative processes will be institutional self-evaluation for the purpose of enhancing quality;

D. In cases where deficiencies are identified, remediation will be expected and aggressively monitored;

E. Appropriate action will be taken in keeping with individual commission policy and procedures in those cases where an institution is found to be demonstrably incapable of effectively offering distance education programming.

The establishment of new criteria for determining accreditation will certainly have a profound effect on the standards for the evaluation of a class. Technology will continue to advance; online teaching will continue to evolve in both how it serves instructors and students alike. And certainly what is learned in the online classroom will translate into the traditional classroom. If anything, education is an exciting field to be involved in, one rich with promise. As more is learned about online technologies and what they are capable of as more and more of us are able to afford the equipment that makes online technologies accessible to us, and as more is learned about how we learn, our structures of education will evolve, will transmute, will continually confirm what the essences of good teaching are all about.

IMPLEMENTATION/EVALUATION

REFERENCES

1. **Talbott, S.** 1999. "The Future Does Not Compute—Transcending the Machines in Our Midst" *Educause*, March/April.

2. **The Institute for Higher Education Policy.** 2000. "Quality on the Line: Benchmarks for Success in Internet-Based Distance Education," April. <http:www.ihep.com>.

3. **Hmieleski, K**. 2000. "Barriers to Online Evaluation: Surveying the Nation's Top 200 Most Wired Colleges." *Interactive and Distance Education Assessment Laboratory*, March.

4. **Hmieleski, K**. **and M. Champagne**. 2000. "Plugging in to Course Evaluation." *The Technology Source*, September. <http://horizon.unc.edu/TS/assessment/2000-09.asp>.

5. **Olsen, F.** 1999. 'Virtual Institutions Challenge Accreditors to Devise New Ways of Measuring Quality." *The Chronicle of Higher Education*, Information Technology, August 6. <http://chronicle .com>.

6. _____ 1999. "Role of Accreditors in Distance Education Is Debated at Conference." *The Chronicle of Higher Education*, Information Technology, February 12. <http://chronicle.com>.

7. **Henry, T.** 2000. "Professors Seek Online Standards." *USA Today Tech Report,* July 10. <http://www.usatoday.com/life/cyber/tech/cti205.htm>.

8. **McCollum, K.** 1998. "Accreditors Are Urged to Prepare to Evaluate Distance Learning."*The Chronicle of Higher Education*, A34, Information Technology, May 15. <http://chronicle.com>.

9. **Carneville, D.** 2000. "Accrediting Bodies Consider New Standards for Distance-Education Programs." *The Chronicle of Higher Education*, Friday, August 11. <http://chronicle.com/free/2000/08/2000081101u.htm>.

10. **Commissions on Higher Education.** 2000. "Draft: Statement of the Regional Accrediting Commissions on the Evaluation of Electronically Offered Degree and Certificate Programs." September, pp. iii-iv. <http://www.wiche.edu/Telecom/Guidelines.htm>.

Glossary

Some of the terms used in this glossary are based on the following sources:

Landon, B. 2000. "Online Educational Delivery Applications: A Web Tool for Comparative Analysis." <http://www.ctt.bc.ca/landonline/uindex.html>.

Willis, B. 1995. "Glossary of Distance Education Terminology." *Guide #14.* Engineering Outreach, College of Engineering, University of Idaho, October. <http://www. uidaho.edu /evo/newhtml/coursoff.htm>.

Accessibility: Accessibility for persons with disabilities entails providing for a universal text version without relying on frames, tables, or images.

ADL Co-Laboratory: ADL Co-LAB was formed to provide the backbone for the development of guidelines, certification procedures, and shared courseware objects in a collaborative environment among government and private groups.

Administration: Administration tools include all those setup and maintenance tasks involved on the server side of the application and extending to setup/configuration of client side software to work properly with the server side application. Some of these tasks may be carried out by instructors in some situations.

Address bar: This is the browser location where the Web-page addresses (URLs) are entered, or paths to documents on your computer.

Analog: A signal that is received in the same form in which it is transmitted, while the amplitude and frequency may vary.

Androgogy: The practice of teaching adults.

Application sharing: Application sharing includes the running of an application on one machine and sharing the window view of the running application across the Web and there may also be provisions for sharing mouse control of the application.

Arithmetic/Logic Unit: This unit of the CPU performs arithmetic operations ($<$, $>$, $=$) or logical operations (and, or, but, not).

Asynchronous: Communication in which interaction between parties does not take place simultaneously.

AU: A format typically used to compress and digitize sound files.

Authorization: tools that assign access and other privileges to specific users or user groups.

Backbone: A primary communication path connecting multiple users. A system of high-speed host computers that connect the Internet.

BBS file exchange: Bulletin Board Service is the facility for downloading files and upload\posting files over the Web.

Best practices: A set of guidelines for online academic programs approved by the eight regional accrediting commissions for higher education in the United States.

Bit: Abbreviation for a single binary digit.

Bitmap images : Bitmap images (often called raster images) consist of dots (pixels) in a grid on your screen. Pixels are picture elements; tiny dots of individual color that make up what you see on your screen. All these tiny dots of color blend to form the images you see. Each dot consists of one or more bits of data. The more bits per dot the more colors and shades of gray that may be represented by that dot.

Bookmarks: Bookmarks identify internet locations and this category covers the creation, display, management, and updating of bookmarks.

Broad bandwidth: The capacity to carry large amounts of information on a communication channel.

Browser: Software that allows you to find and see information on the Internet. Browsers normally have many functions beyond simply reading Web pages and linking to the next one. Included among these functions are email, audio and videoconferencing, saving the URLs of favorite sites with bookmarks, document sharing, Web searching, creating and editing pages, and even Web shopping.

Byte: A single computer word, generally eight bits.

Cable modem: Many cable television (CATV) providers now provide a service and equipment to transmit data over coaxial cables that bring the Internet signal into the home. A cable splitter divides the signal between the television and the cable modem attached to the personal computer. Both internal and external cable modems are available with transmission rates of 500 Kbps to 2Mbps.

Central processing unit (CPU): The processor that manages most of the computer operations and data handling.

Chat: Chat includes facilities like Internet Relay Chat IRC and similar text exchanges.

Chatroom: A location with a website that supports some form of real-time interaction either by typing or voice. This facilitates the ability of a class or group to communicate with one another at the same moment.

Codec (COder/DECoder): Device used to convert analog signals to digital signals for transmission and reconvert signals upon reception at the remote site while allowing for the signal to be compressed for less expensive transmission.

Compressed video: When video signals are downsized to allow travel along a smaller carrier.

Compression: Reducing the amount of visual information sent in a signal by only transmitting changes in action.

Computer assisted instruction (CAI): Teaching process in which a computer is utilized to enhance the learning environment by assisting students in gaining mastery over a specific skill.

Control unit: The component of the CPU that manages most of the computer operations by obtaining an instruction, decoding it, and then carrying out the instruction and storing it if required.

Course planning: Course planning tools are facilities that enable at least initial course layout and or structuring.

Course: Course tools are facilities that facilitate the instructor's tasks related to bringing course materials together and managing the student's use/access of those materials.

Course customizing: Course customizing includes the facility to change the structure of the course and its assignments, exams, etc. This may include guides, templates, and related product support and training.

Course managing: Course managing tools include facilities to enable instructors to collect information from or about students related to their progress in the course structure and to permit/deny access to course resources.

Course monitoring: Course monitoring includes facilities that provide information about the usage of course resources by individual students and groups of students.

Crash recovery: Crash recovery tools include facilities to recover from communications or server hardware failure without loss of data. These are tools in addition to the tools provided by the operating system.

Curriculum managing: Curriculum management includes tools to manage multiple programs, to do skills/competencies management, and to do certification management.

Data: Data tools include tools for marking online, managing records, and for analyzing and tracking.

Desktop video conferencing: Video conferencing refers to the abilty of two or more groups or persons to send images and sound to each other in real time from a distance.

Digital: An electrical signal that varies in discrete steps in voltage, frequency, amplitude, locations, etc. Digital signals can be transmitted faster and more accurately than analog signals.

Digital divide: Refers to the growing disparity among White, Asian, Black, and Hispanic populations who have access to the Internet.

Digital subscriber lines (DSL): Perpetual, high-speed Internet connection allowing both analog and digital transmission. Generally faster than ISDN connections.

Distance education: The process of providing instruction when students and instructors are separated by physical distance and technology, often in tandem with face-to-face communication, used to bridge the gap.

Domain name system server (DNS): A server on which domain names are registered and stored and where the domain names are translated into an IP address for correct routing to the destination computer.

Download: Using the network to transfer files from one computer to another.

Email: Electronic mail using the Internet protocols unless noted otherwise. Sending messages from one computer user to another.

Facsimile (Fax): System used to transmit textual or graphical images over standard telephone lines.

Female connectors: Connectors used to attach peripheral devices to a computer that are configured with holes to accept pins of male connectors.

Fiber optic cable: Glass fiber that is used for laser transmission of video, audio, and/or data.

File transfer protocol (FTP): A standard protocol for the transfer of files from one computer to another using the Internet.

Firmware: Permanent instructions recorded by the manufacturer on a computer chip that a computer must follow to upload the operating system. These instructions remain intact when the power to the computer is off.

Flames: Abusive or insulting messages that get sent back and forth over the Internet.

GIF (pronounced jiff): A compression file format based on the graphic interchange format.

Goal: The intended outcome of an activity.

Group browsing: Group browsing involves a group tour of websites with a shared browser window and some interaction capability between the members of the group and at least the tour leader.

Help desk: Help desk tools are facilities that assist the technical administration personnel in handling trouble calls and requests for technical assistance.

Home page: A document with an address (URL) on the World Wide Web maintained by a person or organization which contains pointers to other pieces of information.

Host: Computers that are directly connected to the network and may store and transfer data at high speed (much like a superhighway) while permitting other computers to connect along the major arteries much like side roads.

Hot plugging: A technology that permits the device to be plugged in while the computer is running and the device will be recognized by plug-and-play so that it will automatically configure the device for immediate use.

Hypertext markup language (HTML): The code used to create a home page and is used to access documents over the WWW.

Hypertext transfer protocol (HTTP): The protocol used to signify an Internet site is a WWW site, i.e., HTTP is a WWW address.

Hypertext: Web pages must be formatted in a set of standard codes collectively called hypertext markup language (HTML). These codes are rules that manage the appearance of colors, fonts, text styles, digital images, sounds, animations, and links within the Web page.

IMS (Instructional Management Project): A global coalition of educational institutions, commercial organizations, and government entities that adopted specifications for the interoperability of distributed learning resources.

Installation: Server installation includes both software setup tools and installations related services provided by the vendor.

Instructional designing: Instructional designing includes facilities to help instructors create learning sequences.

Instructional events: Robert Gagne, a preeminent voice in instructional design and learning theory, suggests there are nine events that prompt the necessary conditions for learning to occur. He calls these instructional events.

Instructor support: Instructor support tools are facilities to assist technical support personnel in providing technical assistance to instructors using the application.

Integrated services digital network (ISDN): A telecommunications standard that permits multiple communications channels that can simultaneously transmit voice, video, and data. It is possible to obtain much faster transmission speed than over conventional phone lines.

Interactive Media: Frequency assignment that allows for a two-way interaction or exchange of information.

Internet: The Internet refers to an international system of interlinked computers that all use a specific set of communication rules known as Transmission Control Protocol/Internet protocol (TCP/IP). The IP address consists of four groups of numbers separated by a period. The numbers in each group may be from 0 to 255. As an example, 206.13504.77 may represent an IP address.

Internet protocol (IP): A universally accepted set of rules provide a naming system to specifically identify any computer in the world. Every host computer has a unique address known as an Internet protocol (IP) address.

Internet service provider (ISP): The ISP has a permanent connection to the Internet and normally charges a fee to the temporary user. In order to connect to the Internet you need a computer that links by cable, telephone lines, or satellite to an Internet service provider (ISP). Every online user must have an ISP.

Interpolation: A computer generated mathematical of the color values of new pixels based on the surrounding pixels usually used when you increase the size of a bitmap image through resizing.

JPEG (pronounced JAY-peg): A compression file format based on the Joint Photographic Experts Group standard.

Local area network (LAN): This refers to computer connections for fast transmission of data within the physical structure of the organization. This is often called a local area network (LAN). Such networks require a network interface card (NIC) that is either an expansion card or a PC card.

Learner tools: Tools/facilities used by the student learner at their location, the client side of distance education.

Learning community: A class where there is substantial quantity and quality of interaction within that class, whether traditional or online.

Learning object: A discrete "chunk" of data that is part of a learning module. It could include video, audio, text, email, slides, case studies, collaborative activities, or any medium that can be digitized.

Lesson: Lessons are those facilities that facilitate the development and deployment of instructional sequences smaller than a whole course, like assignments, modules, topics, etc.

Listserv: An email program that allows multiple computer users to connect onto a single system, creating an online discussion.

Livechat: A computer based conferencing technology that you allows you to use Web-based audio and a microphone to converse with people just as you would a telephone. There are a number of programs that allow you to do this for no cost beyond the Internet connection.

Local area network (LAN): Two or more local computers that are physically connected.

Lossy: Each time JPG files are manipulated and saved they will lose quality.

Mailing list: A mailing list is a collection of email addresses collected under a single name.

Male connectors: Connectors used to attach peripheral devices to a computer that are configured with exposed pins to permit connection to female connectors.

Managing records: Managing records include facilities for organizing and keeping track of course-related information.

Marking online: Marking online includes facilities that support the marking of student generated material while online.

Megahertz (MHz): Clock speed is measured in megahertz. One megahertz (MHz) is equal to one million pulses per second.

Metadata tags: Electronic tags that are currently imbedded in Web materials to permit their retrieval by search engines. The IMS metadata search fields include learning level, users' support, educational objectives, copyright information, price code, learning object, and many other fields in addition to those currently existing such as author, subject, and publisher.

Metasearch engine: Search engines that simultaneously search many engines. Dogpile.com is a leading metasearch service that integrates several medium and large Web search and index guides into a single service by providing a single launch point.

Modem: The modem is a device that converts the digital signal of the computer to an analog signal that can be transmitted across telephone lines (MODulation) and a modem at the other end reconverts the analog signal back to a digital signal (DEModulate).

MPEG: A compression standard for video. The videos are normally compressed into MPEG (Motion Picture Experts Group) format to further reduce the size of video files allowing for faster transmission of digitized video.

Motivation building: Motivation building includes self-help tools and other facilities that provide direct encouragement to overcome difficulties that impede or impair student performance.

Multimedia: Multimedia includes the support for images, audio, video, and VRML files. Any document which uses multiple forms of communication, such as text, audio, and/or video.

Multiplexer (MUX): A multiplexing device that tags each stream of data and then combines those streams into a single stream for transmission across telephone lines. If you have a digital line that carries multiple signals such as an ISDN line, you will require multiplexing.

Netscape: An example of browser software that allows you to design a home page and to browse links on the WWW.

Network: A series of points connected by communication channels in different locations.

Newsgroups: Newsgroups facility includes Usenet newsgroups and like functions.

Online: Active and prepared for operation. Also suggests access to a computer network.

Online fees handling: Online fees handling includes tools to accomplish credit card transactions.

Online learning: It is distance learning modernized with the instructional mediums, computers, modems, and the Internet as the means by which teachers and students connect.

Online learning centers: Online learning centers are pre-formed digital supplements in each of 38 subject areas provided by McGraw-Hill.

Online service: Many of the ISPs provide additional services to their members including chat rooms, information, news, sports, weather, financial information, games, places to create and store your own website, and even travel guides. Such ISPs become identified as an online service.

Operating system (OS): A set of instructions that manage and coordinate the hardware devices and run the applications software. Windows 95/98/2000 and MacOS-9 are examples of operation system software.

PC cards: These are external cards that may be inserted into a laptop computer and can be used to add memory, sound, fax/modem, disk drives, and other capabilities. These cards are often referred to as PCMIA (Personal Computer Memory Card International Association) since they must adhere to a set of standards that allow interchangeability. The PC cards come in three thicknesses referred to as Type I (thinnest cards, usually memory); Type II (modems); and Type III (thickest, usually hard drives).

PDF (portable document format): A type of formatting used by Adobe that permits both graphic and text combinations to be transferred over the Internet while retaining all of the original formatting.

Personal computer (PC): A computer device used in the home or office powered by a microprocessor that includes a control unit, an arithmetic/logic unit, a system clock.

Plug-and-play: A technology that automatically configures expansion cards (or other devices) when the computer is subsequently turned on after the device installation.

Plug-ins: An additional add-on program required by browsers to display many of the more advanced multimedia elements on a Web page including advanced multimedia features including streaming audio and video, and interactive multimedia such as voice.

POP3: The message arriving at your mail server is transferred to POP3 (Post Office Protocol) server that stores the message(s) until opened by the recipient.

Port: Connection points or interfaces from the computer to external devices such as a mouse, monitor, printer, speakers, microphone, scanner, drawing tablet, modem, or other peripheral devices.

Portal: A portal refers to websites such as Dogpile.com, Yahoo!, AltaVista, Netscape Netcenter, and Lycos that offer multiple services such as search engines, weather, news, sports, yellow and white page directories, chat rooms, and emails.

Portfolio: A collection of integrated student work that may include threaded discussions, exams, written papers, and other materials upon which a more comprehensive evaluation of performance may be made.

PPP: A software package which allows a user to have a direct connection to the Internet over a telephone line.

Presenting information: Presenting information includes facilities for formatting, displaying, or showing course material over the Web.

Progress tracking: Progress tracking includes some facility for the student to check marks on assignments and tests.

Protocol: A formal set of standards, rules, or formats for exchanging data that assures uniformity between computers and applications.

GLOSSARY

RAM: Application program instructions (word processors for example) and any data being processed by the application program is stored in volatile memory called random access memory (RAM) which is erased when the computer is turned off or loses power.

Registering: Registering includes online registration and/or linkage with existing registration systems.

Remote access: Remote access tools include facilities to do application system administration from more than one machine.

Resource: Resource tools includes tools for building knowledge, team building, and building motivation among instructors.

Resource monitoring: Resource monitoring includes the facility to display the disk space and CPU resources devoted to the application while it is being used.

RTF (rich text format): A type of formatting used in word processors that preserves most formatting when transferring documents among various word processing programs.

ROM: The system software is normally stored in nonvolatile memory known also as read only memory (ROM) which is maintained when the computer power is off.

SCORM: Sharable Courseware Object Reference Model (SCORM). Standards for Web-based learning that make it possible for a learner to custom-assemble content based on their own personal needs and pace.

Screen area: The area of the computer screen that has to do with the number of "pixels" or dots that make up what you see on your screen. If you increase the screen area, you can have more information appear on your monitor.

Search engine: Search engines are used to locate websites with topics of interest by typing in key words or phrases and then pressing the designated key to submit the search request to the appropriate server. There are numerous search engines. Some are designed to search within a website, while others will search large parts of the Internet.

Searching: Searching includes the facility to locate parts of the course materials on the basis of word matching beyond the users current browser page.

Security: Browser security refers to the support for secure transactions on the Web and to verify the security of downloaded code.

Self-assessing: Self-assessing includes practice quizzes and other survey style assessment tools that may or may not be scored online.

Server: A computer with a special service function on a network, generally receiving and connecting incoming information traffic.

Server security: Security tools are used to prevent unauthorized access and/or modification of data. This can include a wide range of approaches and methods.

SMTP: When you send a message it is transmitted using a protocol referred to as SMTP (simple mail transfer protocol) that manages the routing and delivery of your message.

Small computer system interface (SCSI) (pronounced skuzzy), this is a high-speed parallel port used to attach external devices including printers, disk drives, and scanners. The SCSI port can support up to seven devices that are daisy chained together.

Spams: Unsolicited email messages that are sent to numerous recipients at once.

Streaming audio: A technology has been developed that instantly begins to feed (stream) the audio file into your computer so that it plays immediately from the beginning while downloading the next parts in sequence.

Streaming video: A technology has been developed that instantly begins to feed (stream) the video file into your computer so that it plays immediately from the beginning while downloading the next parts in sequence.

Student support: Student help desk support tools include facilities to facilitate the tasks of an operator responding to requests for help by student users of the application.

Student tools: Student tools include applications that cater to the special needs of tele-learners.

Study skill building: Study skill building includes facilities that support effective study practices, which can range from simple review tools to mini courses in how to study.

Subscribe: A process of adding your name to a mailing list by sending along your name, email address, and other requested information to the person that manages the list.

Support tools: Instructor tools are facilities primarily intended for use by instructors, markers and course designers.

Synchronous: Real-time information exchange. Communication in which interaction between participants is simultaneous.

System clock: A small microcomputer chip that times and synchronizes computer operations.

System unit: The metal or plastic case that holds the electronic components of the computer.

Transmission control protocol/Internet protocol (TCP/IP): A specific set of communication rules that makes possible the transmission of data among most any type of computer and transmission system including cables, telephone lines, or satellite. The TCP/IP standards determine how the digital information is formatted, how the messages find their target, and how widely different computers can talk with each other,

Team building: Team building includes the facility for instructors with common interests to communicate in a way that facilitates their forming a sense of group/team identity.

Telecommunication: The science of information transport using wire, radio, optical, or electromagnetic channels to transmit receive signals for voice or data communications using electrical means.

Teleconferencing: Teleconferencing includes audio conferencing. Two-way electronic communication between two or more groups in separate locations via audio, video, and/or computer systems.

Testing: Testing includes facilities to assist in the making up of practice quizzes, tests, exams, and other assignments.

1394 port: This is a connector similar to a USB and can connect multiple devices with Plug-and-Play capability including printers, digital cameras, CD-ROMs, DVD-ROMs, printers, and hard disks.

Top-level domain (TLP): Every domain also has a **top-level domain** (TLP) that identifies the organizational type operating the site.

Transmission control protocol (TCP): A protocol that makes sure that packets of data are shipped and received in the intended order.

Uniform resource locator (URL): The address of a homepage on the WWW. Internet protocol numbers are usually difficult to remember or associate with a particular recipient so a host name that corresponds to the number is usually used (for example, WWW.eCollege.com). This corresponding text version contains the domain name. This address represents a critical component of the uniform resource locator (URL) that the Web uses to find resources.

Uplink: The communication link from the transmitting earth station to the satellite.

Universal serial bus (USB): A connector that can connect up to 127 different external devices by connecting them serially one to another in a chain sometimes called a daisy chain. Most new digital cameras, joysticks, DVD-ROMs and other devices come with a USB connector and also support plug-and-play technology and hot plugging.

Vector images: Vector images are defined by mathematical equations that make up individual, scalable objects. The objects may be lines, curves, boxes, circles, other shapes, or fonts with editable attributes including line thickness, color, and fill.

Video conferencing: Video conferencing includes broadcasting video to those without a video input device.

Virtual space: Virtual spaces include MOOs, MUDs, and virtual meeting rooms.

Voice chat: Voice chat enables two or more to communicate via microphone and speaker conference call style over the internet connection in real time.

WAV: a format typically used to compress and digitize sound files.

Whiteboard: A window that appears on your computer screen during a videoconferencing session that allows you to draw on the screen much like a chalkboard or whiteboard in the classroom. The notes and drawings you produce may be viewed at once on the screens of all the participants.

Website: A collection of related Web pages accessed by typing in its specific address within a browser.

Wizard: A software program that automatically guides you through the set-up process for programs and applications.

World Wide Web (WWW): A collection of electronic hyper-linked documents residing on computers around the world.

Index